A SHEARWATER BOOK

Seeking the

Sacred Raven

SEEKING THE

SACRED RAVEN

POLITICS AND
EXTINCTION ON A
HAWAIIAN ISLAND

MARK JEROME WALTERS

◐ ISLANDPRESS / SHEARWATER BOOKS
Washington · Covelo · London

A Shearwater Book
Published by Island Press

Copyright © 2006 Mark Jerome Walters

All rights reserved under International and Pan-American
Copyright Conventions. No part of this book may be reproduced
in any form or by any means without permission in writing from
the publisher: Island Press, 1718 Connecticut Ave., NW, Suite 300,
Washington, DC 20009.

SHEARWATER BOOKS is a trademark
of The Center for Resource Economics.

Library of Congress Cataloging-in-Publication Data
Walters, Mark Jerome.
Seeking the sacred raven : politics and extinction on a Hawaiian Island /
Mark Jerome Walters.
p. cm.
Includes bibliographical references and index.
ISBN 1-55963-090-6 (cloth : alk. paper)
1. Hawaiian crow. 2. Hawaiian crow—Conservation—Political aspects.
I. Title.
QL696.P2367W35 2006
333.95'8864—dc22   2005034290

British Cataloguing-in-Publication data available.

For the sake of consistency, the diacritical marks in 'alalā have been
standardized in historical quotations and elsewhere throughout the text.

Printed on recycled, acid-free paper ♺

Design by David Bullen Design

Manufactured in the United States of America
10 9 8 7 6 5 4 3 2 1

TO MY DEAREST NOELLE,

MY WONDERFUL WILLIAM,

AND MY ADORABLE ANNA

CONTENTS

Part III: Last Light

PROLOGUE

BLUE MANGO TREES
in starlight. White oleander in headlights. Having left Hawai'i
Island's King Kamehameha Hotel before daybreak, I head south
through darkness along the Māmalahoa Highway toward Mc-
Candless Ranch in faint hope of glimpsing one of the world's
rarest birds—the legendary 'alalā. Living only in cloud forests on
the leeward side of the great shield volcano Mauna Loa, the 'alalā
once numbered in the thousands. Now—it's May 1996—only
about a dozen remain in the wild, limited to a small tract of mile-
high forest, almost all within the misty mountains of McCandless
Land and Cattle Company.

A little after six o'clock, first daylight touches the hillside pastures of grazing cows and horses. Banana trees, broad leaves
drooping as if bereaved by a passing shower, dot the sloping coffee
plantations. I pass green-and-yellow-hued macadamia orchards
and hillsides shadowed with tamarind and dark-leaved avocado
trees. Roadside hibiscus open pale pink faces to morning light.
Imperceptibly the highway gains altitude, until a break in the trees
offers a panoramic vista of Kealakekua Bay, more than a thousand

feet below. The road continues into a grove of orange-blossomed poinciana trees, opens into a clearing, and then sweeps through a carpet of purple jacaranda blossoms that have fallen on the asphalt.

To native Hawaiians, the ʻalalā—closer to the raven family than to the crow—is a sacred bird, a guardian spirit and a guide to the afterlife. When a Hawaiian dies, the soul travels to a Leaping Place—each island district has one, usually a high ocean promontory—and awaits its guide. For people of the districts of South Kona and Kaʻū on Hawaiʻi Island (also known as the Big Island), one of those spirits is the ʻalalā, and one of the Leaping Places is the volcanic cliff at the southernmost point of the island, Ka Lae. When the guardian spirit arrives at the appointed place, it joins the waiting soul, and together they leap into the afterlife. Without a spirit guide such as the ʻalalā, a soul could lose its way and drift forever through a twilight of ghosts and night moths, with only grasshoppers to eat.

With the ʻalalā on its own way to the hereafter, what will become of those future souls who might have relied upon its protective powers? And who, I wonder, is guardian of the ʻalalā itself? Clearly, the ʻalalā's existence—and its disappearance—is much more than a question of endangered species and biology, important as those are. It is a question of culture, the here and now—and eternity.

As I continue along the highway toward McCandless Ranch, the aroma of roadside plumeria blossoms wafts through the car windows. Morning light softens the shadow of Mauna Loa and washes across the landscape like paint across an artist's palette, mixing vibrant blues and greens with splashes of ochre, crimson, and orange.

Hawaiʻi: the fragrant illusion.

Plumeria and oleander are foreigners here. So are banana trees. As are mango and avocado, monkeypod, macadamia and banyan, tamarind, orange, papaya and pink hibiscus and the amber-draped poinciana tree. It is not that the rare ʻalalā is about to depart from Hawaiʻi. Rather, Hawaiʻi long ago left the ʻalalā. Little remains of the place the ʻalalā of old knew—not much of the original forests, nor the animals. Nor the people. The ʻalalā has become a familiar in a strange land.

By seven o'clock, I've spotted the sign along the highway for the McCandless property. I turn up a steep, narrow road, pass a paddock with several cows, and pull up next to a metal-sided warehouse bright in the morning sun.

"Mornin'!" says the ranch manager as he steps through the door. Wearing blue jeans, a denim shirt, and wraparound Ray-Ban sunglasses, Keith Unger introduces himself. "Welcome to the land where anything grows! Well, anything except what's supposed to."

I had telephoned Unger a few weeks before to arrange a trip to the ʻalalā's cloud-forest home. McCandless Ranch was struggling financially because of the collapse of beef prices, he had said, and visitors paying for a picturesque half-day trip up the mountain supplemented ranch income.

Unger spreads a map on the hood of his van. "We're here at about a thousand feet," he says, placing a finger on the triangular island's southern half. "We'll be heading up here to about five thousand, right into the heart of the cloud forests.

"From sea level, Mauna Loa is more than two and a half miles high," he goes on to say. "Measured from the ocean floor, it's two thousand feet taller than Mount Everest!" Unger pauses to scratch his Adam's apple. "Now, I realize you've come all this way to see the ʻalalā. A lot of birders do. Many leave disappointed. Still, it's a worthwhile drive up the mountain."

I had initially heard about the ʻalalā on my first trip to Hawaiʻi, nearly ten years before. A news account in a Honolulu paper had described this bird—the "Hawaiian crow"—as sacred to Hawaiians and living in the cloud forests of Mauna Loa. The article mentioned ranch owners refusing entry to biologists seeking to study the ravens.

This brief encounter years before had left in memory the image of a bird with a dimension deeper than biology or natural history, if for no other reason than that it figured so prominently in the religious life of Hawaiians. Here was a bird not only of mysterious physical presence but, it seemed, also of luminous metaphorical, even spiritual, possibilities.

For years after learning of this bird, I sought out every word to be found on it. Those being remarkably few, I contacted some of the people who knew about it. What is the ʻalalā like in the forests? Can it truly be as mysterious as people say? How has a bird once so common become so rare? And what do those Hawaiians who might have hoped to rely upon the ʻalalā to reach the afterlife think? Did the bird's decline parallel that of traditional Hawaiian culture? That last question—the potential threads running from culture out into the natural world—was most intriguing; answering it held the possibility of adding another, deeper layer of truth to our usual one-dimensional scientific understanding of conservation and endangered species. The loss of the ʻalalā therefore stood to represent the diminishment of who we have been—and to symbolize what we have become.

My desire to understand the ʻalalā became a quest. I wanted to circle the raven, so to speak, examining it from every possible perspective: those of the ardent environmentalist, the dispassionate (and sometimes passionate) biologist, the native Hawaiian, the lawyer, the "average citizen." The bird, I sometimes imagined, were I to fully comprehend its many dimensions, could deepen my understanding of both culture and biology and, perhaps, even my own evanescent presence on an ancient planet. The 'alalā was thus not only a bird. It was also a mirror, and a window.

As we lean over the vehicle's hood, Unger says, "The 'alalā used to range along here through the band of cloud forests up to about 6,500 feet. Before the Polynesians arrived, the birds may have lived on some of the other islands. But in recent times, they could be found only in a few areas of the Big Island. And now they live here," he says, "on McCandless Ranch."

We climb into the four-wheel-drive van and begin to ascend the narrow private gravel road up Mauna Loa.

"The 'alalā may have once nested in these lowlands," Unger says, pointing into the trees along the road. "Today they visit the lower dry forests to eat fruit and flowers." The forest seems unexpectedly bland in its browns and grays, I comment. Unger replies, "A lot of people envision the original forests as being flower shops. Not true, except maybe when the 'ōhi'a are blooming. Many varieties of the proverbial hibiscus in the Hawaiian woman's hair are actually imports. Many traditional Hawaiian leis were made not from flowers but from nuts, seaweed, shells, or just leaves."

Unger explains that the forest's problems began long before the deluge of exotic species that would be ushered in by the arrival of Captain James Cook in 1778. More than a thousand years earlier, Polynesians, who brought their own plants in their canoes, had burned the lower dry forests, planted crops, and exploited birds for feathers and food. "By the time Europeans got here, the native Hawaiians had already wiped out quite a bit of the lower forests and dozens of species," he said.

It was true. The early Polynesians introduced what would eventually amount to forty or fifty exotic species of plants and animals, including the coconut palm and small pigs. These, along with forest clearing and hunting, eventually contributed to the extinction of many native animals, especially birds. Some sixty animal species became extinct following Polynesian colonization. The new settlers caused many of these extinctions. Others resulted from natural forces—habitat changes in these ever-changing islands, for example.

Since Europeans arrived, late in the eighteenth century, thousands of species have been introduced. It has been estimated that in prehistoric times, a new species colonized Hawai'i about every twenty thousand years. Now several dozen, on average, take root annually.

"You might see a few sandalwood trees, or 'iliahi," Unger says as we continue the climb. Only some species are fragrant, and most of those went for export in the 1800s.

All but gone is the beautiful hala pepe tree, with branch tips hung with whorls of slender, sword-shaped golden yellow blossoms. For early Hawaiians, the hala pepe was a tree sacred to Kapo, goddess of insight and intuition, and to Laka, goddess of dance.

Unger cranes his neck over the steering wheel in search of the once common wiliwili tree. The colorful seeds of the orange or brick red claw-shaped flowers were once strung on twine to make leis. Hawaiians also used the tree's soft, buoyant wood to make outriggers for fishing.

As we climb past four thousand feet into the cool atmosphere, mist emerges among the stands of large trees. The humid ocean air that has been drawn up the mountain by the rising heat of day begins to condense. This leeward weather system has created an emerald forest necklace between about four thousand and six thousand feet around the volcano.

This weather contrasts with that on the other, windward, side of the island, where powerful northeastern trade winds drive moisture-laden air currents up Mauna Loa's eastern ramparts, creating torrential rains. "Our side of the mountain maybe gets thirty or forty inches of rain most years," Unger says. "The windward side can get up to four hundred!"

At about 4,500 feet, the road passes by glistening fern forests and huge old trees, their trunks tufted with mounds of red moss. An infinite variety of green, myriad textures, and a multitude of leaf shapes surrounds us. The smell of decaying wood fills the air. Unfurling fronds of fern arc through light and mist. A lacework of rhizomes crisscrosses the ground like green vessels of vegetal life. The cinnamon brown head of a new fern thrusts its head up through the base of the mother plant.

A light rain begins, even as sunlight still electrifies the forest. Then Unger points out a young man in the road ahead. "John Klavitter," he says, "one of the biologists studying the ʻalalā." Unger pulls to a stop.

Klavitter steps up to Unger's open window: "I saw the ʻalalā not twenty minutes ago! But they've gone down the mountain. Not much chance of seeing them again today." The birds of our pursuit having gone, we stand and chat.

Klavitter reminds us that only a handful are left in the wild this spring of 1996—fourteen, to be exact. "On the other hand, that's the most there've been in the wild in years," he says. Nine of these were hatched in captivity and released. The other five are the only wild ʻalalā that remain.

"The Hoʻokena and Keālia pairs are approaching twenty years of age and are at the end of their reproductive years," Klavitter says. The fifth wild bird is a single young male known as the Bachelor, hatched in 1992. His parents—the Kalāhiki pair—both disappeared in 1995. About two dozen additional ones survive in aviaries.

Lack of birds isn't the only issue. With their habitat infested with disease-carrying mosquitoes and alien predators such as cats and mongooses, the issue is where to release the young ʻalalā. Permanent captivity is ultimately a dead end. Confined to captivity, a species will gradually lose the physical characteristics that permit survival in the wild.

Unger interrupts us to point out a small black silhouette wheeling against the sky—an 'io. "Like the 'alalā, the Hawaiian hawk is also endangered," Klavitter points out. "How do you protect one endangered bird from its endangered natural predator?

"'Io historically always preyed upon 'alalā," he replies to his own question. "But degraded forests over the past century or so have greatly benefited the Hawaiian hawk at the 'alalā's expense."

"Do you let nature play itself out," Unger asks, "or do you intervene and take sides?"

"No matter what you do, you're taking sides," Klavitter replies. "Human conservation is intended to restore the balance among species. At present, we're pulling out all the stops to intervene on behalf of the 'alalā. I mean, when you're on a first-name basis with every remaining bird, that's hand-holding individuals on the short list of extinction."

Speaking of the 'alalā as extinct is, as Klavitter reminds us, premature. The number of birds in the wild is slowly growing, he points out, thanks to the recent releases.

Unger doesn't respond but instead motions us toward the forest's edge. We part the vegetal curtain and enter the cloud forest realm of the 'alalā.

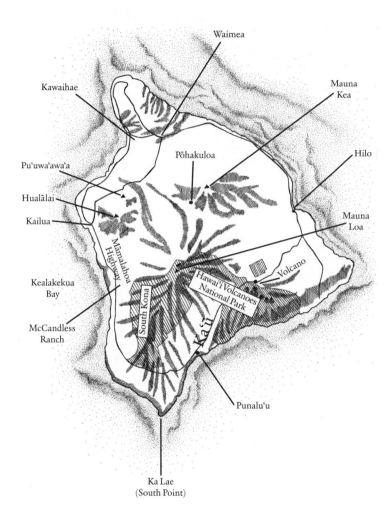

Waimea

Kawaihae

Mauna
Kea

Pu'uwa'awa'a

Pōhakuloa

Hilo

Hualālai

Kailua

Mauna
Loa

Māmalahoa
Highway

Kealakekua
Bay

South Kona

Hawai'i Volcanoes
National Park

Volcano

Ka'ū

McCandless
Ranch

Punalu'u

Ka Lae
(South Point)

HAWAI'I ISLAND

PART I

BEGINNING IN DEEP DARKNESS

chapter 1

MOUNTAIN OF EMERALD LIGHT

STEEPED IN EARLY explorers' descriptions of Hawai'i's dense cloud forests, I've expected to enter an impenetrable thicket. As one explorer in the late 1700s wrote, "the Wood [was] impassable every where out of the common Paths" and "so Immoderately thick & strewed with Under wood & firn that it was totally Impassable." The woods are "very thick and luxuriant," wrote another. "The largest trees are nearly thirty feet in the girth, and these with the shrubbery underneath and the whole intersected with vines renders it very umbrageous."

But beneath the thick canopy of tree ferns and 'ōhi'a trees where we stand is an forest nearly devoid of underbrush.

"Where's the understory?" I whisper.

"Feral cattle, they keep it pretty well mowed down. Pigs dig up a lot of the ferns and trample the underbrush," John Klavitter answers.

Keith Unger, a rancher at heart, bristles at the cattle reference.

"Livestock keep the fire-prone exotic grasses down. 'Fact, we purposely keep a few cattle back here to prevent fire. Sounds like a contradiction, but cattle are one reason some of the best remaining highland forests are on our ranch."

Klavitter adds, "The understory is critically important for the ʻalalā. It protected them from hawks and supplied a lot of fruit and insects. Now there is almost no protection and little food."

Still intent on keeping blame off his cattle, Unger says, "Pigs are just as bad, if not worse. Polynesians brought them here over a thousand years ago."

"I agree, pigs are destructive," Klavitter politely responds. "But Polynesian pigs were probably a lot smaller than the European boars. They knock over native tree ferns to reach the heart. After the pigs eat the core of the fern, a trough is created where rain collects and mosquitoes breed. Mosquitoes carry avian malaria and pox, which are detrimental to forest birds. This isn't even to mention the introduced rats and mongooses, which raid ʻalalā nests and prey upon newly fledged young on the ground.

"And then there are the ʻio, which have capitalized upon the open understories, where the hunting is easier than amid dense ferns and other low-growing native plants. An almost unlimited supply of introduced rats, mice, and game birds has enabled the ʻio population to expand. The ʻalalā, on the other hand, got stuck with a dwindling supply of food. In theory, if enough areas were fenced, the understory would grow back, driving the ʻio to better hunting grounds outside ʻalalā habitat—or at least supporting far fewer hawks within it. Some of the historical balance between the ʻalalā and the ʻio might then be restored."

Klavitter turns his ear skyward. We hear a faint sound like the distant yelp of a dog.

"Maybe the Keālia pair," Klavitter mouths.

The sound rises again. I gaze up as ethereal columns of sunlight splinter through the canopy. I sadly listen to what may be among the last wild calls of ʻalalā. "Not many visitors even get to hear them," Unger whispers. "Consider yourself lucky."

We've now been in the forest for more than an hour, and Unger turns us back toward the road. Then, to our amazement, we hear another ʻalalā, this one closer. Its call is a high-pitched exclamatory note, like a child's yell, followed by a slow, gurgling caw.

Several nearby birds let loose from the treetops with ear-piercing, humanlike shrieks mixed with an occasional crowlike "Cawwwll!" There is yelling, yakking, whooping, barking, and howling—a cachinnation followed by quieter mutterings. We duck into an ʻōhiʻa shadow until the calls subside, leaving an edgy silence. The birds have disappeared, but their eyes still seem to be upon us. We are turned from observers into the observed.

Then suddenly we see it—a spreading fan of black feathers sweeping from a bough, silhouetted against a sunlit gap in the leafy ceiling. Another ʻalalā appears as the first bird levitates from the perch. Like miniature hang gliders, two more birds glide silently through the canopy shadows. The four ʻalalā now surrounding us alternately step from their perches into the air, catching themselves on black wings and arcing upward to a nearby tree. They stare at us and play musical branches, sailing acrobatically from one perch to another.

Unger points out another ʻalalā half hidden twenty feet above the ground behind the glossy oblong leaves of an Ilex or kāwaʻu tree. Klavitter peers through his binoculars and whispers, "Noe, daughter of the Keālia pair."

Noe rubs each side of her beak on the branch as if sharpening her bill. She gazes down at the ground, then into the forest. She works her bill under some loose bark, flecking off a short strip as she searches for insects.

Klavitter whispers again: "The ʻōhiʻa. Thirty feet up. Noe's brother, Paniolo." Paniolo (Hawaiian for "cowboy") tilts his head and gazes at us, then swoops down before arcing up to land in a nearby 'ōhi'a. Cocky, swaggering, he perches ten feet away and climbs, parrotlike, along the branch, calling loudly as his eyes bear down on us.

"Cowboy is brash," Unger whispers, and Klavitter nods in agreement. Paniolo is fond of what biologists nicknamed the John Wayne display, wherein he hunches his shoulders menacingly and extends the whiskerlike feathers, or "beard," on his throat.

As the 'alalā grow used to our presence, our whispers become soft voices. Klavitter says that a wild 'alalā once tried to steal a mouse that Paniolo was carrying in his beak. Both birds flapped wildly as they tumbled downward in a midair tug-of-war. The wild bird gave up, and Paniolo victoriously devoured the mouse on a nearby limb. "Paniolo may be the only captive-reared 'alalā that fought a wild bird and won," Klavitter remarks.

In August 1995, biologists found Paniolo motionless and fluffed up in a tree near the rest of the wild 'alalā. His right leg had been broken in an 'io ambush. Biologists took Paniolo to Kona International Airport, and from there he was flown by helicopter to a treatment facility on Maui. His leg was splinted, and after several months of recuperation he was returned to the forest, where two female 'alalā welcomed him back by preening his feathers.

Perched above, Paniolo, showing no sign of his previous injury, examines us from every angle, pivoting and tilting his head. He climbs and scoots nimbly along the branches, sometimes using his beak as a lever to maneuver his body. Noe and Paniolo are soon joined briefly by their elder brother Kehau, who suddenly takes flight and lands twenty feet above us in a kāwa'u tree. We are surrounded by 'alalā.

We hear among the dark boughs an occasional soft "Whaaa" and "Aaa-wooo" and the more pointed "Aa-waaoop!" At times, the birds seem more at home with us than with each other, as one occasionally delivers a pointed snigger, growl, or throaty "Raa-raa" to a compatriot.

I wade farther into a glen of waist-high ferns. An ʻalalā glides from a tree onto the ground twenty feet away. Soon the Bachelor's siblings join the congregation. Lokahi perches about thirty feet up in a huge ʻōhiʻa tree. Hiwahiwa appears briefly before spreading her wings and gliding into the shadows. In less than ten minutes we have seen not only Bachelor's two siblings but also the three Keālia children — Paniolo, Kehau, and Noe.

Then come others.

"Nānū and Hōkū!" Klavitter points out two more after peering through his binoculars at their colored leg bands. "Hōkū is short for Hōkū lele, which means shooting star." Through my binoculars I can see Hōkū's dark, gleaming eyes.

His sister Nānū, named for a rare and fragrant Hawaiian gardenia, sits beneath the canopy in a spray of light. Once common, only about twenty of the trees remain in the wild — and none on Hawaiʻi Island, where all but one tree of the species were destroyed by a road repair crew in the 1930s.

Nānū and Hōkū's sister Hilu, shyer than the others, barely ventures from the shadows. She flaps across a clearing in the canopy and is momentarily backlit by the sun before perching again and slipping back into forest shadows. She flutters her eyelids and then closes them as if to nap.

"I think that's Mahoa over there!" Klavitter says, pointing out Hilu's brother, who sits partially hidden in a large ʻōhiʻa.

I sit between two large, moss-covered logs, as if in a chaise longue, to expand the family tree in my notebook. The ink on the page is smeared by fog drip. I lie back in the cool wetness, close my eyes, and then inhale deeply the scents of the forest before adding to the family tree.

By noon, mist hangs from the scarlet-blossomed ʻōhiʻa boughs. As we continue our trek back, a few ʻalalā follow. Then, about a half mile from the road, pandemonium erupts in the treetops. The Hoʻokena pair appears, and the other birds noisily respond to the

Hilu

Nānū

Mahoa

Hōkū

Kalāhiki Pair

Umi's Descendants

Ho'okena Pair

Hiwahiwa

Keālia Pair

Lokahi

(died in 1995)

Paniolo

Noe

The Bachelor

Kehau

'ALALĀ FAMILY TREE
May 1996

wild birds with a cacophony of wails, caws, and trills. As the Bachelor debuts nearby with a loud, harsh "Aaaaa-whoooopp!"—a
series of forceful slurred whole notes that fill the canopy—other
calls subside. We watch him, perched in a dark-leaved kāwaʻu, dip-
ping his bill into a fruiting ʻieʻie vine brocading the branch. He
draws out a small berry, holds it down with one foot, and spears it
with his bill.

It's been an extraordinary morning: we have seen twelve of the
last fourteen ʻalalā in the wild, the most ʻalalā, Klavitter says, he's
ever seen in a single day. Only the Keālia pair remained out of sight
—and those two we believe we heard.

On the drive back down the mountain, we meet up with Donna
Ball, a young woman with light brown hair who heads the team of
field biologists. In a clearing behind her, a short distance back in
the woods, is the dome-shaped tent, nicknamed the Hula Dome,
where the biologists live. I open my door and put a foot on the
ground as she steps forward.

"Any luck?" she asks.

"Twelve!" Unger says.

"Wow! That's good!"

"Does it bother them that they're followed by biologists all the
time or have visitors like us?" I ask.

"We try to follow each individual less than two hours a day.
During the breeding season, nesting birds are monitored only
from a blind. They don't seem to mind our presence. You probably
noticed that being around people doesn't seem to bother them!"

"Do you go to sleep worrying about them?"

"Sometimes," she says as a droplet of water falls from a tree and
lands in her hair.

Then she says, "I do worry about them, all the time," as if
relieved to share the burden.

Unger and I drive in silence down the mountain. Once back at the warehouse, I bid Unger farewell and head down the steep drive in my car and back out onto the Māmalahoa Highway.

My time on Mauna Loa already seems like a dream. But no longer is my imagination required to conjure up images of forests or the raven of my quest. Part of me wants to return. Another wants to preserve the experience in memory as it is, fearing, perhaps, what may come in the months and years ahead.

2

IN THE BEGINNING

IN THE BEGINNING
were coral polyps and starfish, sea urchins and limpets. Of hot
darkness they came: crabs, conch shells, and mother-of-pearl. The
sacred essence entered all things. Then swam the spinner dolphin
through the dark sea, home of the silver albacore, the stingray, the
octopus. On land, Hula winds stirred the 'ie'ie vine, and blossoming 'ōhi'a trees stretched their boughs. In the Third Era of
creation came the 'alalā.

> A male this, the female that
> A male born in the time of black darkness
> The female born in the time of groping in the darkness
> Overshadowed was the sea, overshadowed the land
> Overshadowed the streams, overshadowed the mountains
> Overshadowed the dimly brightening night
> The rootstalk grew forming nine leaves
> Upright it grew with dark leaves
> The sprout that shot forth leaves of high chiefs
>
> . . . .
>
> The rootstalk sprouted, the taro stalk grew
> Born was the 'alalā. . . .

Growing from one another, all species were siblings. Indeed, the land itself was considered a member of the human family. These views of creation figured into the way Hawaiians exploited and conserved the islands' animals and other living resources.

The Hawaiians' view of the 'alalā began with their creation story, as told in the Kumulipo, or "Beginning in Deep Darkness." Here, Earth was not made by a creator but spontaneously arose from nothingness. Earth was then swept by a chaotic whirlwind of god-inspired life—plants and animals of sea and land—a world where every leaf expressed the face of the divine, every wind spoke the voice of spirits, and every forest fragrance breathed the supernatural. In this world there were no natural occurrences, only supernatural ones: the rainbow, the wind, a sudden call or flight of birds, unexpected ocean waves, cloud formations, the behavior of animals. What was not divine was an earthly sign. Noisy flocks of 'alalā screaming down from the uplands of the gods and across the lowland villages warned that lava from Mauna Loa was on its way, and ancient Hawaiians knew that when the wiliwili bloomed along the coast, sharks would bite.

In line with these beliefs, the early Hawaiians based land management on both scientific and anecdotal knowledge. And their practical understanding of natural phenomena merged with their spiritual beliefs. This blend of mind and spirit, antithetical to most Western approaches to natural resource management, brought me to the heart of the question about efforts to preserve the 'alalā. In the Hawaiian view, did the presence of the sacred in the 'alalā and other animals bestow upon them a powerful, implicit claim to existence? If the 'alalā's spiritually fortified existence did contribute to its preservation in the old days, could such intangible values likewise help in modern times—given half a chance? Have such beliefs been permanently supplanted by the traditional Western view that animals are objects first and beings last—if at all? Or is the whole notion of "spiritual ecology"—the belief that spiritual values drove conservation among the early Hawaiians and other indigenous peoples — our own romance with what never was? Such questions haunted me because whatever conservation values most of us practice today, they are insufficient to save many other vanishing species. Without a fundamentally different model of belief — and behavior — what possible hope can we offer to the ʻalalā, to other species, or to ourselves?

I thought, with some comfort, about the *seemingly* secular foundations of our own Endangered Species Act of 1973 (ESA). While on the surface the law can be overwhelmingly technical, a closer look reveals a faint echo within it that bestows upon all plants and animals, no matter how small, a powerful right to exist. The law does not say, "Save only those species from which we stand to materially benefit"; it says to save them regardless of the cost. The ESA, as Holmes Rolston III said, is "a congressional resolution that the nation and its people ought to live as compatibly as they can with the fauna and flora of their continent (and abroad), and it deplores the fact that we are now not doing so."

While I knew that many of my questions would never be fully answered, I felt that the complex values reflected in the ancient Hawaiian code of behavior toward the land and the many animals that dwelled thereon might, if nothing else, yield scattered insights into the struggles of our dark time of vanishing species. The questions could help me to better understand the global web of social, ecological, and political forces in which so many vanishing species like the ʻalalā are trapped.

In the traditional Hawaiian world, four major gods reigned: Kāne, god of sunlight and freshwater; Lono, god of harvest, peace, fertility, and the winter wet season, who spoke as thunder, lightning, and rain; Kū, god of war and chiefs; and Kanaloa, god of the ocean, whose breathing created the tides.

These major gods were composed of a multitude of lesser ones, many of whom were ancestral spirits known as ʻaumākua.

Hawaiians addressed these spirits not in fear but as respected, dependable compatriots in life. Unlike the more powerful gods, 'aumākua were actual members of one's family. They were also guides to the afterlife.

Ancestral spirits could assume many forms, including birds, sharks, turtles, limpets, mud hens, lizards, eels, field mice, caterpillars, even wind or rocks. To do physical harm to or to eat one's 'aumakua could bring death. A family had several or even many different 'aumākua. The 'alalā would most likely have been 'aumākua for those families whose ancestors lived in Kona or Ka'ū, the only districts where the bird itself lived. It would very likely have been the 'aumakua of those whose professional trades — such as canoe making — regularly took them into the high forests of the 'alalā.

The omnipresent 'aumākua guided nearly every act and thought. For early Hawaiians it was kapu, or forbidden, to hit anyone in the face or head because that was the body's entrance for good spirits, including 'aumākua. Picking a blossom from the 'ōhi'a tree or other plant required a prayer for dispensation, lest the act offend a lesser god. Hence, there were myriad prayers for fishing, planting, harvesting taro, cutting certain trees, even burying a newborn's umbilical cord.

The divine presence in trees and elsewhere in the natural world evoked reverence, as well as fear of potential punishment — these gods could deliver both reward and retribution — that may have mitigated exploitation of the island's resources. The possibility of retribution must have permeated Hawaiians' thinking. After all, they believed themselves related to the land through Earth Mother Papahānaumoku and Sky Father Wākea, whose union gave birth to the islands. They believed that Earth nurtures and feeds people as a mother nurses her child; the Hawaiian word for land, 'āina, comes from 'ai, "to eat." The term aloha 'āina, "love of the land," implies a deep physical dependence. The phrase's existence in thousands of ancient Hawaiian sayings suggests that these feelings for land as family are part of an ancient Hawaiian core of beliefs.

As much as religious belief, practical experience and knowledge were core to how Hawaiians managed natural resources. In ancient times Hawaiians divided the islands into narrow, pie-shaped slivers running from near the sea toward the center of each island. Because these slices, or ahupua'a, traversed a range of topologies — sometimes all the way from the ocean to the highlands — each offered a cross section of resources, including products of coastline, lower cropland, and highland forest. This meant that the families, no matter what part of the ahupua'a they happened to live on, had fish, crops, and forest resources. These large tracts also reduced the likelihood that the land would become ever more fragmented in the future. Each ahupua'a was overseen by a highly skilled land management expert, or kahuna. In the Hawaiian view, technical training and expertise alone did not make kāhuna; they needed to possess practical knowledge, wisdom, and spiritual strength.

It was technical expertise and hard work that turned the wet valleys into fields of kalo, or taro, a root crop that became a staple of which the Hawaiians reportedly developed three hundred distinct varieties. Hawaiians integrated bananas, sugarcane, and other basic crops into the kalo paddies — not to mention several species of fish, much as ancient Chinese agriculture integrated carp production into rice paddies. Every stage of kalo planting, harvesting, and production was ushered in with chants or prayers. And so it was with other crops, such as the sweet potato.

Practical and spiritual considerations in land use were supplemented by strict laws, or kapu, that regulated the use of natural resources. Fishing for some species was banned during spawning. Laws set certain places, such as the upland forested realm of the gods, off-limits to ordinary Hawaiians. Before a canoe kahuna went into the highland forest home of the 'alalā to find a tree for a canoe, he spent days preparing spiritually, and his chosen party would enter the godly realm with ceremony and offerings, including pigs, coconuts, red fish, and 'awa, a sacred drink derived from the root of the 'awa plant. Once the gods had ordained the visit, the kahuna and his canoe-making party took signs from the forest birds. If an 'alalā or an 'elepaio was seen scouring a koa tree or flecking off bark in search of insects underneath, the kahuna might deem the tree unsound.

With a conservation ethic based upon spirituality, knowledge, and law, Hawaiians managed to keep these ever-changing islands productive for more than 1,500 years before the Europeans arrived in the late 1700s. Indeed, the visitors were amazed by the abundant crops, wild-caught or gathered food, and other resources that supported thriving villages and a burgeoning population. But if the nature-loving Hawaiians of the Kumulipo were not living in perfect paradise when the first Europeans arrived, it could well be—to borrow Alan Moorhead's phrase—that they were happier than they would ever be again. And the 'alalā living in the highlands of restricted human use had little to fear.

c h a p t e r 3

CAPTAIN COOK

I N JULY 1776, TWO
ships departed from England, bound for the Cape of Good Hope
and on into the Pacific, where they would seek a shorter route
between Asia and England by way of the legendary Northwest
Passage. As charged by the Admiralty, upon each landfall the
explorers were "to observe the nature of the soil, and the products
thereof; the beasts and fowls that inhabit or frequent it . . . you are
to bring home specimens of each . . . that we may cause proper
examination and experiments to be made of them."

In early 1779, the *Resolution* and the *Discovery* reached Kealakekua Bay, on the southernmost island of a mid-Pacific archipelago.
Save for one stretch of sandy beach, the bay's shoreline consisted
mostly of black rock and a sheer precipice that rose nearly a thousand feet. At the bay's southern end the explorers saw several
grass huts tucked in groves of coconut palms near the village of
Kekua, which today is known as Nāpōʻopoʻo. The smaller village
of Kaʻawaloa stood at the northern end of the beach. On the higher
land beyond each end of the cliff rose tiers of hills where rock walls
partitioned cultivated fields. In the uplands, grass huts were
scattered among palm groves, and in the higher hills grew trees

that the explorers recognized as breadfruit. Still farther inland they found numerous kukui trees, whose nuts and wood were being used for making everything from candles and leis to canoes; paper mulberry trees, from whose bark kapa cloth was made; pili grass for thatching dwellings; ti for food wrapping, rain capes, sandals, and thatching; and bamboo. Fields of sweet potato, dryland taro, and other cultivated crops may well have covered more than sixty square miles, from the bay as far north as Kailua, nearly twenty miles away.

Countless canoes filled with the curious greeted the ships. So many Hawaiians climbed up the side of the *Discovery* that the ship began to heel over. Some chiefs and a high priest, Koa, eventually came aboard. Later that evening, the priest escorted Captain James Cook to shore, while other members of the crew set up iron instruments and an observatory in a sweet potato patch and began collecting specimens of plants and birds to be described and classified once they reached natural history museums in England and continental Europe. There the specimens could be disassembled, as if they were clocks, and each part measured and described. To the visitors, these specimens were reducible objects of nature, not ineffable vessels of spirit, as the Hawaiians saw them.

Cook was escorted to a temple, or heiau, at the southern end of the bay, consisting of a large mound of stones about twenty yards wide and forty yards long, with a top paved with flat stones and surrounded by a railing whose posts were crowned with twenty human skulls. Below the temple's northern wall was a sacred stone-lined pool. Koa laid a red cloth over Cook's shoulders, stepped back, and handed him a pig. The priests then bestowed upon Cook the rare honor of chanting to him the story of Hawaiian creation, including the birth of the 'alalā and all of Hawai'i's other animals and plants. This was, tradition holds, the Kumulipo, the lengthy chant of more than six hundred lines, not including a genealogy of chiefs that contained more than a thousand names.

This would have marked the first time in the 1,500-year human habitation of the islands that the word 'alalā fell upon the ears of westerners. So began the bird's remarkable journey from a shining spiritual presence within an isolated Pacific culture to a sharply demarcated object within Western intellect and scientific thought.

Only days after first hearing its name, westerners saw the raven for the first time when James King, an officer on the *Resolution*, came upon two 'alalā kept as pets in the village of Kekua. King tried to buy them, perhaps as scientific specimens, but the Hawaiians warned him "not to hurt or offend them." The Hawaiians, King related, "refus[ed] everything I offered for them." He wrote that the ravens were "kept about their houses, & they had some superstitious notions about them, for they calld one an Eatooa." *Eatooa* was probably King's rendering of the Hawaiian *he akua*, "a god," which would include an 'aumakua. "I am led to believe," wrote King, who had witnessed elsewhere in the Pacific a similar adoration of particular birds, "that the same custom prevails here; and that, probably, the raven is the object of it."

The Europeans' view of the raven was so different from the Hawaiians' that it might as well have been a different species. When King recorded his encounter with the raven in the ship's log, the bird was abstracted from everyday experience and rendered for the first time as mediated by written characters, *a-l-a-l-a*. These letters, recorded in unalterable ink symbols upon a page, tended to divorce the bird from its living presence. And so perception of the bird began to subtly change. Within the oral Hawaiian culture, the 'alalā was a daily revelation. To the westerners, it was more of a static object to be studied for what it was, and, to them, always would be — a species of bird. And what would become of a bird torn from the context of spirit and belief in which it had, for more than a thousand years, existed and evolved in the Hawaiian mind?

After several days of exploring the lowlands and shore, several parties of the European visitors hiked up the slopes of Mauna Loa.

They confirmed that the lower elevations thrived with cultivated breadfruit trees, plantains, sweet potatoes, taro, gingerroot, and sugarcane. Climbing still higher five or six miles inland, they saw cultivation decreasing and breadfruit and other trees intermingling at the edge of the native forests.

In the forests, the visitors "shot a number of fine birds of the liveliest and most variegated plumage that any of us had ever met with." Along the way they met bird hunters who captured their prey by coating branches with a gluey substance made from juice of the "Kepaw" (pāpala kēpau) tree and breadfruit. The visitors managed to secure a few specimens from the bird catchers, who collected birds for food or for brightly colored feathers to use in ceremonies or in making cloaks or leis. Feathers from an estimated eighty thousand mamo, or black Hawaiian honey creeper, would be used to complete the feather cloak of Kamehameha the Great—he was a young man at the time of Cook's arrival—and as many as two hundred birds were required for a single small feather lei.

It is not known how well those birds that were captured and plucked of their feathers fared upon release. In many cases, they may have been plucked completely—the different colors of feathers put to various purposes—and the birds' flesh eaten, given that many of the old descriptions from the bird catchers end with the Hawaiian phrase meaning "They were delicious!" Perhaps, when faced with a declining number of forest birds because of overhunting, Kamehameha the Great ordered plucked birds to be released—for he is said to have proclaimed at some point during his reign, "The feathers belong to me, but the birds themselves belong to my heirs."

By most accounts, Cook and his crew had a paradisaical sojourn at Kealakekua Bay in those early weeks in 1779, having arrived during the thanksgiving festival of Makahiki, presided over by the god Lono. After spending nearly three weeks at Kealakekua Bay, in

February 1779 the ships left. Encountering foul weather a few days later, however, the *Resolution* sprung her foremast and had to return to Kealakekua for repairs. This time, the two ships were met by no jubilant crowd, perhaps because the festival had ended and the respect—if not adoration—that had been afforded Cook had ended with it. The bay was nearly deserted, and the cordial relations between the hosts and the visitors were about to end.

The crew accused a Hawaiian of stealing some blacksmith's tongs and a chisel from the *Discovery*. After the tools were recovered, Cook's men seized the canoe of the accused thief. As it happened, the canoe belonged to the chief Palea, who had just come ashore after a visit to the ship. Denying that he had stolen the articles, the chief tried to get his canoe back. A sailor then struck him on the head with an oar.

The next morning, Sunday, February 14, Captain Clerke of the *Discovery* noticed that his large cutter was missing. Cook schemed to take the great chief Kalaniopu'u hostage until the cutter was returned. As they were escorting him to the *Resolution* under the pretense of a friendly visit, one of Kalaniopu'u's favorite wives intervened, crying and begging her husband not to go. Kalaniopu'u sat down on the ground about thirty yards from the water. Because a crowd of several thousand Hawaiians had gathered on the beach, Cook abandoned his hostage-taking plan. More trouble loomed: a native messenger from across the bay brought news that some sailors had fired upon a chief. As the messenger carried the report to the village of Ka'awaloa, at the northern end of the beach, fighting began. Cook's men fired, and Cook himself killed a man. When the explorers stopped to reload their muskets, the Hawaiians attacked. As Cook headed to the water, he was struck from behind and stabbed in the back of the neck. He fell facedown in the shallows, where he was stabbed again and clubbed to death.

Several days later, the crew having recovered only a few charred bones of their former captain, the *Resolution* and *Discovery* sailed for England. In addition to dispirited sailors and the remains of their famous commander, on board were more than 120 crates of bird skins and other specimens that had been collected during the Pacific expedition. Somewhere among these was a specimen with glossy black feathers and black wings and tail, with a toe tag that identified it as a "Tropic Crow" from the island of "Owhyhee."

c h a p t e r 4

FOR LOVE
OF THE GODS

N O LONGER A CHAIN
of emerald islands lost in the vast Pacific, after Cook Hawai'i
became a regular port of call for whaling ships and other vessels.
This infusion of foreigners happened to occur as the traditional
laws and mores of the Hawaiians had begun to falter as a result of
internal strife. Economics, politics, religious beliefs, and culture
at every level were altered in the decades that followed. With
these transformations came a profound change in the land itself.
As entrepreneurs began to mine the forests for sweet-smelling
sandalwood and other products, a group of missionaries set sail
for Hawai'i from Massachusetts on the *Thaddeus*, destined to rescue native islands from their nature-worshipping ways. Among
the beliefs the newcomers brought was their own creation story.

   In the beginning this time, there were no limpets or dolphins,
only a lonely abyss swept by a mighty wind. The missionaries' God
made night and day. He made fruit trees and the moon and stars,
and into the seas he put monsters. He made cattle and reptiles,

birds and wild things. It was a creation story that, while filled with animals, spoke not of kinship and the spiritual standing of animals but of human dominion.

In the Christian creation story, God did not inhabit features of the world. But he did create the world, and it therefore belonged to him; the animals and plants were not God; they were *God's*. In the end, perhaps what most separated the beliefs of the missionaries from those of the Hawaiians was the concept of possession or ownership—an apostrophe, so to speak. To the missionaries, this distinction was the difference between worshipping nature idols and honoring the sacred presence. If the world belonged to God, he was free to bequeath it to his children, who then gained rightful dominion—or domination—over Earth. Ownership offered a sense of superiority and a confidence to dominate the natural world that Hawaiians apparently lacked.

For better or worse, these were the views upon which much of Western culture was based—a world that I myself had inherited. It was a pervasive view that, if I could never fully and truly escape, I was determined to at least peer beyond and experience, with the help of the ʻalalā.

Far from being honored as a guardian of the human spirit, the ʻalalā and all other animals adored by the Hawaiians would over time become spiritually demoted in the period of Christian conversion. They would in effect be purged of their godliness and therefore, at least in the eyes of many Hawaiians, of their greatest significance. Lacking a spiritual sheen, the ʻalalā would be relegated to a kind of lower world.

Upon their arrival into this nature-worshipping culture, the missionaries rejoiced in song, offering a taste of what was to come:

Wake, Isles of the South! your redemption is near,
No longer repose in the borders of gloom;
The strength of his chosen in love shall appear

. . . .
The heathen will hasten to welcome the time,
The day spring, the prophet in vision once saw,
When the beams of Messiah will 'lumine each clime,
And the isles of the ocean shall wait for his law.

Hiram Bingham, an ordained minister from Vermont, wrote of his arrival, "The appearance of destitution, degradation, and barbarism, among the chattering, and almost naked savages, whose heads and feet, and much of their sunburnt swarthy skins, were bare, was appalling. Some of our number, with gushing tears, turned away from the spectacle. Others, with firmer nerve, continued their gaze, but were ready to exclaim, 'Can these be human beings!'"

Among those aboard the *Thaddeus* were two native Hawaiians who had earlier made their way to the United States on the whaling or merchant ships that by then regularly called at the islands. Both had become devout Christians and were eager to return to their native land to share their faith. One, Thomas Hopu, among Hawai'i's first Christian converts, would become an influential voice for the newly arrived missionaries.

As the *Thaddeus* anchored in the waters off the village of Kawaihae, some thirty-five miles north of where Cook had anchored in Kealakekua Bay, Hopu went ashore and proclaimed, "These white people are kahunas of the most high God who have come to tell us of the One who made heaven and Earth. Hereafter will come the great day when all will be judged before God."

The timing of their arrival must have struck the missionaries as miraculous. Only a few months before, the Hawaiian king Kamehameha the Great, whom Cook had met years earlier when the future king was a young man, had died. As an ardent defender of Hawaiian traditions against the simmering rebelliousness of some in the younger generation, he might have imprisoned or expelled the proselytizers. But when Kamehameha's son Liholiho had assumed power, several months before the *Thaddeus* arrived, he, now free of the old ruler, ordered Hawaiians to abandon their old beliefs and destroy their temples. The missionaries' work was half done. Even the major temple at Puʻukoholā, built by Kamehameha the Great near Kawaihae, had just been pillaged, within sight of where the *Thaddeus* would soon anchor.

The newly arrived missionaries wasted no time in reshaping Hawaiian perspectives on life, spirituality, and the world. They dismissed the Hawaiian deities as "little gods who made not heaven and earth." As a first step in bringing Christianity to the natives, the missionaries redefined Kāne, Kū, and Lono as the Holy Trinity. The presence of a fourth major god, Kanaloa, might have posed a problem in theological transition — until the missionaries turned him into the devil.

Whereas Hawaiians had always honored their gods by feasting, the missionaries introduced fasting, although hunger, to the Hawaiians, was synonymous with hell. The hula, a sensuous dance and a ritualized reflection of the divine and, often, of the lilting movements of palm trees or ocean waves, was prohibited.

The missionaries discouraged or banned other spiritual interactions with lesser gods as well. Without this infusion of revelation from everyday encounters with the ʻalalā and other animals, the Hawaiians' source of spirituality slowly shifted from life to written Christian texts, which the Hawaiians soon memorized or learned to read. The fire of mysticism that had molded their spiritual imaginations faded to embers of original belief. As the scholar Martha Beckwith wrote in the 1930s, "It is highly probable that the almost complete absence of cosmic imagination already noticed is due to suppression under the influence of the hard-headed incredulity of the literal-minded English and Americans who became their mentors."

A hallmark of the traditional Hawaiian way of life was absence

of explicit property ownership. This permeated Hawaiians' atti-
tude toward land, which was the child of Sky Father Wākea and
Earth Mother Papahānaumoku, who were the ancestors of
humans. And how could one buy or sell one's own ancestors?

The missionaries considered an individual's ability to own, buy,
and sell land not only a right but virtually a religious value. In 1848,
less than three decades after the *Thaddeus* arrived, Calvinist missionaries helped to oversee the distribution of land into private
ownership. During the so-called Great Mahele, ordinary Hawaiians received about 3 acres of land each, while each missionary
could claim up to 560 acres. The island's ten high chiefs, twenty-
four lesser chiefs, and two hundred or so land stewards were all
required to give half of the lands they managed to the missionaries.
Most of this land was then sold to foreigners. And what foreigners
did not own they came to largely control. By 1893, non-Hawaiians
owned or controlled 90 percent of the lands of Hawai'i.

Privatization of property, in turn, gave rise to plantations and
other commercial enterprises that directly benefited missionary
families. Within a generation or two of the *Thaddeus*' arrival, at
least one direct descendant of a missionary sat on the board of
each of the island's five largest sugar companies. By 1910, the same
five sugar companies controlled 75 percent of the sugar crop. Some
twenty years later, they controlled 96 percent. These companies
ultimately came to control nearly every business associated with
sugar, including banks, insurance companies, utilities, and mer-
chandising, not to mention railroads and shipping.

The Hawaiian historian S. M. Kamakau wrote in the mid-
1800s, with understandable resentment, that many descendants
of the missionaries "have bought land and become owners of stock
farms and sugar plantations and have made slaves out of some of
the people with work. . . . The Hawaiian people welcome the
stranger freely; rich and poor, high and low give what they can. The
strangers call this love ignorance and think it is good for nothing.

The love upon which they depend is a love based upon bargaining, good for nothing but rubbish blown upon the wind."

In 1848, a scant thirty years after the *Thaddeus'* arrival and the ensuing onslaught of whaling, merchant, and military ships and disease, one observer lamented,

> It can scarcely be said that there is any Native population at all. The hill sides and the banks of watercourses show for miles the ruins of the "olden time"—Stone walls half sunk in the ground, broken down and covered with grass.—large broken squares of trees and imperfect embankments.—remains of old taro patches and water runs now dried up and useless, and many other such tokens that like old coins—old Castles and old books, impress one with a melancholy curiosity about a people that cannot now be found.

Had all earlier convictions of the 'alalā as 'aumakua vanished in this cultural upheaval and its aftermath? Had the sacred 'alalā long since been replaced by the simplified avian object of field guides and natural history museums? Not long after my first visit to see the 'alalā on McCandless Ranch, I began to find out.

It made sense to concentrate on regions where the 'alalā lived— leeward Mauna Loa. Despite countless phone calls and numerous conversations, I could find not a trace of living knowledge of the raven's spiritual significance. Discouraged, one morning I sat on the shore of Kealakekua Bay near the ruins of the temple where the priests were said to have recited the Kumulipo to Captain James Cook more than two centuries ago. Today Nāpō'opo'o is a collection of modest homes, with the spires of two Christian churches rising above the palms; only remnants of the temple's eastern and southern retaining walls remain. Stiff grass grew from the mud at the edge of what was once a sacred pool. An upholstered sofa, minus seat cushions, was half submerged in stagnant green water.

At the northern end of the beach stands a small white monolith marking the occasion of Cook's death. I was amazed to find myself standing amid ruins at this very spot, where the Kumulipo had been recited to Cook. Stones endure; beliefs do not.

It happened to be a Sunday morning, and soon the bell chimed at Kahikolu Congregational Church, not far away across the bay. Taking this as an opportunity to continue my heretofore fruitless quest, I drove over to find a picturesque stone and white plaster structure behind some trees. Men in bright flowered shirts and women in mu'umu'u had just begun to enter. Inside, the congregants sang "He Hemolele 'Oe, Iehova"—the Hawaiian version of "Holy! Holy! Holy!"—as two guitars and a ukulele were strummed.

Then the minister entered. There was much singing and holding of hands among the congregants as the minister took the podium, each side of which was graced by spear-shaped kāhili, or feather standards. For the next half hour the minister spoke of love and trust. The service included the ordination of three new deacons. Afterward, the congregants filed out and gathered in an open-air hall adjoining the church for lunch. It was there that I met a woman named Joanna Gaspar, whose family's roots stretched back many years in the area.

"My grandmother lived in Ka'awaloa before the town was abandoned," she told me, speaking of the town that had stood at the bay's northern end before it was abandoned at the beginning of World War II. "I've heard of the 'alalā being 'aumākua for some people, but I don't know any still alive." Then she added, with a hint of defensiveness, "Besides, Christianity has replaced the old beliefs!"

Gaspar directed me to Elsie Thompson, a woman in her eighties, who sat at one of the long lunch tables. Her maiden name was Ackerman and she had grown up at Kealakekua Bay, although she now lived in Keālia, several miles south, she said. "The 'alalā was ʻaumakua for my father-in-law," she said. "He's passed away. He talked about the ʻalalā, but not a whole lot. I never asked him about it. It was a personal thing."

I spoke to several other parishioners, each one with seemingly less information to offer. After the gathering, I left the churchyard with the lilt of Hawaiian hymns still running through my mind. My gaze up the lower flanks of Mauna Loa evoked vivid memories of the ʻalalā from my earlier visit. So little left, indeed.

As I sat there once again, not far from where James King had first witnessed the ʻalalā more than two centuries earlier, echoes of the Kumulipo being chanted in the temple seemed to emerge. In coming here to try to discover the pre-Western concept of the ʻalalā and to understand the bird's re-creation in the Western mind, I had arrived at the place where the ancient story of the ʻalalā seemed to have all but ended and where the modern began.

chapter 5

PANIOLO, HŌKŪ, AND MAHOA

SOME SIX MONTHS, thousands of miles, and many hours of research and contemplation have passed since I first saw the wild 'alalā on Mauna Loa. Today, memories of the ravens drift through my mind like falling leaves. Scarcely a day passes without a thought of them, no more so than now. Donna Ball, the biologist we met on our way down the mountain back in May, has just e-mailed: "Paniolo has vanished and we've given him up for lost. Haven't found a trace. We have no cause of death, but we suspect an 'io." I am brought back to her earlier warning, "Everyone knows there will be some bad news along the way. It's heartbreaking, but we do our best not to lose heart." Only thirteen 'alalā—five wild and eight captive-reared— now remain in the wild.

She soon writes again with more news: "A biologist found the carcass of Hōkū partially pulled through a small entrance at the base of a large boulder, possibly a rat or mongoose den. . . . The transmitter was found nearby. The head, both wings, tail and a large portion of body feathers were recovered, but many of the ribs, along with both feet, were missing." Twelve 'alalā—five wild and seven captive-reared—now live in the wild.

With each reported death, memories of that magical day in May return: a spreading fan of black feathers sweeping from branch to branch, silhouetted against a break in the sun-dappled canopy; 'alalā playing musical branches, stepping into midair and sailing upward in a gentle arc to the next perch. Paniolo cocking his head to gaze down at us, swooping overhead, and arcing up again to land in another 'ōhi'a.

And the bad news continues. Ball writes in early 1997: "Mahoa is gone. A large cat was also caught in a trap placed near the kill-site the night following the carcass recovery."

Three 'alalā deaths just between late 1996 and early 1997; two—possibly all three—caused by 'io attacks. I open my notebook and sadly strike out the names of Paniolo, Hōkū, and Mahoa. Now only eleven 'alalā—five wild and six captive-reared—remain in the wild.

At some point—usually long before all the individuals are gone—a species becomes functionally extinct. In some cases, this is because the survivors are too old to reproduce. More often, as the remaining individuals pass away, the gene pool becomes so small that the species risks becoming inbred, with offspring lacking the vigor and genetic diversity to carry the species into the future. With each death, how much closer to that threshold has the raven moved?

Hilu

Nānū

Mahoa

Hōkū

Umi's Descendants

Kalāhiki Pair

Hiwahiwa

Ho'okena Pair

Lokahi

(died in 1995)

Keālia Pair

Paniolo

Noe

The Bachelor

Kehau

'ALALĀ FAMILY TREE
January 1997

chapter 6

SEARCHING FOR
THE 'ALALĀ

IN EARLY SPRING OF
1997, a year after my first visit to see the 'alalā and 198 years after
the *Resolution* and *Discovery* arrived back in England with thousands of specimens from the third Pacific voyage, I boarded an
Amtrak train in New York City and headed to the Academy of
Natural Sciences in Philadelphia, once a world center for the study
of natural history, to learn more about the "tropic crow" said to
have been procured on Hawai'i Island.

That particular specimen had long since been lost somewhere
in Europe. Fortunately, before the "tropic crow" was lost, several
descriptions of it were published, and several of the works that
contain the description are housed at the academy's library. Upon
arrival, I set to work at one of the long wooden tables, filled out
several book request forms, and handed them to the librarian. Ten
minutes later, she rolled out the first book on a heavy wooden dolly
and presented me with a pair of white cotton gloves to use when
handling the fragile works.

I opened the 1781 book by John Latham called *A General Synopsis of Birds*. Latham, who lived from 1740 to 1837, was a practicing surgeon at Dartford, England, when he undertook his decade-long project to describe the birds then known to Western science. For this work, Latham, using the "Tropic Crow" from the collection of Sir Joseph Banks, described this species scientifically for the first time:

> LENGTH twelve inches and a half. Bill an inch and a quarter in length; at the base pretty broad, and the tips of both mandibles notched: the plumage is of a glossy black above, but of a dull black on the underparts: the wings and tail are black with a gloss of green; the last rounded: vent and side feathers tipped with dusky white: legs and claws black. From O-why-hee, one of the *Sandwich Islands*, in the South Seas.

Several years later, German naturalist Johann Friedrich Gmelin undertook a work even more ambitious than Latham's. Gmelin would seek to create an "improved, corrected, and enlarged" edition of *Systema Naturae*, by his famous mentor, the taxonomist Carl Linnaeus. Gmelin's work had a bemusing, moralizing introduction — a common practice of scientific writers of the time. Only much later did its prophetic relevance to the modern story of the 'alalā become clear:

> Man is placed at the head of the animal creation . . . who has power of changing his place upon earth at pleasure; and who has dominion over all other creatures on the face of the globe. . . . Instead of following that which . . . is right . . . instead of endeavoring to secure those things which are most advantageous and truly beneficial, he, infatuated by the smiles of fortune, anxiously collects her gaudy trifles for future enjoyment, and neglects her real benefits; he is driven to madness by envious snarlers; he persecutes with hatred the truly religious for differing from himself in speculative opinions; he excites numberless broils, not that he may do good, but for a purpose that even himself is ignorant of.

Gmelin does eventually describe the "Tropic Crow," but his rendition is almost verbatim from Latham's description. Latham himself, meanwhile, had outlived his fortune, and at the ripe age of eighty-one, desperate for an income, had begun another work on birds, this one even more ambitious than his earlier work. Published between 1821 and 1828, *A General History of Birds* would became a touchstone for generations of ornithologists. By its inclusion in this influential work, the "Tropic Crow" from "O-why-hee" had been given an enduring presence in the scientific literature. But, as accident would have it, the ʻalalā actually had not yet arrived.

Latham's descriptions of the Tropic Crow had struck ornithologists as peculiar. By then, it was assumed that only one crowlike bird lived on Hawaiʻi Island at the time of Cook's arrival—the ʻalalā. And from everything that ornithologists had subsequently learned about it, its wings did not have "a gloss of green," nor were the "vent and side-feathers tipped with dusky white," as was the so-called Tropic Crow. The average ʻalalā was about twice as long as the specimen Latham described. Whatever the Tropic Crow was, it wasn't an ʻalalā, and it hadn't come from the Hawaiian Islands. The toe tag of the crowlike specimen brought back by the Cook expedition had apparently misrepresented the place of its collection.

In fact, Cook's third Pacific expedition did not procure a specimen of the ʻalalā. After all, the Hawaiians had admonished one of Cook's officers for trying to purchase two tame birds at Kealakekua Bay. Aside from the few words about the ʻalalā found in the journals of this expedition, firsthand knowledge of the sacred raven would remain with the Hawaiians alone for decades to come.

Not until 1825—some forty years after Cook's visit—would another ornithological "investigation" of the islands take place, lifting the birdlife there from more than forty years of scientific neglect. The forty-six-gun frigate HMS *Blonde*, commanded by Lord George Byron, a cousin of the poet, had come to Hawaiʻi to return the bodies of the Hawaiian king Kamehameha's heir, Liholiho—the breaker of the kapu—and his wife to their homeland. Both had contracted fatal cases of measles while visiting England.

Aboard the ship was the "somewhat of a naturalist" Andrew Bloxam, who would collect twenty-five different kinds of birds there. He later published an account of the voyage that included the first list of all Hawaiian bird species known to westerners at the time. What might have been a landmark contribution turned out, however, to be so mistake ridden that a later ornithologist would declare it "a disgrace to all concerned, since, so far from advancing the knowledge of the subject, it introduced so much confusion as to mislead many subsequent writers." While Bloxam listed the ʻalalā, he had not collected one. Half a century after Cook's departure from the islands, an actual specimen of the ʻalalā had yet to make it across the Pacific, and its presence in the scientific literature remained obscured by error and doubt.

A little more than a decade after the *Blonde* expedition, J. K. Townsend, a private collector from Philadelphia, traveled to Hawaiʻi and managed to procure a true specimen of the ʻalalā from the missionary Cochran Forbes, in February 1837. Back in Philadelphia, Townsend was apparently unaware that he held a ticket to ornithological fame—that is, the chance to describe a new species.

At the time, Europe was the global center for the study of natural history. It was from Europe that virtually all major natural history explorations were mounted, and it was in museums of England, Germany, and elsewhere on the continent that almost all the specimens were housed for further study. In the United States, the Academy of Natural Sciences of Philadelphia was already one of the premier American institutions for the study of the natural sciences. But it wasn't until 1838 — nearly sixty years after Cook's famed exploration of the Pacific — that the United States challenged the superiority of European exploration. This was a four-year voyage to the Pacific, spearheaded by the U.S. Navy, called the United States South Seas Surveying and Exploring Expedition.

The USS *Peacock* was one of several ships in the fleet, and aboard it was American naturalist and artist Titian Peale. While in Hawai'i he managed to procure several specimens of the 'alalā, apparently unaware that Townsend had also gotten one the year before. One can only imagine Peale's delight and enthusiasm in looking forward to one of the golden moments of any naturalist's life: publishing the first account of a species. But in July 1841, several months after departing Hawai'i, Peale's ship foundered in a storm at Cape Disappointment, at the mouth of the Columbia River. He and the crew survived, but the *Peacock* and thousands of its scientific specimens — including the 'alalā — did not.

After returning to Philadelphia and Washington, D.C., Peale received Townsend's 'alalā specimens. Peale published the description of the bird in his 1848 account of the expedition, *Mammalia and Ornithology*. But deep professional and personal disappointment followed what should have been the height of Peale's career.

After some reverie into the distant past, my senses returned to the books before me. The library's copy of *Mammalia and Ornithology* is a large volume with a rough black spine and a deep blue-green and black mottled cover. "Extremely rare book," the librarian whispered, almost daring me to touch it with my bare hands. "Not even the Library of Congress has a copy."

A trace of gold lettering was still visible on the cracked spine. I opened the volume, quite by chance, directly to page 106: "'Alalā of the Hawaiians." The account began with the customary Latin description, followed by the English. With words like *irides* (plural of iris) and *setaceous* (bristlelike in form or texture), parts of the description might as well have been in Latin:

In form like the Raven; colour nearly uniform, sooty brown; the quills somewhat lighter; all the feathers of the body lead-coloured at the roots; bill, legs, and claws, blue-black; irides brown; setaceous feathers, covering the nostrils, black and glossy; three first quills graduated, fourth longer; shafts black above, white beneath; tail rounded, consisting of twelve feathers; shaft black above, sooty beneath.

One specimen measures 18⅞ inches total length; bill, 2³/₁₀ inches; tarsus, 2½ inches; hind claw, ⁸/₁₀ inch. Male? A second: total length, 17¼ inches; bill, 2 inches; tarsus, 2²/₁₀ inches. Female?

Peale bestowed on the bird a scientific name: *Corvus hawaiiensis*, or Hawaiian Crow. So it was, I mused, some seventy years after Cook's journey to Hawai'i that the actual 'alalā had finally made its first appearance in Western scientific literature. And with its first mention in this literature, the 'alalā was well along its circuitous journey through Western scientific thought.

Peale continued with his description of the 'alalā:

Like most of its congeners, this species is noisy; its voice closely resembles that of the North American Fish-crow, C. ossifragus. It was observed in small societies on the Island of Hawaii, where it is known to the natives by the name of 'alalā. They frequent the woody districts of the interior, seldom, if ever, visiting the coast. We noticed that the smaller species of birds were kept in great terror by the presence of the 'alalā: from this we infer that, like other crows, they will rob nests of their eggs, and when an opportunity offers, eat the old birds also: such is their character as given to us by the natives.

The specimens were obtained a few miles inland from the village Kaawaloa, celebrated as being the spot where the renowned Captain Cook was killed: — a camera lucida sketch is introduced on our plate, as a background to the bird. Our specimens, collected by the Expedition, of the Hawaiian Crow, or 'alalā, with many important notes attached, were lost in the wreck of the U.S. Ship Peacock; but we are happy to acknowledge our obligations to Mr. J.K. Townsend, who has kindly loaned us others, collected at the same place, and sent to him by the Rev. Mr. Forbes, missionary at Karakakoa Bay.

No sooner were the first few copies of *Mammalia and Ornithology* published than more troubles began. Charles Wilkes, commander of the U.S. Exploring Expedition, was competing to have his own account published in a book authored by John Cassin. Angry that Peale not only had beat him to the press but also had published an unauthorized account of the expedition, Wilkes managed to have Peale's publication suppressed. Consequently, today Peale's *Mammalia and Ornithology* is one of the rarest of all books, while Cassin's version remains the voyage's official account.

Wilkes accused Peale of being little more than a practiced observer of nature rather than a true scientist or trained taxonomist. Indeed, Peale was a naturalist, a layman's profession that would be increasingly criticized for lack of empiricism. During the second half of the nineteenth century, the once highly respected profession of the American naturalist had come to be seen by many scientists as an amateur's trade. Sadly, Peale's standing went the way of his fading profession, and no amount of quality or originality on Peale's part could, in that climate, compensate for his lacking academic credentials. The battles between the specialist and the generalist, in which Wilkes and Peale were engaged, would linger, even to reemerge in the bitter disputes that would inflame the history of the 'alalā in the century to come.

Nevertheless, as Cassin himself mentions in his introduction, in his own account with Wilkes he relies heavily on Peale's observations of the voyage. Indeed, he depends upon Peale's descriptions for almost every entry, and his description of the 'alalā is taken almost verbatim from *Mammalia and Ornithology*. Cassin's account, however, has an appendix and additional plates and is supplemented with notes from another naturalist on the expedition, making the account the more comprehensive of the two.

The loss of Peale's specimens, the suppression of his book, his failure to secure his longed-for curatorial appointment to the Smithsonian Institution in Washington, D.C., and the illness and death of his wife, daughter, and young son, all within a period of about three years as he was preparing the book, all but broke Peale's spirit and ambition.

This unexpected history of the 'alalā was deeply moving. Long after the books had been carted off and returned to their protective tombs, the voices of history kept sounding. It was as if the words of Peale, Townsend and Wilkes, and others had joined the noisy chorus of 'alalā I had heard in the cloud forests of Mauna Loa the year before. And little did I know that these early conflicts were but a prelude for much greater ones to come.

Soon the museum's ornithological collections manager, David Agro, came to escort me to see the actual specimens Peale used in his description. We walked up the stairs and through a labyrinth of hallways to the room where the specimens were stored. Agro unlocked a metal drawer, handed me the 'alalā tray, and offered me a table to work on at the end of his office. There before me they lay, cotton bulging out of eye sockets. I looked at the stiff, charcoal-colored 'alalā for a while, thinking about how far removed a specimen is from the living bird. Memories arose of Noe and the others flitting among the old 'ōhi'a trees in the deep forests of Mauna Loa, where light cartwheeled through the leaves with every breeze through the canopy. It didn't take me long to reach my limit for staring at the dead. But that didn't stop me, after thanking Agro and the librarians, from catching a cab across town to visit Peale's grave at Laurel Hill Cemetery.

"Once you get past the death end of it, this is a very interesting job," Joe Direso, the cemetery's general manager, volunteered as we drove along a winding road to the plot. "We've almost reached educational status, where the burials aren't as important. Just like the reason you're here. I'm a keeper of history and memories."

Soon we came to a small white marble slab inscribed with Titian

R. Peale's name. "This is a big plot," Direso said. "They must have been somebody." We got out and walked around. A tall yew tree presided over the plot.

As I stood beneath the yew in a cold, brisk wind, I could imagine Titian Peale walking the warm shore of Kealakekua Bay or climbing to the heights of Kīlauea, collecting his specimens and scrawling in his notebooks. Probably never did a life more filled with professional promise end in greater disappointment. The Hawaiians named the ʻalalā. Latham and Gmelin had identified the wrong bird, and Titian Peale finally got it right. For at least one bird, he had succeeded in Adam's task — naming one of the "fowls of the air."

But he occupied a spot of bitter irony. Western scientists such as Peale brought new dimensions of awareness and understanding to the Hawaiians' mystical view of the ʻalalā. At the same time, it was the arrival of westerners that ultimately led to the bird's decline. Was eventual exploitation the price of Western knowledge of, or enriched perspective on, the ʻalalā?

Surely it was, the scientist's voice in me kept saying.

But another voice calling from deep within told me that science is but one of many ways to know the ʻalalā. And so I stood there in wonder.

THE RAVEN-WARRIOR

As the 'alalā's presence in Western scientific literature grew, its spiritual essence among Hawaiians, in life and in memory, ebbed — or so it seemed to me. For all that my library visit had revealed about the raven as known by Western science, discovering the lost 'alalā of the Hawaiians would be far more difficult. Such were the faint traces of the 'alalā left by the oral culture among which the species lived — knowledge tenuously impermanent to begin with, and upon which numerous layers of belief had been subsequently deposited. And in failing to discover this aspect of the Hawaiian past, would I be left with an empty outline of the bird? What I had hoped would be a window into their perception of the 'alalā seemed to be a wall.

If anything of the traditional Hawaiian view remained today, one might reason, it would be among the few Hawaiian elders and their protégés who have consciously nourished and sheltered knowledge of the ancient ways. And that meant exploring knowledge and feelings secreted away in the minds of several living Hawaiians I had known only by reputation.

When I telephoned the renowned Hawaiian hula master and chanter Pualani Kanaka'ole Kanahele at her office at the

University of Hawai'i at Hilo to ask about the 'alalā, she engaged in some small talk before politely asking, "Why do you wish to write about this?"

"Because there's still time," I said, as if to evoke the old Hawaiian phrase "Ke nae iki nei nō"—"Some breath remains"—that is said about someone on his deathbed.

She chuckled warmly. "Yes, I suppose it is good to write about it before it's gone. What would you like to know?"

"What does the name 'alalā mean?" I asked.

"As with many Hawaiian words, it has many meanings," she explained. "One meaning is the Hawaiian word for the cry of a child—'alalā. That's how it is said the 'alalā got its name. But the word also refers to a specialized style of chanting, a style I sometimes use myself. You open your mouth very wide and create a sound by vibrating the vocal cords. The 'alalā style projects your voice farther than other chanting styles. It makes a different sound because you use a different space in your head to create the resonance. Maybe the Hawaiians learned this style of the chanting by mimicking the bird. I don't know. Hawaiian words invite many meanings, not all of them explicit."

Kanahele said that she believes the 'alalā is a very powerful bird, powerful enough to bring death, but suggested that others probably knew much more than she did. "Explain to them your interest in the Hawaiian view of the 'alalā," she advised. "That will mean more than if you had come to do a scientific study."

Later, another elder advised, "If you want to learn more about the 'alalā—the real 'alalā—you should talk to some of the chiefs on Hawai'i Island. Put your questions in a letter to me and I will take it to them."

Several months later, my Hawaiian acquaintance called to say that he had arranged for me to visit some chiefs and officials associated with Pu'ukoholā Heiau, a revered temple in Kawaihae. Originally built by Kamehameha the Great for the war god

Kūkā'ilimoku, it was one of the sites destroyed during the revolt against the old beliefs after the king's death. The structure is now being restored as a national historic site by the National Park Service and restored for use as an active temple by a group of Hawaiian elders. In August 2000 I drove to the heiau to meet some of the chiefs and others — at least one of whom was a descendant of the heiau's original royal court.

One of the current temple chiefs, Daniel Kawaiaea, is the superintendent of Pu'ukoholā Heiau National Historic Site. Although he was not there for me to meet that day, William Akau, a direct descendant of Kamehameha, and the mō'ī ali'i, or high temple chief, was. He welcomed me warmly, introduced the others, and spoke freely in answer to my questions.

"Some people have the mistaken idea that the recent Hawaiian renaissance is about trying to relive the past, but that's such a shallow view," he began as we sat in the hot early afternoon sun near the heiau. Mauna Kea loomed to the east, and to the south, the slopes of the volcano Hualālai rose like a dark, deep green mound above the town of Kailua. Beyond, Mauna Loa was lost in the haze.

"At Pu'ukoholā Heiau we're not necessarily trying to preserve the past. We are seeking to reestablish, best we can, the royal court in a way appropriate to our times. The era of the court was a time of war. Ours is a time of peace, which came about from the wars of Kamehameha the Great when he united all the islands."

Mel Kalāhiki Sr., one of the standing chiefs, explained that one of the societies of chiefs employed by the court during Kamehameha's time — which the present chiefs are attempting to resurrect in modern form — was a specialized group of chanters known as 'alalā.

"The 'alalā belonged to the class known as ali'i koa, or warrior chief," he said. "Their task was to chant in a style that used a quivering of the vocal chords to produce a stylized, haunting, melodious chant."

"The ʻalalā inherited his role as a specialized chanter along bloodlines, assuming he could perform well enough," Maʻulili Dickson, the ilāmuku, or marshal, added. "This type of chanting required both talent and skill. There were many ceremonial occasions, such as the ʻawa ceremony, when the ʻalalā would be called upon to perform these chants. There are many, many chants, but the ʻalalā was called upon only on selected occasions.

"Often a chief might want to deliver an address, and he might call on the ʻalalā to put the message into a chant and deliver it. The ʻalalā also needed oratory and poetic skills, something which most all Hawaiians were born with but which the ʻalalā was especially good at.

"The ʻalalā—the bird, that is—is a gifted orator. No wonder the ʻalalā chanters took their names from the bird. The word also describes a gurgle in one's throat, and it was used to describe a technique for reciting mele, or songs, even the Kumulipo. Some called for a monotone recitation, with breaths drawn at precisely the proper time. Some recitations required a skilled ʻalalā. A single misspoken word could bring bad luck. During wartime, another job of the ʻalalā was to shout the chief's commands to large groups of warriors. The ʻalalā had to have a strong and loud voice, a gift reserved for a special few. No bird in the forest can shout like the ʻalalā.

"Here at the heiau we also use ʻalalā who write and deliver special chants, just as in former times. The ʻalalā in our assembly are amazing. You give them a message to deliver, even a few words of it, and they can create a chant or rhyme right on the spot, with many different meanings.

"The ʻalalā must be a sort of poet as well as a skillful performer in order create the trill deep in his throat. That is also known as an ʻalalā. The word literally means to cry or wail, but it designates other specific things, such as the ʻalalā class. The wail that women once expressed at the death of a loved was also known as ʻalalā.

"Many things of old Hawai'i are gone, but many more we have resurrected in a modern form. The vessel, or form, may be different, but the spirit it contains is the same. We were an oral culture and we still are, although most of us now read and write. The 'alalā is that oral culture in us that still lives."

After our meeting, I gave Chief Akau a lift to his home in Waimea on my way back to Hilo. As the road ascended from the coast, we passed through fog, and it soon began to drizzle.

"Kamehameha's time was not so long ago," he commented. "Consider that Kamehameha died in 1819. That's just a few generations past. The islands were not united until 1810, and Pu'ukoholā Heiau was built to the war god and was the center of Kamehameha's efforts to unite the islands.

"Kamehameha was a powerful supporter of the kapu system, the sacrosanct system of laws by which the royalty ruled. He supported the class system in Hawaiian society, which was composed of the ali'i, or ruling class; the kahuna, or 'priests' and 'experts'; the maka'āinana, or commoners; and the kauā, or slaves. When Kamehameha died, much of old Hawai'i died with him. The funeral was held in Kailua. His flesh was burned off the bones, and the bones were secreted away to secret burial so that no enemy could find and desecrate them."

Chief Akau continued: "I had never experienced just how close Kamehameha's time was to my own life until the 1980s, when a Japanese company bought a stretch of coast north of here, in Kohala, to build a resort. I knew, from my grandparents, who were descendants of Kamehameha, that his bones had been buried in a cave on that land. The curator of the royal mausoleum near Honolulu arranged a meeting with the governor of Hawai'i, who was part Hawaiian, and so understood immediately. He got a law passed in the legislature that condemned that land immediately. So stories such as I am telling you are not ancient history. They are barely old. Surely your father told you the stories his father told him. And you will tell your children those same stories. Those stories are still very young, as are the stories of Kamehameha. Now, tell me this. What story will you tell of the 'alalā?"

Several months later, with an introduction from these chiefs, I was able to meet the high priest of Pu'ukoholā Heiau, Kahuna Nui John Keolamaka'āinana Lake. Lake, who has a degree in Spanish linguistics and is an authority on Hawaiian traditions, language, and protocol, spent years poring over Hawaiian texts and other sources in an effort to rescue the dwindling knowledge of Kamehameha's royal court at Pu'ukoholā Heiau. A scholarly, soft-spoken man who chooses words with care, Lake spoke with warmth and spontaneous humor over breakfast not far from his Honolulu home.

"Much has been lost from the time of Kamehameha," he told me. "By taking bits and pieces of knowledge from here and there, much of it from untranslated Hawaiian manuscripts written by ethnographers who worked right after the time of Kamehameha, we have drawn a rich picture of the workings of Kamehameha's court and even strategies in battle. We have gained quite a bit of knowledge about the 'alalā.

"The first warriors to advance were sling bearers who formed a long line opposing the enemy. Directly behind and parallel to them were the spear carriers. Their spears were eighteen feet long. They were used for tripping up the enemy in close combat. Off to the side of these frontline forces stood an 'alalā. At the 'alalā's command, the sling bearers and spear carriers would trade places. First the sling throwers would loose their stones, and then, upon the 'alalā's command, they would fall back and the spear carriers would advance. The sling bearers would reload and, once again upon the 'alalā's command, they would move to the front.

"As these forces advanced onshore, they were backed up by

well-organized groups of waʻa kaua, or war canoes. There were typically a thousand canoes in each group, and a full force might consist of five to eight thousand waʻa kaua. It was not unusual to have a force of between five thousand and ten thousand warriors for a major assault. To communicate the commander in chief's orders amidst the melee must have been a considerable challenge. That's why the ʻalalā were crucial to winning a battle.

"Each island is now responsible for building up these ranks, and we periodically gather at the Puʻukoholā. It is magnificent. Among those being developed are the ʻalalā. There are very few people who can chant in the ʻalalā style. But in time we will have many again. My adopted son chants in that style. I can also do it. George Manu, of Hawaiʻi Island, is also an ʻalalā, although he is not formally associated with the heiau.

"The bird may have been ʻaumakua to the ʻalalā warriors of Kaʻū and Kona. What we can be sure of is that the ʻalalā warrior class took their name from the bird. ʻAlalā the bird is a heralder in the forest, and the warriors were the heralds in battle and chanters in Kamehameha's court.

"It would have also been natural for the warriors and chanters to have called upon the bird for strength and ability, to rely on the bird to provide the gift of heraldry and chant. It was not in the Hawaiian way of thinking to take a namesake from an animal and for the connection to end there. There is almost always a connection in spirit and a sharing of soul, so to speak. In this case, there was probably a sharing of voice, a strong and gifted voice."

And so, I began to learn, the ʻalalā still existed in spirit, if not in body, in Hawaiian culture. The ʻalalā of spirit and metaphor remained even as the species struggled to maintain its tenuous hold in the cloud forests above. In taking on a cultural presence, the ʻalalā had become an indelible part of Hawaiian identity, spirit, and soul.

chapter 8

ABUNDANCE
AND LOSS

IN THE 'ŌHI'A FORESTS, a few miles above Ka'awaloa (celebrated as being the spot where Captain Cook fell), I found this bird numerous in the month of June, by which time the brood had already left the nest," wrote Scott Barchard Wilson, an ornithologist who spent several months collecting and studying Hawaiian birds for his 1887 work *Aves Hawaiienses*. His was the first notable ornithology to come out of the islands since the U.S. Exploring Expedition, more than three decades earlier — and, in fact, the first serious ornithological exploration since Captain James Cook landed more than a century before. Wilson had traveled to Hawai'i with the support and encouragement of his mentor, Alfred Newton, a professor of zoology at Magdalene College in Cambridge, England. Wilson would remain there for a decade. Although many of the subsequent publications on Hawaiian birds appeared under Wilson's name alone, his mentor may in fact have written many of them. Such was the

competitive get-my-name-in-print nature of ornithology then—
and now.

With Wilson's—or Newton's—work, Hawaiian ornithology
had been roused from long slumber. The work inspired another of
Newton's students, the wealthy and eccentric Englishman Lord
Lionel Walter Rothschild. Fascinated by the islands and barely in
his twenties, he sent a cadre of collectors there, including H. C.
Palmer and his assistant, George C. Munro. Wilson wrote:

> A friend, extremely clever at imitating sounds, was able, by carefully
> concealing himself and then mimicking the cry of the young ʻalalā, to
> collect round him in a short time many of the old birds; he had found
> a nest at the end of April, which he informed me was a large loosely-
> fashioned structure of dead sticks, resembling that of Pigeon, placed
> in a Pandanus. The ʻalalā seems to feed principally on the fruit of the
> ʻieʻie, but no doubt, when occasion serves, takes the young of the vari-
> ous forest birds. . . . I was assured by the islanders that [the birds] con-
> gregate in large numbers and feed on the sheep occasionally found
> dead from natural causes or killed by wild dogs.

In the twenty or so years following the publication of *Aves
Hawaiienses*, far more would be written about the ʻalalā than during
the entire preceding century. More than anything else, this new
cadre of bird collectors and ornithologists would comment on the
ʻalalā's abundance.

In 1891, Munro saw "numerous" ʻalalā throughout Kona, especially in the forest and open country, flying above the treetops and
frequenting the "vegetation from the highest trees to the ground.
Its call is a harsh caw repeated rapidly. A flock calling in unison
made a great hubbub." Munro characterized the ʻalalā as the noisi-
est bird in the lower Kona forests at daybreak, yet able to remain
"entirely silent as they sail from tree to tree on motionless wings."
He wrote:

They went in flocks and were most inquisitive, following the intruder with loud cawing. The least imitation of their cry brought them close in. We saw an amusing instance of this. A tethered horse on the mountain of Hualālai, neighing for company brought a whole flock down around it. This trait has no doubt been exploited to their undoing. In the early 1890's as Kona became more closely settled the farmers, exasperated by the depredations of the crows in feed pens and poultry yards, made war on it, capitalizing on its well known traits of curiosity. By imitating its call many birds would easily be brought to gun.

Their food was originally largely the fleshy flower bracts and ripe fruit of the 'ie'ie vine . . . , the berry of the ohelo and other berries. The 'ie'ie was very common and flowered and fruited at different elevations at different seasons, so furnished food most of the year. Later as the county developed and new fruits and livestock were introduced, their food habits changed to include the imported berries and carrion of dead animals.

Between 1893 and 1900, Lord Rothschild published *The Avifauna of Laysan and the Neighbouring Islands*. In this work, he drew much of his account of the 'alalā from the earlier work of Titian Peale and Scott Barchard Wilson.

A few years after Palmer and Munro's sojourns in Hawai'i, the ailing archeologist Henry W. Henshaw, who had come in the hope of regaining his failing health, took up ornithology. While he noted that "certain Hawaiian birds are dying out," the 'alalā was not one of them. He was optimistic for the birds that were in trouble, but already he was alert to the birds' declining habitat:

> The necessity for the preservation of large forest tracts for the retention and preservation of rain has recently become so manifest that effective legislation in this direction is sure to follow soon, with the important secondary effort of affording safe shelter for the birds. The preservation of the forest in large tracts will in all probability insure the perpetuity of a greater or less number of species of the latter; so

that opportunity will be afforded for an acquaintance with a study of the birds for an indefinite number of years to come.

Like Munro before him, in the late 1800s or early 1900s Henshaw saw 'alalā abundant throughout and beyond the Kona district. He wrote:

> Though called the Kona Crow, the alala is numerous in the forests of both the Kona and Ka'ū districts of Hawaii, outside of which island it has never been found. This locality brings the bird within sight of the Hilo district, into which the bird seems not to desire, or perhaps to be able, to pass. As food suitable for the crow abounds in the Olaa woods, the only apparent cause for the bird not spreading further northward would seem to be the more abundant rainfall on the windward side of Hawaii.
>
> It would be difficult to imagine a bird differing more in disposition from the common American crow than the Hawaiian 'alalā. The bird, instead of being wary and shy, seems to have not the slightest fear of man, and when it espies an intruder in the woods is more likely than not to fly to meet him and greet his presence with a few loud caws. He will even follow the stranger's steps through the woods, taking short flights from tree to tree, the better to observe him and gain an idea of his character and purpose.

In the 1890s, not long after Wilson's book was published, entomologist R. C. L. Perkins, sponsored by the British Association for the Advancement of Science, came to the islands. While there he also commented on the abundant 'alalā, which he witnessed in Kona. The 'alalā "feeds largely on the 'ie'ie flowers, more especially, I think, when decayed. In the interval between the disappearance of the old and the opening of the new flowers this bird came up the mountains in large numbers . . . where they fed freely on the fruit of the poha. With the opening of the fresh flowers of the ['ie'ie] they disappeared again."

After this brief twenty-year burst of light cast upon the raven and other Hawaiian birds by Wilson, Palmer, Munro, Henshaw, and others from the late 1800s through the early 1900s, the study of Hawaiian forest birds again fell into slumber—a sleep sealed for decades by world war. When, in time, the raven would be rediscovered, ornithologists would look back with sadness and dismay at the bygone days of its abundance.

When Munro returned to Kona in 1937, nearly fifty years after his first visit, he lamented: "I found a great change. The birds were greatly reduced in numbers. I saw no flocks, only a few scattered individuals. The birds refused to answer my call, perhaps having learned the danger of it, thus proving the 'sagacity of the crow.'" Munro ventured no guess as to the cause of this rapid decline. But something had occurred between 1900 and 1937, he surmised, that had begun to wipe out the 'alalā. By the early 1940s the 'alalā was thinly scattered, and then in only parts of its former range.

The decline was so considerable that in 1944, on the northwestern slope of Hualālai, it was a matter of surprise and excitement to ornithologist Paul H. Baldwin that he saw "at least six or eight in one day."

"The 'alalā were quite tame. . . . They exhibited enough curiosity and lack of fear to come to trees 20 feet from us while we sat under ohia trees. They would retire then to 30 feet away and remain 10 minutes or so looking us over," he wrote. "They originally caught sight of us while soaring over the trees, came down, and without hesitation dropped in close. Their manner expressed great curiosity, especially when we talked or handled carrots, notebooks or lunches." Baldwin described how one of the curious onlookers "erected his forehead and crown feathers when perched but flattened them when he took off in flight. The crows uttered no sounds while near us but screeched in air." He described one 'alalā call as "a grossly magnified 'meow' of a cat, as the relatively high resonant beginning dropped off to lower pitch."

While the ʻalalā continued to survive in pockets on Mauna Loa, five years later, in March 1949, Baldwin neither saw nor heard a single ʻalalā during a three-day search on a twelve-mile trek through forests of the volcano's southeastern slope. And in other trips he made to areas where, a century before, ornithologists had witnessed an abundance of the birds, few, if any, were to be found:

> Unquestionably, some areas within this range were vacated by the crow subsequent to the early 1900's. The withdrawal from lowest elevations was especially complete and probably was in progress in the early 1900's.
>
> Shrinkage of the occupied areas in upland Kona and Kaʻū certainly also occurred by the late 1940s. . . . It may be assumed that reasons for change in distribution and in numbers at the upper elevations were in part different from the factors operating at the lower limits of ʻalalā range. It is not explained as yet why ʻalalā populations should not have maintained themselves satisfactorily at the upper areas in their original range.

As for their disappearance at lower altitudes, Baldwin wrote, "The effects of avian malaria on populations of resident Hawaiian birds at low elevations . . . may have contributed strongly to an early disappearance of the ʻalalā from the Kona lowlands." The devastating effects of avian malaria and other diseases became increasingly clear to the ornithologists who followed him: mosquitoes had also invaded the cloud forests of the ʻalalā.

The ʻalalā's mysterious decline continued unabated, and by the 1960s the bird's tenuous existence yielded but an eerily few glimpses. In June 1960, a party that included Roger Tory Peterson, who was finishing the Hawaiian section of the new edition of his *Field Guide to Western Birds*, was with a party blessed with the rare experience of witnessing four ʻalalā at once, near the rim of Kīlauea Crater in Hawaiʻi Volcanoes National Park:

During our first night, in the pre-dawn hours of June 18, we felt two earthquakes. Along the road were beautiful tree ferns, and almost everywhere the remarkable 'ōhi'a Lehua tree . . . which grows even on the raw lava, showed scarlet flowers. . . . Mr Walker then took us down the Kona road to the Dillingham Ranch. In the woods of this ranch . . . we were able to find the almost extirpated Hawaiian Crow. In the woods of the Dillingham Ranch, one of the few places where this endemic survives, we saw at least four and heard others. The first two were together; one was apparently hunting for food about the crotch of a tree, while the other was on the ground feeding on a dead Mynah, which was covered with ants. These brownish crows answered readily a crow-call obtained from the mainland by Mr Carlsmith. Yet their voice was different, a crrraw, which Peterson characterized as a "cracked caw."

Encounters grew rarer by the year thereafter; recorded sightings in the 1960s amounted to a roll call of the damned: "An 'alalā here; no 'alalā there. A. Johansen, Jr. saw one on Hualālai's southwest slope. R. Williams saw up to six, driven off the mountain by a winter storm. E. Molcilio twice saw 'alalā around 1964 near the Ka'u Forest Reserve."

In March 1964, biologist P. Quentin Tomich described the 'alalā's nesting behavior for the first time when he closely watched a nest with five eggs—none of which subsequently hatched— above the Māmalahoa Highway, northeast of Pu'uwa'awa'a. All the nests "were in ohia trees, and were generally built where the largest trees occurred in clusters with adjacent glades. They were constructed of [coarse] sticks, and the linings that remained were of stems and glades of grasses, a few small twigs, and some lengths of slender vines. Nests were placed in forks near the tops of trees, supported each by two or four branches that divided repeatedly to form the leafy canopies of the trees." Tomich was among the last to observe 'alalā in that traditional breeding area.

On December 20, 1965, seven 'alalā were seen, one of which was begging for food. A biologist heard several during a hike on January 30, 1966. N. Carlson heard them along the upslope edge of the Hōnaunau Forest Reserve. G. Knight heard 'alalā eight miles east of Keālia village. A ranch manager recalled seeing "plenty"—fifteen to twenty—in October 1960, but he found only two—one of them sickly—when he searched in 1966.

In June 1967, P. Crosland spotted one, twig in bill, winging its way over the Māmalahoa Highway near an old jeep road on Hualālai. On November 8, 1967, about a mile from the Hualālai Nānū Sanctuary, N. Santos saw and heard one along the Judd Trail. J. W. Aldrich saw two on January 16, 1967.

Rancher P. L'Orange sighted three between January 1968 and June 1969. G. Ackerman reported several at the Papaloa-Pauahi area on Easter Sunday 1969. D. Kalealoha saw a half dozen 'alalā while he was working on a boundary survey in April 1969 south of McCandless Ranch. Four were found on September 17, 1969, in a survey from Po'ohoho'o to Pu'u Henahena, but none were recorded in repeat searches. S. Montgomery heard a single call at Po'ohoho'o on December 21, 1969.

Nearly every year from 1969 to 1974, witnesses saw nesting 'alalā in the Honomalino area, especially in Alika Homesteads. In 1973 there were six documented nesting attempts in the area, but only a single fledgling survived.

In June 1970, R. Keakealani and S. Yano saw several near the Stone Corral and Pu'uiki areas. E. Molcilio heard 'alalā in the Kiolaka'a forest in October, but not a single one was seen there during a survey the following year.

In the summer of 1970, near Kīlauea, Samuel M. Gon III, now a senior scientist and cultural advisor for The Nature Conservancy of Hawai'i, saw his first 'alalā: "It was my very first multi-day back-packing hike and we were having a bento lunch in Kīpukapuaulu before continuing up the Mauna Loa Strip Road to the Mauna Loa trailhead for our first leg up to Pu'u'ula'ula Cabin," he recalled.

"While we were eating, an ʻalalā quietly flew in, landed on a fence post perhaps 12 meters away, and regarded us calmly. Lorin Gill, our hike leader, pointed to it without much excitement, and I remember thinking: ʻAh, so this is the ʻalalā.' After a few minutes of preening and head-tilted looks at us, the bird took leave of us. At the time I was ignorant of the declining numbers of ʻalalā, and did not recognize how fortunate I was to see one of the Kaʻū birds. Little did I know that in a few more years, Kaʻū would be graced by ʻalalā no more."

Most of these parting glimpses were painstakingly compiled by Winston Banko and his son Paul during extensive searches for the raven, both in forest and in memory. They interviewed hundreds of ranchers and others. Many people scoffed at their claim that the bird, once common, verged on being extinguished.

One skeptic was Bill Benham, a reporter for the *Hawaii Tribune-Herald*, who in 1971 wrote that "the bird may not be as rare as was thought." He claimed that the ʻalalā might threaten the forests by spreading seeds. He quoted Norman Carlson, a "conservationist" from the Bishop Estate: "The birds seemed fairly tame and seemed to have an appetite for the banana poka vine, a nuisance which is threatening forests above Laupāhoehoe."

In fact, out of hundreds of people interviewed, only one island resident, George Schattauer, a second-generation German who managed a macadamia nut plantation in Kona, seemed to genuinely share the Bankos' concern for the ʻalalā.

"Most of the land was private, and I had to find a way to get on the land to talk to people," Banko said. "George knew most of the people and got a lot of locked gates open for me. . . . George seemed to have a memory of the changes that were undistorted by his expectations of how things were supposed to be. He had the capacity to accept the seemingly impossible because it was true."

In 1972, Winston Banko warned that midnight for the ʻalalā was not far off. The ʻalalā had plummeted from hundreds to a scattered few within memory [of] many living residents. . . . Something must happen besides an annual count-down of dwindling numbers. . . . The plight of many species dictates that no time be lost. A comprehensive program [must be] built around the sanctuary concept, captive breeding projects, and beefed-up conservation and research manpower. . . . There is no tomorrow for species reduced to a few scattered individuals. . . . Midnight for the Hawaiian crow, at least, is not far off. . . . History is not kind to those who misjudge priorities.

Several years later, in January 1975, the last documented sighting of the 'alalā in Ka'ū was made. By this time, fewer than fifteen birds were known to exist in the wild.

chapter 9

'UMI'S CHILDREN

I
T IS 1997 AND ONCE AGAIN I
am on Mauna Loa. Since the deaths of Paniolo, Hōkū, and Mahoa
the previous fall, no more 'alalā have perished. Better yet, four new
captive-reared 'alalā have been released, bringing the total number
in the forest up to fifteen.

Today I am accompanied by Peter Harrity, the biologist responsible for guiding the 'alalā from the safety of captivity to the wild,
where diseases, Hawaiian hawks, and alien predators—rats, feral
cats, and mongooses—abound.

While working with the new releases, Harrity lives in a trailer
more than five thousand feet up on Mauna Loa's slopes, next to
the aviary where the young birds live prior to release. The aviary is
formed of woven polyethylene netting draped over a large wooden
structure, like skin hanging on a haggard body. The behemoth
bird-jail, nearly the size of a gymnasium, is an odd, almost ghost-
like human artifact set incongruously in a cloud forest.

Cynthia Salley, the owner of McCandless Ranch and on whose
leased land the aviary sits, has given me a ride up the mountain.
When she drops me off, Harrity is sitting pensively on a fern-

covered koa log outside his trailer. He wears a green baseball cap with "Keālia," the name of a nearby ranch, stitched in white across the front. Harrity has blue eyes, a slender nose, and a spry, happy face. He stands up, introduces himself, and then invites me to sit down on the log. He's silent for a while, and then, as if anticipating my question, says, "It feels sometimes like we're swimming against the tide. But little by little the numbers are increasing in the wild."

After a brief conversation, we drift into a comfortable silence as trees fade in and out of the mist. Intermittent high-pitched calls arise from the forests. As Harrity listens, his lips hint of a smile. Earlier that morning, at breakfast with Salley, she had told me, "Peter's one of the first environmentalists willing to listen to all sides. A listener is a rare thing among people working on the 'alalā. He has a deep spiritual connection with the birds."

Harrity breaks the silence to talk about the recent releases. "They all have Hawaiian names," he says, pointing out that it is unusual for scientists to name the objects of their study. "There's something about the 'alalā, or maybe being in Hawai'i, where the birds had such a personal connection with the people." The four new ones are Uila, which translates as Lightning; 'Ele'ele, Dark Black; Kona Kū, Wind-borne Rain; and Makani, Wind. All are the great-grandchildren of 'Umi, the captive flock's patriarch, who had been captured as a fledgling in 1973.

The captive-hatched birds live in the safety of the aviary for several weeks before they're released, Harrity tells me. For a while, the aviary remains open, and they're allowed to come and go. On a platform outside the aviary he places eggs, papaya, or honeydew melon, with some hand-collected native fruits, such as 'ōlapa. Gradually the young 'alalā are weaned from the handouts and begin to forage on their own. "Right now the 'ōhi'a flowers are in blossom, and the young birds are beginning to drink a lot of nectar," he says.

Harrity's biggest worry is that young birds may need to learn a lot of their survival skills from wild birds—especially when it comes to avoiding predators. But the young 'alalā don't have much of a relationship with the older birds, making the transfer of knowledge difficult.

For example, in the past the 'alalā managed to coexist with the 'io, or Hawaiian hawk. "But when you're down to so few 'alalā, all the defense dynamics change," he explains. "Maybe a lot of ravens could ward off the hawks or maybe they posted sentinels that would warn of an 'io's approach. Or maybe there were enough 'alalā to spare a few."

While pinning the blame on a natural predator would be easy, it's not that simple, he says. Habitat loss to cattle ranching, logging, and diseases such as bird malaria and pox, not even to mention exotic predators such as cats, mongooses, and rats, are all killing 'alalā.

His own theory—one harkening back to the early part of the twentieth century—is that loss of the forest understory has been the single greatest factor in the 'alalā's decline. In most places, it's dangerous for a young bird to be on the ground. "But in Hawai'i it's different because originally there weren't any mammalian predators. So a young 'alalā could safely spend time near the ground foraging for fruit and berries and then venture into the canopy. If any 'io came, a young 'alalā could dive back into the underbrush."

Over the past two centuries, much of the forest was cleared for cattle—descendants of which still wander, wild, through the cloud forests. "It's almost like a park," he says, echoing my earlier experience. In addition, feral pigs uproot tree ferns, leaving depressions where water collects and malarial mosquitoes breed. The mosquitoes infect 'alalā. "We can hatch and release all the baby birds we want," he says, but without healthy habitat to put the birds in, "we can't win."

Although it's impossible to determine exactly what initiated the 'alalā's downward spiral more than a century ago, most of the forces working against them now also existed then. Most biologists agree that the raven's current plight is an accumulation of past problems—but problems now exacerbated by more alien species and even less suitable forest to escape to as their best habitat declines. And their declining population has become its own problem, since their strength lay partly in their numbers. As a species divided, the birds no longer have one another to warn of 'io and other predators.

"It's no longer a race to save the 'alalā but a race to save its habitat. And nobody is doing that. It's expensive to install fences to keep predators out. You can't fence out mosquitoes. People really relate to releasing birds and all that, but it's a stopgap measure."

Indeed, the state had made little or no effort to protect 'alalā habitat. A publicly appealing stopgap measure was both cheaper, at least in the short term, and politically feasible. Not only was it expensive to secure habitat; often such efforts ran afoul of powerful ranchers and other private landowners—an area where the state feared to tread.

"Why not wait until the forests have been restored," I ask, "and then release more 'alalā?"

"Keeping birds in the wild is the only way to preserve their culture," Harrity replies. "Ideally we'd keep the wild birds handing down skills to a new generation, because once that knowledge is lost, it will be much harder to reestablish the bird in the wild, even if we have good habitat."

By culture, he means that there might be a complex set of behaviors that a particular group of birds has developed through their own experience—a knowledge, held in the memory of the adult birds, that would then be passed down to their children, and without which a young bird would be hard-pressed to survive.

As an example, Harrity explains a sophisticated enemy avoidance strategy that he believes is learned. When a young bird is released into the forest, the wild birds will often track it. While one of the wild birds serves as a decoy by calling loudly in the distance to distract the young 'alalā, another bird, a scout, secretly moves closer, often at ground level, to get a closer view of the interloper. The scout then suddenly flies up and loudly screeches or calls, terrifying the surprised young bird. "They could use a similar decoy-and-reconnaissance strategy to monitor the whereabouts and activities of 'io. You can't just release captive-reared 'alalā into the forest and expect them to automatically possess these sophisticated survival skills."

Harrity falls silent as the sisters Uila and 'Ele'ele appear twenty feet away in a kāwa'u tree. Two other young 'alalā call in the distance. "Those are their brothers, Makani and Kona Kū, calling," Harrity whispers.

He picks up a small aluminum antenna, and we walk through the clearing and farther into the forest. A loud ping beams from the receiver hanging from his belt. Some of the birds have miniature transponders attached to their backs that transmit a locator signal, and Harrity's receiver is set to different frequencies to identify particular birds. The faster the beep, the closer the bird. If the electronic backpack detects no motion for twelve hours, the "mortality signal" goes off — the rapid pings of death.

It is evident that Uila is missing some tail feathers. "They got pulled out in a scuffle with one of the wild birds," Harrity says. "They'll grow back."

Makani suddenly sweeps into the scene, perching on a branch about thirty feet away from us and letting loose with a loud caw. "Makani, a big, bad male," Harrity says with a smile. The raven pries bark off his perch, probably looking for insects and grubs. Kona Kū, meanwhile, perches barely ten feet above us.

As an 'apapane sings its sweet melody in the distance, a soft splat lands on my shirtsleeve. "It's starting to rain," I say. "No,"

Harrity corrects, glancing over with a laugh. "Kona Kū just shit on your sleeve. It's a sign. I'm not sure of what."

As we move into a gap in the canopy, Harrity points out two tiny moving specks against a momentary break in the clouds. "See those 'alalā, how high they are?" I could barely make out the tiny figures, ethereal and dreamlike, gliding on the slow flap of wings. "That's got to be a wild pair — probably the Ho'okena pair — doing the territorial thing," he says. "In two or three months it will be breeding season. Typically you'll have birds hatching in May. But they're too old. They just go through the motions of building a nest, mating, and sitting on infertile eggs."

We are distracted as two adult 'alalā pursue the recently released 'Ele'ele and Uila. "The older birds don't have much heart in it," Harrity explains. "They just lazily flap through the air in the general direction of the scrambling young birds," he explains. "A kind of gingerly getting to know you, each observing certain rules of etiquette. But if these were wild birds doing the chasing, it'd be high speed, hard swerves, and nonstop. No mercy! But birds released several years ago, they have sympathy for the newcomers."

'Ele'ele and Uila, meanwhile, glide to the screen atop the aviary. "It's home free," Harrity says. "The adults won't venture there."

I ask him about the birds' Hawaiian names. "A matter of respect, I guess, and to acknowledge that the birds are a part of the culture," he says. It strikes me as ironic that little about the efforts to save the bird is in any way Hawaiian. Then again, sadly little about the islands actually is. Other than the occasional blessings bestowed by native Hawaiians upon the recovery efforts, the 'alalā and efforts to save them are defined by the scientific culture of Cook, Latham, and Peale. Whether that is to the birds' benefit or their detriment I cannot say. In many ways it does not matter, for the Hawaiian system of beliefs that might once have sustained the 'alalā has, in many ways, shared the unfortunate fate of the bird.

Along the way, Harrity frequently pauses to point out various fruiting plants. "I eat all the fruit the crows eat," he says, reaching up to point out some pea-sized green berries. He also points out the scarlet veins spreading gracefully across the leaf of a māmaki, from which he sometimes brews a tasty tea. "The plant has a white mulberry-type fruit along the twigs that tastes real nutty. The crows just love it, but it's kind of off peak season now.

"This is 'ōpala, a member of the ginseng family. The 'alalā love 'em," he says.

Uila and 'Ele'ele, perched on the aviary, each emit a soft, throaty "Raa-raa." "That submissive call is a kind of helpless thing," Harrity explains. "It's a signal to the wild birds to back off. The older the released 'alalā, the more aggressively it seems the wild birds will chase them. They'll respect submissiveness, at least with new birds. But a wild adult bird will take one of the older released 'alalā almost to the ground before letting him go. It's a game of chicken to show who's boss.

"Before Paniolo disappeared, Makani was always at him because he sensed a challenge. The dominant Makani would sweep onto the food tray outside the aviary and just knock Paniolo and the other birds right out of the way. He wouldn't do that with the more submissive Kona Kū. The birds know who's a potential threat to their dominance. It's amazing. To return the favor, when the wild birds turn on Makani and start chasing him, Kona Kū tries to help out by running interference. But you can bet that Makani would never do that for Kona Kū!"

A loud, sharp call arises from near the clearing's edge. An adult bird sweeps down before disappearing deeper into the forest. "Hear how different that is from the young birds?" Harrity asks. "The wild birds have a sharp yelping, almost scolding sound. The breath of their calls can be haunting. Sometimes it's like they're angry, and at other times it's as if they're moaning or crying. You'd almost swear their calls expressed different emotions."

As the wild bird vanishes into the distance, the young 'alalā surrounding us begin their late morning roost. "They're usually active from about six or seven in the morning until about eleven o'clock," Harrity says, glancing at his watch. The 'alalā, now perching quietly in the trees nearby, begin softly cooing and mewing. "They'll be active again before settling down for the night in the same places they're roosting now."

"See this fresh green color here? This is 'ōhelo, one of the 'alalā's favorite foods," he says. The shrub is related to the blueberry and cranberry; in summer, islanders harvest the sweet, juicy fruit for jelly and jam. The 'ōhelo is sacred to the fire goddess Pele, and branches with berries are sometimes thrown into the volcano at Kīlauea.

Harrity points out kōlea, another plant beloved by the 'alalā, its berries growing along the branches between the flowers. Then he reaches out and bends a slender branch of a *Clermontia*, or 'ōhā, toward me, saying, "I've tasted it, and it really is a peppery flavor. The 'alalā just love it!"

A soft churring arises from a nearby 'ōhi'a embraced by an 'ie'ie vine. A drizzle begins. Harrity is ready to head into town for supplies, and we climb into his truck for the forty-five-minute drive back down the mountain. We don't speak much along the way. After a while, he ventures, "The unexpected deaths of Paniolo, Hōkū, Mahoa two months ago were terrible. It seems like overnight, three of the birds were just gone! But I'm optimistic about the 'alalā because I think we have a good young group coming up in captivity. On the other hand, when you think how quickly the three vanished, you know it could happen again."

But for now, life is good, and Uila, 'Ele'ele, Makani, and Kona Kū join the family tree.

Hilu

Nānū

Mahoa

Hōkū

Uila

‘Ele‘ele

Makani

Kona Kū

Hiapo

Umi's Descendants

Hiwahiwa

Kalāhiki Pair

Ho‘okena Pair

Lokahi

(died in 1995)

Keālia Pair

Paniolo

Noe

The Bachelor

Kehau

‘ALALĀ FAMILY TREE
March 1997

PART II

NIGHT

DAWNING

YESTERDAY

chapter 10

ESCAPE
TO CAPTIVITY

At twilight on June
18, 1970, high on the slopes of Hualālai, biologist Winston Banko
stumbled upon a sickly 'alalā fledgling perched on a fallen tree. In
the entire year before, Banko, who worked for the U.S. Fish and
Wildlife Service, a bureau in the U.S. Department of the Interior,
had found only twelve adult ravens in the wild, scattered in four
small groups around Mauna Loa and its ancient sister volcano
Hualālai. He estimated that no more than two dozen 'alalā remained in the wild. (None lived in captivity at the time.) So rare
was the 'alalā that, until that morning, he had never even before a
fledgling.

The young bird had sores at the base of its bill and on its head.
"Fearing the sick bird might fly away, I returned to my vehicle to
wait for darkness after which I returned with my battery lantern to
pick this bird off its perch," Banko wrote of the incident. The next
morning, he found another young raven similarly afflicted. He
flushed it from its low perch and captured it as well.

Banko temporarily placed Makai and Mauka, as he named them, both suffering from bird pox, in the laundry room of his family residence at Hawai'i Volcanoes National Park, near his office. "They had enough room to fly a bit, and it seemed to work out pretty well. I didn't know exactly what to feed them, but they were fruit-eaters, so I fed them papaya and cut up guava."

Banko hoped to nurse the birds back to health and then release them, but when he notified Ray C. Erickson, his supervisor at the U.S. Fish and Wildlife Service's Patuxent Wildlife Research Center in Maryland, of the situation, Erickson told him to send the birds there for keeping. "I wasn't keen on sending them because I thought they'd be even more susceptible to mainland diseases than in Hawai'i. At the same time, they had daily attention from me and it was something of a distraction," Banko said. A short time later the rare birds were put in cages and flown five thousand miles to their new, better equipped home at Patuxent. So began, more by accident than by design, the captive effort to save the vanishing 'alalā.

Not everyone was happy to see these "Hawaiian birds" falling under the care of the federal government. Historically, jurisdiction over fish and game fell to individual states. In 1966 the federal Endangered Species Preservation Act, however, brought the federal government more to the center of endangered species conservation than ever before.

But jurisdiction, at least for now, became moot. In early August, Eugene H. Dustman, the director of Patuxent, wrote to Michio Takata, director of the Division of Fish and Game of the Hawai'i Department of Land and Natural Resources (DLNR), the state agency that oversaw endangered species, "It is with regret that we must inform you of the death of one of the Hawaiian crows." Makai had begun to show signs of shock almost immediately upon arrival, he explained. The bird became unsteady on its perch and was transferred to a veterinary hospital for further care and observation. "It appeared to recover and become normally active and vocal . . . when it suddenly died," Dustman wrote. "The remaining bird is doing well. It has eaten canned dog food and cantaloupe. We do not anticipate further problems." Three years later, Mauka, too, died.

News of the deaths saddened but didn't discourage Banko. As one of the country's first endangered species research biologists — a position he had assumed when he arrived in Hawai'i in 1965 — he had the authority to set his own work priorities. And set them he did.

"Once I found that the 'alalā used traditional roosting areas, places they always returned to roost, I would get there at sunup and follow their movements all day. They were noisy. One reason I made the 'alalā a priority was that it was a bird I could easily track and study."

Banko's son Paul, who had just begun high school and was always eager to help his father with fieldwork, was mesmerized by the 'alalā and felt deeply connected to them. Being in the wild with the 'alalā was, he said, an "incredible experience," and he was amazed at the way the charismatic birds would play tricks on him by swooping or calling loudly to startle him.

"I remember searching for quite some time for an individual in its territory, when suddenly it shrieked from a perch right over-head," he said. "It seemed as if it had been silently stalking me, waiting for just the right moment to startle me out of my wits. There was no nest nearby, so it was not defending eggs or off-spring. They are irresistible to watch also because they often 'mutter' and 'growl' as they poke under bark for invertebrate prey, and they sometimes move in ways or strike poses that virtually anyone would agree is amusing."

Like his father, Paul was also drawn to the 'alalā partly because they were easy to track. "Despite being able to blend into the forests and avoid detection, 'alalā are large and relatively slow-moving, so when they allow themselves to be seen, they are easier to track than the smaller forest birds that flit about quickly before disappearing into the canopy," he said. "Although 'elepaio often fly to low perches to 'scold' people, the 'alalā seems sometimes to follow people and to react to them with unusual curiosity.

"Although they can be cryptic when it suits them, they sometimes surprise visitors in their territories by appearing suddenly. It's not possible to take them by surprise, and they are keenly aware of their surroundings."

While they can be gregarious and noisy, they can also blend into the forest unheard and unseen. This stealth may have evolved, Paul Banko thought, because among the three native crow species that lived on the leeward side of Hawai'i Island before it was colonized by Polynesians, the 'alalā was the smallest. "They may have become clever at detecting and avoiding trouble from interlopers and at insinuating themselves into territories that perhaps were co-occupied by the larger, presumably dominant corvids," he said.

By the mid-1970s, Paul Banko was conducting his own studies of the 'alalā, including monitoring of the rapidly declining number of nests. He soon came to know the location of nearly every remaining 'alalā nest—not that there were all that many by then. He could also walk the perimeters of their territories from memory. Encouraged by his father, Paul, who was by then working with the federal government, tried to rekindle the informal captive program that had prematurely ended with the deaths of Makai and Mauka.

On June 9, 1973, Paul came upon an 'alalā at Hōnaunau Forest Reserve on Mauna Loa. He named her Kona—a name that would later be changed to Hina. "This bird had just fledged and couldn't fly; she was perched near the ground and was easily caught by hand," Paul recalled. "At the time, we assumed that she was sick, but we later discovered that 'alalā routinely fledge a week or two before they can fly level or upward. For days after leaving the nest, they spend their time napping, being fed by their parents, and launching clumsy, short-distance flights that typically end near the ground. They gradually climb and hop to higher perches before flapping off again."

On June 22 of that year, he and his father found another young ʻalalā in a nest on Hualālai, south of where Kona was captured. The capture of this second bird, Alika—later renamed ʻUmi—was almost Paul's last. He had climbed a tree to photograph the chick in its nest forty feet up in a vine-covered ʻōhiʻa when he felt a strange tingling spreading across his face: he was swarming with gray mites. Paul was so alarmed that he nearly fell from the tree. Finding the young ʻalalā also swarming with mites, he slipped a sock with the toe cut off over the head of the chick and down along its body, thus snugly encasing its wings and legs. With the head poking out the open toe, he attached a line to the sock's other end and gently lowered the chick to his father on the ground. A short time later, Alika was dusted with a pesticide and sent to Hawaiʻi Volcanoes National Park, where Mauka and Makai had lived before their one-way journey to Maryland.

These two new birds fared well. Within a week or two after capture ʻUmi became demanding and boisterous and screeched when hungry. On July 10, Paul and his father captured yet a third chick from Hualālai just as the chick was fledging. He was called Mahana—a name later changed to Kekau—and introduced into the aviary with the other two.

One visitor to the park, who stopped by the aviary to observe the three ʻalalā on a clear, brisk morning in September 1975, wrote that they were "doing well in captivity with excellent appetites and glossy, smooth plumages. . . . Although very little is known of the life history of the Hawaiian Crow, biologists had hoped these individuals [would reach] maturity this spring, with a chance for reproduction even though the sex of the birds is unknown. Two of them exhibited behaviors that could have been incipient courtship and they were separated from the third bird."

The sexes can be very difficult to tell apart by sight alone, though the adult male is generally slightly larger than the female and has a longer bill. In the wild, their calls and behavior often offer a clearer distinction, with the males waking up early to spar verbally with other males nearby in loud "Aaoow-whop!" cries.

As the captive flock grew, so did disagreement about who had official jurisdiction over the birds — the state of Hawai'i or the federal government. As an endangered species, the 'alalā fell primarily under the purview of the U.S. Department of the Interior rather the state of Hawai'i. That bred resentment in some DLNR employees. While they rejected federal jurisdiction over the birds on principle, they also feared the loss of potential funds — that is, federal support. In the early 1970s, a time of generous federal support for endangered species, caring for an endangered species could be highly profitable.

For the previous two decades, the Department of Land and Natural Resources had been successfully raising and releasing the endangered Hawaiian goose, or nēnē. The breeding project on Maui had brought in hundreds of thousands of federal dollars to DLNR. State biologist David Woodside and several of his DLNR colleagues were confident that an 'alalā project would do the same — assuming the state could get control of the birds, which were now housed by the Bankos at Hawai'i Volcanoes National Park under the auspices of the federal government. Win Banko was well aware of the growing resentment at DLNR, and before his retirement in 1976 he warned that the federal government and the state of Hawai'i were on a collision course over the 'alalā. "The state expressed strong interest both in 1970 and 1972 in obtaining a breeding nucleus of Hawaiian crows for Division of Fish and Game," the federal biologist wrote. "[They] are strong State's

righters. . . . Obtaining such stock would have considerable publicity value and help meet criticism that the State is not doing what
it should in saving native birdlife from extinction. My feeling is
that Crows . . . would be used in the end to pry loose increased
monies from Congress to fund what will prove to be an inadequate
program." In other words, he feared that the state would exploit
the ʻalalā for its financial and public relations potential and miss
the point that the purpose of involvement was, after all, to save the
species.

At the time, the National Park Service, a subdivision of the Department of the Interior, was aggressively trying to remove feral
pigs and cattle from Hawaiʻi Volcanoes National Park—a similar
challenge that DLNR would never accept when it came to state
lands. With the National Park Service itself very keen to restore the
ʻalalā—a desire being backed up by action—relinquishing control
to a questionable state-run program seemed tragic and short-
sighted to Paul Banko and his father. They didn't hesitate to
say so. Some biologists branded the outspoken father and son
troublemakers.

But with the success of the nēnē program, the state could make
a strong case for taking over the program, and in 1975 a U.S. Fish
and Wildlife Service official, weary of advocating for what was
probably a lost cause, wrote to Michio Takata, director of DLNR's
Division of Fish and Game, that "we would welcome your assuming responsibility for a Crow propagation project." DLNR wasted
no time in taking the Service up on the invitation: "We would be
more than willing to accommodate the birds at our facilities on the
Island of Hawaii. . . . [We] would very much like to begin the ʻalalā
propagation program at an early date."

The three captive ʻalalā would be housed at the same facilities
where the nēnē had been successfully raised: a place called Pōhakuloa, near a U.S. Army bombing range high on Mauna Kea, in
northeastern Hawaiʻi Island. The high slopes of Mauna Kea may

have been suitable for the nēnē, but this cold, dry, and windswept mountainside was no place for these 'alalā, which lived in warming, moist cloud forests.

Nevertheless, early one March morning in 1976, state biologist Ernest Kosaka drove a Jeep Cherokee to Hawai'i Volcanoes National Park, caught 'Umi, Hina, and Kekau, and, with the federal government's blessing, placed each in a two-foot-long box with ventilation holes. Two of the boxes were secured on the rear seat of the vehicle and one in the front. The windows were opened a spread-hand width to allow for a flow of fresh air. "The crows were very quiet inside the boxes," Kosaka noted. "Their presence was evident if you stuck a finger in a vent hole to carry the box and they bit you."

As the birds departed, a saddened Paul Banko took their photographs, as if to create a keepsake of departing loved ones. "It was a very disappointing day for me," he recalled; he believed that "a valuable opportunity for restoration was being postponed if not foreclosed."

He and his father feared, among other things, that the state would model the program after the nēnē project, wherein birds were bred in captivity and released into the same poor habitat that had made their survival in the wild such a struggle in the first place. Without serious attempts to improve the habitat, releases would at best constitute a costly, unsustainable race to try to make up for the unnaturally high mortality of the birds in the wild.

Kosaka, as if recording the details for posterity as much as to defend his handling of the birds in the politicized atmosphere, wrote of his release of the birds into their new cage:

All three crows bit me as I gently carried them out of the box, releasing their bite when I placed them on the ground. They immediately flew to a perch on the side of the pen; then all three crows settled on a mamane "tree" put into the pen as a perch. Within 15 minutes they appeared to be calm and were observed preening. There was also a lot of pecking at the branches to remove bark and possibly search for insects. . . . I would like to emphasize that the crows were successfully transported from the Park to Pōhakuloa without mishap. Their acclimatization and adjustment to their new environment will be monitored closely.

As DLNR took control of the small captive flock, the 'alalā remaining at large continued their struggles in the wild.

11

MOUNTAIN
OF SORROW

O NE OF THE LOVELIEST
and largest ahupua'a, or ancient land divisions, on all of Hawai'i
Island was a place called Pu'uwa'awa'a, Hawaiian for Furrowed
Hill, located on the northern slope of the ancient volcano Hualālai. Stretching from shore to mountain, as these ahupua'a usually
did, the uplands of Pu'uwa'awa'a included expanses of open fields
interspersed with islands of trees and bordered by rich native
forests.

If the scattered historical reports are any indication, the forests
of Pu'uwa'awa'a were a veritable delight for the 'alalā. As one of the
only remaining Hawaiian native dry forests surviving into the
twentieth century, Pu'uwa'awa'a represented one of the world's
rarest of ecological jewels. This sub–cloud forest terrain may also
have been among the best feeding habitats the 'alalā ever knew, as
it was rich in many fruits.

The district's most prominent feature is a huge cinder cone
mound, pushed by volcanic forces out of Hualālai's northern slope

more than a hundred thousand years ago. Over the millennia, before magnificent forests and their tangle of roots had time to grasp the rocky volcanic earth, the slopes had eroded into a series of deep gullies, like pleats of a taffeta gown. White settlers called the mound Muffin Hill. Puʻuwaʻawaʻa might have remained a reminder of what even a land of volcanic stone can become, given enough time and tended only by sunlight, rain, plants, and animals. Today, instead, it stands as a monument to a man who helped to destroy what he could not create.

For thousands of years prior to the modern calamity that has befallen Puʻuwaʻawaʻa and the ʻalalā living there, forests of almost indescribably intricate patterns and designs grew there. In 1913, Joseph F. Rock, sometimes referred to as the father of Hawaiian botany, called these forests of Puʻuwaʻawaʻa "the richest floral section of any in the whole Territory." In 1932, the botanist C. S. Judd called them a "botanical mine" and wrote, "For some reason or other, known only to Providence, our rarer and interesting native trees have been concentrated in certain places where they form a veritable bonanza for the delight of the delving botanist."

It was in the vicinity of Puʻuwaʻawaʻa, on April 11, 1941, that the ornithologist Paul H. Baldwin saw his first ʻalalā. "A crow was heard to give a two-tone ʻcaw', quite unlike the raucous ʻcaws' of California crows," he reported. Three years later, he hiked across the northern side of Hualālai with ranger Arthur L. Mitchell, who lamented even then the sad decline of the once beautiful native dry forests. Nevertheless, Baldwin reported that "many sightings" were made of the crows, which were "conspicuously present from 3750 feet upwards in the vicinity of the cinder cone Poohohoo." He continued:

> The ʻalalā were quite tame on the forested northern slope of Hualālai. They exhibited enough curiosity and lack of fear to come to trees 20 feet from us while we sat under ʻohiʻa trees. They would retire then to 30 feet away and remain 10 minutes or so looking us over. . . . They

originally caught sight of us while soaring over the trees, came down, and without hesitation dropped in close. Their manner expressed great curiosity, especially when we talked or handled carrots, notebooks or lunches. The one seen at 6300 feet erected his forehead and crown feathers when perched but flattened them when he took off in flight.

Baldwin's hikes in the region took him through open country in which thimbleberries abounded, whose fruit, Baldwin surmised, was a principal food of the ʻalalā. "Some trees with berries were present, notably kolea . . . which was common, and ʻolapa . . . less common. At least four crows flew around overhead at 8 A.M. by twos and threes calling frequently," he wrote. "The trail continued upward and westward to the 'tank' hill (4300 ft.) and emerged into dry koa . . . forest suddenly; here and to the northeast there was less thimbleberry, and the crows were lacking."

At one point, near Puʻuwaʻawaʻa, Baldwin and Mitchell encountered "a healthy population of the scarlet, sweet-melodied apapane and numerous iiwi." As for the ʻalalā, "we saw six to eight on the way up. At the summit two crows flew up and over the cone immediately adjacent to Hainoa Crater, putting their range up to the top of the mountain at 8250 ft." Because Puʻuwaʻawaʻa happened to be spared from the lava flows of Hualālai, a collection of rare and unusual species had taken root, grown, and thrived there — trunks, bark, stems, and leaves of improbable textures, shapes, colors, and scents, bearing fruits and flowers of orange, yellow, and stunning crimson, seeds and pods in a fantastic variety of shapes and sizes, and textures and densities of wood to suit the imagination.

Among many others there was the lama, a native persimmon, in winter garlanded with a bright reddish yellow fruit that was sought by the native Hawaiians and the ʻalalā alike. Often found in the dry forest in the company of the lama was the hōʻawa, which Rock saw "loaded" with fruit. Around 1909, he found abundant ʻalalā near

Puʻuwaʻawaʻa, industriously mining the seed capsules. "Nearly 80 percent of all the capsules of this species examined by the writer were eaten out by these birds, which are still very common."

While the ʻalalā did not eat the seeds or fruit of every tree, each played a part in helping to create the understory, protective canopy, or other habitat in which the raven lived. And what the ʻalalā did not use, the Hawaiians probably did—or read in it signs.

There was also the thorny wiliwili, bursting in spring with clusters of claw-shaped light orange, green, or blood red flowers with bright orange seeds; the naio, with fragrant pink blossoms and with seeds so hard that when the Kona grosbeak finch— a species that has long since vanished—cracked them with its immense beak, the sound ricocheted through the forest; the hau kuahiwi, already extremely rare when Rock visited the lava fields of Hualālai in 1909 (specimens today can be found only in botanical gardens or under cultivation); and the native red cotton tree with its bright red flowers. Like the hau kuahiwi, today the once common cotton tree survives only in botanical gardens. The ʻaiea, whose globose orange fruit was favored by the ʻalalā, produced a sticky sap that early Hawaiians applied to branches to catch birds.

By 1910, cattle, sheep, pigs, and other mammals had already destroyed much of the forest. Clearing of the land and logging also played a role. And so went the story of decline for many forests in Hawaiʻi—and with them the bird species that once thrived. But Puʻuwaʻawaʻa was singular in that much of its spectacular diversity remained late into the 1900s. And it was tragic in the premeditated means by which much of what remained was recently destroyed.

These forests of Puʻuwaʻawaʻa were as slow growing as they were diverse, and like human elders, the ancient trees were among the first to go in the face of physical stress. And because they grew slowly, the dry forests were also slower to recover from disruption than the higher cloud forests.

While the native dry forests had been shrinking ever since the arrival of the first Polynesians, even in the 1950s L. P. Richards reported that the 'alalā were "quite plentiful" around Pu'uwa-'awa'a. Once he saw eight and heard a dozen more on the ranch. Up to this time 'alalā also commonly nested in the dry 'ōhi'a belt and up to the base of a place called Potato Hill, a few miles south of the Furrowed Hill.

While often cited in the literature as a major modern problem for the 'alalā, the elimination of the forest understory actually began centuries ago. In 1794, British explorer George Vancouver brought several cattle to the island of Hawai'i, and the king at the time, Kamehameha the Great, released them on the slopes of Hualālai above the town of Kailua and placed a ten-year kapu, or prohibition, on them, allowing them to freely breed. Descendants of these cattle have lived in the forests there ever since. Botanist C. S. Judd wrote, "The toothsome 'ie'ie vines, the ti and banana plants, some of the ferns and native grasses afforded very attractive pasturage for the descendants of the cattle."

Not long after Cook's visit, seafaring traders discovered the alluringly fragrant sandalwood in the dry forests, and there was such a rush by Hawaiians to harvest and sell the trees that the taro fields suffered for want of workers. On Hawai'i Island, one missionary reported meeting a chief with about four hundred people returning with sandalwood trees. Elsewhere, mention is made of parties three thousand strong gathering sandalwood in parts of the island. By the mid-1800s, the largest accessible trees had been cut. Then, with the arrival of whaling vessels beginning in the 1800s, the forests were further exploited for timber to repair ships; fiber plants such as the olonā, prized by the whalers for harpoon lines; and other products.

While there were no recorded observations, let alone formal studies, during the time that described adverse effects upon the 'alalā, one can surmise that many of the bird species in these heavily logged areas had already seen their better days.

In the wake of logged sandalwood, by 1850 the abundance of free-ranging cattle supported "boiling plants" for the extraction of tallow, the only part of the animal, besides the hide, having any value. Fire-fueling exotic grasses overran the cleared or grazed lands. Goats and sheep browsed on trees and bushes and, like cattle, prevented regeneration of koa trees and wiped out many native understory plants. It was as if the underbrush had been cleared to create a shaded park.

Since the late 1800s, cattle, sheep, and goats had freely grazed more than a hundred thousand acres of Pu'uwa'awa'a. Even in the late 1950s, the commissioner of public lands of the Territory of Hawai'i argued that, with proper actions, the "carrying capacity" of the area could be increased by a thousand head of cattle. "In general, this area needs more sunlight by clearing out more of the native trees in some areas and elimination of dense patches of brush weeds in other areas," he wrote. Many of his recommendations were carried out.

Despite the terrible toll, patches of native forest perservered, and in 1905 District Forester J. A. Maguire for the first time argued for their protection. Maguire knew that ranchers would never cede private land for protection, but he reckoned that state-owned land could "be easily reserved."

There are many time gaps in the history of Hawaiian ornithology often spanning decades, voids of knowledge, the consequence of war and other events that curtailed travel to the islands. And so it was that Pu'uwa'awa'a was subsequently forgotten.

Then in 1945, as World War II wound down and the island again became a subject of biological interest, Arthur L. Mitchell echoed in a National Park Service report that many plants and trees at Pu'uwa'awa'a were the last of their kind. He argued, "If we are to be assured of success in preserving these tree species, it seems as if the only solution will be to protect these trees in their natural habitat." The National Park Service recommended "that an area be selected of fifty to one hundred acres where a representative population of native trees exists and be turned into a 'Sanctuary of Native Trees.' . . . It will afford a place where native species can be replanted or encouraged to propagate themselves." Despite the ravages thus far, such a reserve would also have been the first safe haven for the dwindling ʻalalā.

Much of the land was owned by the state—including a sprawling and breathtaking area known as Puʻuwaʻawaʻa Ranch. Reclassifying the land to protected status would have cost little. The gesture would have stood for more than protecting plants and animals alone. The establishment of a sanctuary—the word comes from the Hebrew for a sacred place set aside for God—would have signaled an intent that the early Hawaiians would have appreciated: land as a source of spirit rather than material profit alone.

But such a sanctuary was not to be, and cattle, sheep, and feral pigs continued to freely roam. With logging, ranching, and other activities making money, voices on behalf of the area's native plants and animals were barely audible. The long history of state-assisted destruction of Puʻuwaʻawaʻa continued.

Then, in 1972, F. Newell Bohnett, cofounder of the once popular Sambo's restaurants, leased 108,000 acres of Puʻuwaʻawaʻa Ranch from DLNR. The tract encompassed almost all of the most biologically sensitive areas in the region, including some of the most valuable remaining ʻalalā habitat. The lease, in word, prohibited Bohnett from making any change to the land not directly related to improving pasture. Even then, any alteration of the land required DLNR's prior permission. Improvements that increased the value of the property would also lead to a commensurate increase in leasing fees. Fallen trees in pastureland could be removed, but logging within the forest was prohibited, and selling of any timber was illegal. No sooner had Bohnett signed the lease than he began "improving" the ranch.

In 2000 and 2001, editor and reporter Patricia Tummons conducted a painstaking investigation of Bohnett's activities at Puʻu-waʻawaʻa. She told of his land depredations in a series of articles in the newsletter she founded, *Environment Hawaiʻi*. If the forests were already in decline by the time Bohnett gained control, giving him stewardship was, according to Tummons, like "entrusting the welfare of a beloved invalid, whose best hope for recovery depends on tender care and aggressive medical treatment, to Jack the Ripper." She called the Furrowed Hill the Hill of Sorrows.

In early 1976, Bohnett cut a fence line right through a koa forest and the heart of the important breeding area of the region's ʻalalā and cleared extensively on both sides of the cut, without having obtained the required permit. Paul Banko had been monitoring ʻalalā in the immediate vicinity. One pair built a nest in 1974 and produced three chicks, with one fledgling surviving. In 1975, the pair built a second nest less than a quarter mile from the first one and produced yet another fledgling. When Banko visited the site on May 26, 1976, after the cut had been completed, he was shocked to find that "the territory has been bisected with a new 150–200 foot bulldozer cut & fenceline. . . . [The] 1974 nest tree still stands but [the] 1975 tree apparently has been destroyed." The next morning, however, Banko was able to locate the intrepid pair, in yet a third new nest about a half mile from the old one. In mid-June, he returned to find the female of the pair sitting in the empty nest. In late July, he returned and heard the pair calling some distance from the still barren nest. It was the last nesting pair ever reported seen at Puʻuwaʻawaʻa.

Faced with continuing, if less dramatic, decline of habitat elsewhere, by 1974 only two ʻalalā were documented on Hualālai, the ancient volcano on whose slope the bulge of Puʻuwaʻawaʻa was located. And by every indication, the remaining population on the island was rapidly collapsing.

Bohnett then cleared land for a paved airstrip and built a seven-million-gallon reservoir without notifying the state, let alone obtaining the required written permission. Bohnett maintained that his actions were legal because they were all in the interest of improving pasturage. His only fault, he said, was in overlooking a technicality—getting the state's written permission.

Herbert K. Yanamura, an agricultural specialist with the Division of Land Management (DLM)—the division of DLNR responsible for managing land leases—inspected the ranch and confirmed that the construction, including that of the reservoir, paved airstrip, and new airplane hangars, had been done without permission.

Yanamura was also baffled by why such a huge water supply and large delivery pipe were needed for "irrigation," as Bohnett claimed. The proposed irrigation site wasn't even located on the ranch; rather, it was on an adjacent twenty-acre tract privately owned by Bohnett.

According to Tummons, with the unauthorized work already completed, DLM asked Bohnett merely to submit plans for the improvements—after the fact. A few weeks later District Forester Tom K. Tagawa wrote to DLNR's deputy director dismissing Yanamura's complaints and recommending that "the matter be filed."

When former state representative Jean King, long an advocate of protecting Puʻuwaʻawaʻa, heard of the suspicious goings-on, she pressed DLNR for an explanation. Tagawa drafted a response to King for Christopher Dobb, DLNR's chair, to finalize and sign. In a cover memo to this draft, Tagawa—whose motives for protecting Bohnett remain a mystery—wrote, "We believe that this response to Senator Jean King will answer her request without providing her details of the circumstances surrounding the unauthorized improvements being made by Puʻuwaʻawaʻa Ranch."

The lease gave the state the right to conduct research on the ranch, with or without the lessee's permission. Nevertheless, as a neighborly gesture, in 1976 DLNR biologist Jon Giffin wrote to Bohnett seeking permission to look for ʻalalā that might remain at Puʻuwaʻawaʻa. Bohnett immediately wrote to Ernest Kosaka, who by now had risen in the ranks and become Giffin's boss at DLNR, okaying the research but instructing Kosaka to "please contact your friend Giffin and suggest he keep his findings quiet, until we can find out if our crows here are actually an asset to the area or a liability." Bohnett had already concluded, "They are still killing crows in Iowa because of the damage they do to crops. So why are we so overly concerned over their preservation in Hawaii?" In Bohnett's view, apparently, disappearance of the birds would only prove that the ʻalalā was an unfit contender in the modern world. As reported in the newspaper *West Hawaii Today*, Bohnett believed that "grazing of cattle was in accordance with the theory of evolution's basic premise of survival of the fittest—which he thinks the conservationists must believe in—[and] was working in that cows are stronger than the crows."

In 1978, the Natural Area Reserves System Commission, established by state legislation in 1971 to advise DLNR on conservation matters, proposed a 3,300-acre sanctuary at Puʻuwaʻawaʻa Ranch —a small fraction of the leased land. In response, Bohnett bitterly complained to DLNR: "I do not know what these plants look like, nor do I know their location. I am certain that the beauty of our area would not be [affected] in the least if these plants did not exist. This proposal is a classic example of an irresponsible suggestion by an overzealous bureaucrat that has gotten completely out of hand." Setting aside land was a "sacrifice that is too great a price to pay for the pleasure of such a small interest group." DLNR summarily rejected the sanctuary recommendation.

In 1979 Bohnett gave a friend permission to harvest koa on the ranch, permission that was not legally his to give. Such illegal incursions were reported to DLNR in September 1982, but that was not exactly news within the agency. Jon Giffin, the biologist who was conducting the ʻalalā census, had already reported that "'Alalā habitat at Puʻuwaʻawaʻa Ranch was seriously damaged as a result of the koa harvesting. Both dead and live trees were removed and skid trails cut. . . . This operation effectively destroyed the only known ʻalalā nesting site on the ranch. Native forest vegetation at Puʻuwaʻawaʻa deteriorated to a point that it is unlikely that crows will nest there again."

In April 1983, state wildlife biologist Ronald Bachman wrote to his superiors that "rather serious and extensive habitat alteration has occurred within the koa belt as a result of logging and clearing in the area." He also wrote in a memo to the files that hundreds of acres were involved, that native understory was being bulldozed, and that a portable sawmill had been set up. Trees were being sawn into planks and shipped to Honolulu. Bohnett was receiving a share of the profits.

Not until August 1983 — a decade after the lease had been signed — did DLNR issue its first warning. "You are hereby ordered to immediately stop all koa logging operations on land covered by the subject lease and on land classified as a conservation district," DLNR chair Susumu Ono wrote. A few days later, Bohnett replied, curiously: "We received your letter . . . in which you recommend that we cease 'logging' operations . . . logging will cease until we can get official approval from your department."

On November 10, 1983, Ono shot back: "We sincerely urge that you discontinue the logging of koa. . . . Should you disregard this request, we may have no recourse but to institute termination proceedings for breach of lease conditions."

Two months later, state biologists were still finding "evidence of recent logging activity," including a new logging road and fresh stumps of cut koa trees. Not until September 1984, though, did DLNR vote to remove 80,000 of the 108,000 acres covered by his lease. Bohnett paid the state a penalty of $34,600 for 173 trees that had been illegally cut and another $8,541 for the commercial value of the logged trees. DLNR also voted to set aside between three thousand and four thousand acres traditionally used for nesting by the 'alalā. But by that time, the only 'alalā remaining in the area was a single aged female.

With the withdrawal of land from Bohnett's lease, Natural Area Reserves System (NARS) commissioner P. Quentin Tomich was sure that the dream of a sanctuary for native plants, first suggested nearly eighty years before, was at hand: "I felt comfortable and confident," he wrote after submitting a proposal. But DLNR rejected the idea and recommended only that Bohnett "give his full cooperation" to working with NARS to build fences around individual rare trees.

Bohnett then requested and received from the district planning commission approval to build a road from the main highway to his private twenty acres—the land to which he had earlier built the illegal pipeline to deliver water from the illegal reservoir. In his request for the road easement, Bohnett revealed his master plan: a subdivision of luxury houses on his private, water-poor parcel. The "irrigation" pipe would bring water from the ranch to his new luxury housing development, which he would call Pu'ulani, Hawaiian for Heavenly Hill.

The *Honolulu Advertiser* reported that Bohnett later "told the Land Board he had 'admittedly been indiscreet' in doing things with the land. But such indiscretions were because of his role as 'a doer.'" In November 1984 Bohnett took out a full-page advertisement in *West Hawaii Today*, addressed to the people of Kona, asserting that his "most serious concern is for those of you who desire to have a better and financially independent Kona."

If his alleged concern lived, dreams of a sanctuary for native plants and the 'alalā at Pu'uwa'awa'a would not. On September 6, 1986, between half past three and four o'clock in the morning, three suspicious fires were set at different places in the vicinity of Pu'uwa'awa'a, in the dry brush just below the Maui scenic lookout along the main road. By the time the fire was brought under control, three days later, among the last remaining tracts of native dry forest in the Hawaiian Islands lay smoldering. Today the area has a few lonesome lama and wiliwili trees, thick tussocks of alien fountain grass that quickly invaded after the fire, and a parched land that will almost certainly never again welcome the 'alalā.

By then, only a few 'alalā stragglers still came and went about Pu'uwa'awa'a Ranch. There was momentary hope in 1990, when an 'alalā was unexpectedly spotted there. A July 7 headline in the *Honolulu Advertiser* reported, "Holdout crow spotted: Pu'uwa-'awa'a discovery is big surprise." The bird's presence was not so much a hope as a sad reminder: one more sighting of the same aged female who briefly came to visit her old nesting grounds.

With the birds all but gone at Pu'uwa'awa'a, they fared little better elsewhere on Hualālai. And they continued to decline on Mauna Loa, fifteen miles to the south. By 1990, fewer than a dozen 'alalā remained in the wild.

Late on a winter afternoon in 1998, driving along State Highway 190 toward Pu'uwa'awa'a, I think of my journey into the world of the 'alalā and how far I have traveled since first reading about the bird. More than ten years later, driving toward the Furrowed Hill, I am still in pursuit.

All roads leading into the ranch are gated. So I drive to Pu'ulani, the site of Bohnett's luxury development. As luck would have it, real estate agents are holding open house, and the gate is open. The crowds of visitors will hide my wandering presence. At the far end of the partially built development, I drive around the chain posts of an unpaved road. Worried about drawing attention, I park in a secluded spot behind a half-built mansion. From here the Furrowed Hill is visible several miles away. A detailed topographical map before me, I identify certain features of the landscape, including the paved landing strip. I mark my parking spot on the map and with my compass calculate a bearing toward the summit. With evening approaching, I fear becoming lost in the dark in a land of wild pigs and feral dogs. I park the car facing Puʻuwaʻawaʻa, activate the emergency blinkers, and, in an abundance of caution, carefully position a sheet of plywood to conceal the back blinkers. With front beacons to lead me home, I set out down a steep hill with map, compass, flashlight, and bottled water in a day pack.

The hillside underbrush is a mix of exotic brushes and trees clinging to a steep slope that has apparently eluded cattle or other grazers. I burrow my head in my nylon parka and blindly plow through the brush, whacking my head on large branches and against a tree. After an hour of bushwhacking, the landscape opens up. It is easy going through the pasture toward the massive cinder cone. It is another hour before the ground steepens underfoot. The sun has already fallen behind the steep slope I earlier descended. There is little time. I struggle up the steep hillside, gaining perhaps only a couple hundred feet before late evening convinces me to return. The rolling hills sweep toward Kawaihae Bay. Exhausted, I lie in the grass.

My eyes open to a sky of diamond dust. My heart pounds. Startled by a sudden baying of dogs, I lunge up. The water bottle in the crook of my arm flies off into the darkness. I dash down the slope. I drop my parka and my feet get tangled in it, sending me flying. The baying of dogs surrounds me, and I expect to feel teeth puncturing my leg. There is nothing but a small tree ahead. I climb the trunk, which bows under my weight, and soon the baying ceases. I scan the horizon for the top of the hill I had first descended. I slide down the tree and search for a stick to fend off any attacking dogs. The barking begins anew. I sprint toward the beckoning lights high in the distance. Soon I am at the brush-covered slope leading up Heavenly Hill. By now the baying has receded into the distance, but I still have to struggle through the brush, now exhausted by fear and physical exertion.

When I reach the car, blood pumps audibly through my temples. The lights of the ranch's outbuildings below glow faintly. There is the outline of Puʻuwaʻawaʻa's rounded summit under starlight. Canis Major wheels overhead. I climb into the car and rest my head on the steering wheel. My body shakes, and I realize that all I have learned of Bohnett and Puʻuwaʻawaʻa must have become man-ifest as a profound physical fear. My mind keeps turning over lines from the Kumulipo:

> Fear falls upon me on the mountain top
> Fear of the passing night
> Fear of the night approaching
> Fear of the pregnant night
> Fear of the breach of the law
> Dread of the place of offering and the narrow trail
> Dread of the food and the waste part remaining
> Dread of the receding night

The gate to Heavenly Hill has not been closed, and I drive out and down to the scenic overlook a few miles along the main road. Across the ʻAlenuihāhā Channel, the faint blue face of the volcano Haleakalā rises on distant Maui. I turn, my back to the sea, and stare at the naked silhouette of Puʻuwaʻawaʻa.

CHAPTER *12*

BARBARA
CHURCHILL LEE

I N LATE 1976,
when 'Umi, Hina, and Kekau, the three fledglings captured by
Paul Banko, were ensconced at their new home in the shadow of
a bombing range, fate showed up at their door. Or that is how
Barbara Churchill described her arrival at Pōhakuloa.

In her thirties, with long chestnut hair and dark, intelligent
eyes, Barbara came to the front entrance of the facility unan-
nounced. She must have been a welcome sight to Ah Fat Lee, the
short, handsome man who stepped out of the main building to
greet her. Lee was considered the grand old man of the Hawaiian
endangered species program—such as it was—having successfully hatched and reared thousands of endangered nēnē, or
Hawaiian geese, over his thirty years at Pōhakuloa. Yet he had
received no formal training in breeding birds. As a state worker,
he had just happened into that position—much as the visitor
was about to do—and he had succeeded brilliantly at his largely

self-taught undertaking. But raising the adaptable nēnē would prove to be far easier than breeding ʻalalā.

Sixty-five-year-old Lee gazed at the visitor, musing on the purpose of her visit to this out-of-the-way place. They soon struck up a conversation. Churchill had recently moved from the West Coast to Hawaiʻi, she explained. Lee said little at first, and when he spoke he stuck mostly to talk of the nēnē. Finally, Churchill asked, "Need any extra help up here?"

Lee was skeptical that this visitor could manage the demanding work. But with the recent arrival of the three ʻalalā—the first ever held at the facility—he needed help.

"You put on rubber boots?" he asked.

"Sure," she said.

"And sweep?"

"Of course."

"Without pay?"

She nodded, and he handed her a broom and pointed toward the nēnē pens, which she swept to Lee's satisfaction. He took her on as a volunteer.

Through that winter, beneath Mauna Kea's silvery summit, Churchill and Lee shared with each other the private details of their lives. Lee confessed, his voice reflecting his shame, that he had only a high school education and had never married.

Churchill in turn revealed that she had returned to Hawaiʻi a couple of years earlier after having been diagnosed with leukemia. Her family had a very long history here, she said, and she had come back to find peace. She told him that she was a descendant of early missionaries in Hawaiʻi. She said that her first husband had been killed in the Korean War, and she had spent the next twenty years on the West Coast raising their two young sons and earning her law degree from Stanford Law School. Soon she threw herself into caring for the ʻalalā, making the long drive from the Kohala Coast at sunrise and returning home after dark.

"I fell in love with the 'alalā from the very beginning. They were my family and my children. It was love at first sight—with both the birds and Ah Fat," she would later recall.

Less than a year after Churchill and Lee met, they married. Barbara Churchill Lee, still a volunteer, had, by luck and by marriage, become the de facto director of the state's 'alalā recovery program—and overseer of one of the world's rarest birds.

Confined to a single, cramped pen, 'Umi, Hina, and Kekau often fought until Lee placed the aggressive Kekau in a separate aviary. By observing their solicitous preening and noisy communication and their mutual defense of territory when rats entered their cage, Lee concluded, accurately, as it turned out, that 'Umi and Hina were a pair. Unaware that rats could attack and kill nestlings, Lee thought that the 'alalā "had a fine time" chasing away or sometimes catching and killing the long-tailed marauders. "One time 'Umi nailed one!" she said, meaning he stabbed a rat to death with his bill before then eating it.

Respectful of Hawaiian culture and, by her own admission, always trying to compensate for the "missionary guilt" left by her proselytizing ancestors, Lee bestowed Hawaiian names on the birds, often after great chiefs or legendary figures of Hawaiian history.

"'Umi, he was the son of King Līloa," she related. "'Umi grew up to become a kind king himself, revered for caring for old people and fatherless children. He was so respected that rulers of other islands offered their favorite daughters to him as wives. In time, King 'Umi had numerous children, giving rise to the common expression that 'no commoner could declare that 'Umi was not his ancestor.'" The name was prophetic, it turned out. In time, 'Umi the 'alalā would also father so many that few captive birds were unrelated to him.

"'Umi was my favorite," Lee confessed. "Very male and an adventurer. From the time he was brought to the project, he was boss, always trying to go further, dig deeper, break off every branch; he just tried everything. When he took a bath he'd splash all of the water out before Hina had a chance to bathe. Finally they worked it out so that Hina bathed first. I'd put more water in and . . . leave it overflowing for ʻUmi, who then had a marvelous time. He was a clown. . . . This was in sharp contrast to the quiet and shy Hina. At one point ʻUmi and Hina had eggs and young. The young disappeared one night," she continued, blaming it on rats, which now she recognized as a potential threat.

Lee's responsibilities grew in 1977 when three more wild fledglings joined ʻUmi, Hina, and Kekau. Lee named the new captives Ulu ("to grow" in Hawaiian), ʻEleʻū, and Luʻukia (named after a queen from Kona, according to Lee). With six ʻalalā now under her care—the most ever in captivity—the long-haired stranger who had shown up at Pōhakuloa just a year before was now practically in charge of a species.

Lee hand-fed Ulu, ʻEleʻū, and Luʻukia, barely out of the nest, and kept them in the bathroom at her home until they were old enough to move to their pens at Pōhakuloa. She often cuddled them in her arms, feeding them fruit and other morsels from her fingertips, talking to them. So closely did Lee tend the birds that Luʻukia came to display sexual behavior in her presence.

"The crows are imprinted on me," Lee innocently boasted to a reporter for *West Hawaii Today*, unaware that sexual identification with a human would interfere with the birds' natural mating behavior. "They know I am their source of food. This is a luxury I can afford, since these ʻAlalā will remain as breeding stock. If they were going to be released in the wild, I couldn't become this friendly with them."

Lee had no formal training in biology, ornithology, or the care of captive birds. "I didn't know a thing about ʻalalā," she said. To her credit, Lee personally bought virtually every book she could find on crows and sought the counsel of renowned ornithologists.

In choosing Lee to fill an immediate need for a volunteer, the state had unwittingly begun to fulfill Winston Banko's prophecy: that the Department of Land and Natural Resources would try to garner as much federal support as possible for the program while spending as little of it as possible on the ʻalalā. As for Lee, in 1978 DLNR promoted her to "biological consultant," and she would soon be on the state payroll for the first time.

Lee, meanwhile, had visited the mainland to see her oncologist, who told her that the leukemia was in complete remission. If caring for the vanishing ʻalalā had given her a new life, her hope and joy would not last.

In August 1978, Lee was visiting Honolulu while Ah Fat remained behind. One morning as he sprayed the weeds in the aviaries with the herbicide Roundup, Ah Fat noticed that ʻUmi and Hina were uncharacteristically quiet. He brushed it off as the stress of their molting. The next day, he returned to the pen and discovered the unthinkable. He immediately telephoned Lee. In a shaky, soft voice, he said, "Barbara, Hina died last night."

"My God!" Lee cried. "How did it happen?"

"I have no idea," Ah Fat replied. "I'm going to send her down to the main office now. We got the ants off."

"You've got to get it necropsied as soon as possible to see what's wrong! I'll be on the next flight."

She arrived at Pōhakuloa that night in a state of near hysteria. Cringing at the memory, Lee later recalled, "When Hina died, I suddenly realized, my God, this isn't the place for an endangered species!"

Lee drove Hina to a veterinarian in Kailua for a necropsy. She remained throughout the procedure, taking detailed notes as the doctor cut through Hina's body with a scalpel and narrated his findings into a tape recorder: a discolored kidney here, an abnormality there; a swab of this, a swab of that.

"Standing there and watching Hina get cut open wasn't easy

because these birds were my children. Luckily, I've never had to go through necropsies with my human children, but, ah, I went through three of them with the 'alalā!" she recalled.

The necropsy was inconclusive.

Her nightmare continued. In June 1979, Kekau grew gravely ill. Lee's journal entry for the day seems to describe a tragedy of such proportions that every historical detail should be recorded:

> [Kekau] found on ground under bushes (near pond). 1 P.M. Lethargic, non-responsive to food including mealworms, watermelon and puppy chow. Crouching stance under bushes wings dropping loosely, eyes half-closed—crest up when approached. At 1:30 P.M., offered live sparrow to Kekau to test reactions (also entered pen alone). He grabbed for the bird but caught only feathers—hopped a short distance toward released sparrow, then gave up attempt. Seemed quite weak. Came back to edge of pond, stood on edge and drank two sips from pond. Stood for approximately 15 minutes before squatting down. Accepted two mealworms and one small bit of watermelon but without interest. Wings still drooping. Discoordinated in walking/hopping way to food stand perch (approx. 20 feet) while on rim of pond Kekau slowly dropped until his head and neck were hanging down into the pond with tip of beak in water.

Lee pronounced Kekau dead at 8:45 P.M.

Then, reliving the painful experience of Hina's death nine months earlier, Lee carried Kekau to the veterinarian for necropsy, maintaining her composure as she once again took detailed notes. The veterinarian took tissue from the lungs, stomach, liver, gizzard, kidneys, spleen, and intestines. When he cut away the delicate skull with scissors to remove the tiny brain, he saw a bruise that suggested severe trauma to the right side of the head.

"Wouldn't he have died instantly?" Lee asked.

"Maybe. Maybe not," the vet said, according to Lee.

Lee added the note to her copy of the necropsy report: "Possible —army maneuvers may have caused disturbance at night and possibly trauma by causing him to bash against wires." She also noted that she had seen "cats on top of cage," suggesting that the bird could have injured himself in a frenzy to escape.

Less than two weeks after Kekau's death, ʻEleʻū died. The cause of death in this instance was bird malaria, spread by infected mosquitoes.

Three deaths within twelve months had halved the size of the captive flock. By then it had dawned on both Lee and DLNR that breeding the hardy Hawaiian goose was one thing, and caring for the less hardy and less adaptable ʻalalā was something else. The fact that three surviving ʻalalā would soon be joined by several new captured fledglings was little consolation. Living in captivity was beginning to look almost as dangerous as living in the wild.

Lee could barely muster the courage to watch another post-mortem, least of all on ʻEleʻū, whom she called "Mama's girl." After the necropsy, Lee carefully picked up ʻEleʻū's mangled body and caught a flight to Honolulu. She had already relinquished the body of Hina to the Bishop Museum there, for supposed scientific purposes. Despite having promised to "take care of her," museum officials left Hina's carcass in a freezer in the main office for almost a year, explaining that since a "study skin" couldn't be made out of the dissected bird, the museum "had no use for her," according to Lee.

As Lee carried ʻEleʻū's body through the front doors into the Bishop Museum, she broke into sobs and suddenly turned away and returned to her car. A short time later, she was on a return flight to Hawaiʻi Island, with ʻEleʻū in a small cardboard box clutched at her lap.

As evening clouds formed over Hualālai, the mountain of ʻEleʻū's birth, Lee drove up the winding road toward its summit. She parked her car at a turnoff and hiked into the forest near where ʻEleʻū had been captured as a fledgling six years earlier.

"It was not dark, nor fully light," she recalled. "My emotions

were swinging between guilt and relief. Could I have done more?
No, I had done all I could do. But could I have done more? No. Did
I do something wrong? Yes. No! Yes! No!"

Exhausted from the emotional struggle, she dug a hole near the
nest tree and laid down 'Ele'ū's body as if burying her own child.
She prayed for 'Ele'ū, covered the body with handfuls of earth, and
drove down the mountain in darkness.

Several days later, state officials began asking Lee what had
become of 'Ele'ū's body. "Only the morning star knows," she
replied. And so began what would become known as the "Bones of
Contention" affair.

Federal biologist Ernest Kosaka, who was based in Hawai'i,
telephoned Lee to follow up on the matter. She confessed but
refused to disclose 'Ele'ū's burial place. In notes he made about
their conversation, Kosaka wrote that Lee had "become more of a
hindrance to the propagation project, but we are leaving it to the
State to resolve this problem because it is theirs! (Thank God.)"

The affair escalated, and in July 1979 Ronald L. Walker, chief of
the Wildlife Branch of DLNR's Division of Fish and Game, sent
Lee a memo titled "Your role in the recent disposition of an
Hawaiian crow . . ." Walker stated what he viewed as the facts:

1. 'Ele'ū died at approximately 11:40 P.M. Thursday, June 21st and
   that the death was a "hard" one.

2. The next day, Friday, June 22nd at 6:00 A.M. you became aware that
   Ah Fat Lee was planning to prepare and send the carcass to
   Honolulu for transshipment to mainland laboratories via the local
   office of the U.S. Fish and Wildlife Service.

3. You felt that this procedure was not the right one and that it would
   be better to get the carcass analyzed locally, because of the more
   rapid response from the local veterinarians. You felt that by freez-
   ing the body, and sending it to the main-land, a determination of
   the cause of death would be more difficult.

4. Therefore, without notifying Mr. Lee, you took the carcass from the Pōhakuloa project and flew with it to Honolulu where you contacted Dr. Allen Miyahara and Dr. Sawa. An autopsy was performed on Eleu at the Halawa Quarantine Station and tissue from various organs was retained by Drs. Miyahara and Sawa for future analysis.

5. Upon completion of the autopsy, you took the remains of the bird and informed David Woodside that you would take it to the Bishop Museum for deposit there. However, upon reflection, you decided that there was no need for another specimen at the museum, and that it would be better to return the carcass to the Big Island.

6. You then flew back to Hawaii with the remains and took them to Kona and hid them away somewhere on Hualālai mountain.

7. At no time did you either contact or consult with Ah Fat Lee, the Endangered Species Project Supervisor at Pōhakuloa, Ronald Bachman, the District Wildlife Biologist in charge of the Wildlife Branch on Hawaii or myself. . . .

The death of even one bird is extremely important and decisions made as to follow up to determine the cause of mortality may affect all of the other birds at the project. . . .

I must state that in this instance you were wrong. May I have your assurance that in the future this will not happen again?

Walker cc'd the memo widely.

The memo genuinely baffled Lee. If the ʻalalā were so important, why hadn't the state hired a professional bird person to run the propagation program at Pōhakuloa? And what business, she wondered, did Ron Walker have preaching to her about giving a bird a proper burial? On July 22, Lee let him have a piece of her mind in a memo she titled "ʻEleʻū, Hawaiian ʻalalā, and the Bones of Contention," which she cc'd to a raft of people in and outside Walker's department: "The actions of . . . your office . . . regarding the determination and supervision of the disposition of dead 'alalā, nene, kola and Laysan teal have been 'improper and regretful' at best and negligent at worst."

Lee accused the state Division of Fish and Game of routinely doing far worse in disposing of dead specimens than spiriting away a carcass for a proper Hawaiian burial. Lee pointed out that the state often dumped dead specimens in the freezer and left them there for a decade or more—without necropsies or other studies. Sometimes they used the specimens as study skins or mounts or skeletal specimens for display at Fish and Game offices —also without postmortems or even a record of the approximate time of death. Other specimens had been dumped in the manure trench at the Pōhakuloa project or in the army dump without examinations having been made.

A graduate of Stanford Law School, Lee went on to point out specific evidence for her claims:

August, 1978—An unnamed 'alalā fledgling, found dead near its nest in the field by Jon Giffin, F&G Wildlife Biologist on Hawaii, was sent to the Honolulu F&G office. No necropsy was performed, nor were tissue samples taken. The assumed cause of death, strangulation by hanging, was never verified. The fledgling remained in the F&G freezer for 10 months.

October 1978, A refrigerator-freezer, crammed full of bird specimens . . . was sealed tightly and taken, intact, to the Army's sanitary land-fill, dumped and buried. Both the freezer and the refrigerator compartments contained frozen, partially frozen, desiccated and rotting carcasses which had been there for from five to ten+ years. Aside from an occasional gross exam by Ernest Kosaka or Ah Fat Lee, no necropsies were performed, nor were laboratory tests done.

Also in June, 1979—Following 10 months of my persistent inquiries and remonstrances, the official approval necessary was presumably received and two 'alalā specimens were taken from your office to the Bishop Museum by David Woodside, about a week after Kekau's arrival there. The two 'alalā (Hina and the wild fledgling) were so desiccated by their 10 month stay in the F&G freezer that they were unfit for any purpose other than skeletal remains.

June 21, 1979—'Ele'ū died, as did Kekau, following an alarmingly short and irreversible illness, only 2½ days. She did indeed, die 'hard': the final four hours of her life included weakness so pronounced she couldn't stand or crouch comfortably—so I held her; unremitting diarrhea; inability to breathe or swallow easily, and wrenching, painful convulsions every 10–12 minutes. The name 'alalā also means "the cry of a young child" and I sincerely hope you never have to experience what 'Ele'ū or I or Ah Fat went through for four hours.

Now we come, quite literally, to the bones of contention:

June 22, 1979— . . . There was no doubt in my mind that 'Ele'ū's fate, through the "chain of command," was a freezer for an unspecified period of time and eventual transshipment to the mainland at some future date. . . .

The living 'alalā at Pōhakuloa could not afford to take a chance on leisurely bureaucratic delay. 'Ele'ū's death, the second in a ten-day span, clearly indicated a perilous and urgent problem, or series of problems, at Pōhakuloa.

I now had less than complete confidence in the people involved in the decision making process governing the disposition of "such precious resources as the captive nene, 'alalā and other endangered birds." I can't imagine where your "coherence and coordination" can be— I see very little of it in State or Federal agencies in Hawaii. I see a good deal, however, of inter-agency jealousy, lack of communication and apathy.

Once again, I brought a dead 'alalā promptly to Honolulu, through independent, and this time unilateral, action. Once again I helped arrange swift and thorough pathological examinations with the distinct advantage in having the same pathologist and histologist doing comparative value studies on the three dead Pōhakuloa 'alalā. Duplicate fresh and fixed tissue samples were carefully prepared by Drs. Sawa and Miyahara and delivered to the local office of USFWS.

After all this was *pau*, my maternal and ancestral feelings took over: Eleu is not in a freezer; not stashed away in one of . . . [the]

numerous cubby-holes in the Bishop Museum; not in some strange corner of the nation's attic, the National Museum; not in a sanitary land-fill or manure trench; not in whatever mainland laboratories use these days for antiseptic carcass disposal.

'Ele'ū's bones are, with dignity and love, in a place known only to the morning star.

In response to Lee's seven-page memo—or "memoranda," as one DLNR staffer wryly called it—Kosaka circulated an urgent memo of his own, warning biologists and researchers to clean up their own messy act when it came to the disposition of endangered species specimens. Clearly, Lee had touched a nerve.

Despite the reprimand, Lee seemed at first to prevail. A year after the debacle, she was portrayed in a highly positive feature article in *West Hawaii Today* titled "Saving Hawaii's Endangered Birds." "She has had remarkable success getting all six crows currently at the facility to pair up and mate," the reporter wrote. "She also is the first person ever to succeed in getting 'alalā to breed and lay eggs in captivity." A photograph on the page portrays a smiling Lee, offering Hi'ialo, one of the wild birds brought into captivity, a drink from a garden hose as the bird perches on her left shoulder, its beak agape.

Still, the article concludes with Lee stating that the future of the 'alalā depended upon two big ifs: "If we're successful in raising the 'alalā to the release stage and if we can restore their habitat, then maybe the 'alalā won't be the next extinct bird on the island of Hawaii."

On February 27, 1981, however, the state fired Lee and restricted her access to the 'alalā. The state then hired a professional aviculturist, Fay Steele. After discovering the shoddy conditions and charged situation at Pōhakuloa, within days of his hiring Steele gave notice that he was quitting at the end of March.

But on the seventh of that month, his belongings still packed,

Steele discovered Lee standing in one of the aviaries with an ʻalalā perched on her shoulder. The bird pecked at food held between Lee's lips. Steele immediately resigned. Even though Lee's husband, Ah Fat, still worked full-time at the facility, her visitation rights were revoked. She would never again visit the birds at Pōhakuloa. Ah Fat himself, now seventy, soon retired and joined his brokenhearted wife at home behind a tangled thicket of vines and tree trunks in Hāwī, near Waimea, in the Kohala hills at the northern end of the island.

In 1984, five years after the state's heady victory to gain control of the ʻalalā propagation program from the Bankos and the federal government, officials took stock of a failed program. There were none of the expected accolades and public relations coups, only embarrassments. Little federal money had been forthcoming. In the five years since the captive breeding program had been established, nine ʻalalā had been captured, three had died, and no offspring had been reared. The captive flock stood at six, with the birds having cumulatively aged by fifteen years.

At that time, fewer than thirty ʻalalā were believed to remain in the wild.

It's 1997, and I am visiting Barbara Churchill Lee in the ramshackle two-story house where she lives with her husband, Ah Fat. The house is located in the northern reaches of Hawaiʻi Island, among the worn-down hills of an ancient volcano, now mostly covered in the green of pasture and exotic forest trees or grasses. She greets me at the doorway, offering a shy smile before opening the screen door. We have spoken by telephone several times, and it is only after some convincing that she has agreed to meet and talk about a subject that still causes her deep pain and humiliation. Ah Fat, who has been snoozing on a sofa just inside the door with a newspaper spread across his chest, stands up and offers a warm smile and handshake. Lee gazes about the cluttered dining room as if to apologize. She makes two cups of tea, and we sit down at the table. She rests one slender elbow on the smooth wooden arm of the chair and the other on the table, then places her chin in the palm of one hand—a lean and forlorn Modigliani sculpture.

"I don't know where to begin," she confesses in bewilderment.

"I used to be more outgoing. I'm more reclusive these days since all that with the birds. The press said horrible things about me. I was treated like an outcast. *Environment Hawai'i* called me an 'unprofessional, overzealous volunteer' and accused me of using my political connections to turn the state's captive 'alalā propagation program at Pōhakuloa into my private petting zoo. There comes a point you can't fight it any more. It just wears you down."

As she speaks, she turns to stare out the window onto a dilapidated wooden porch, where birds swirl around a dozen or more feeders. "Most birds are very territorial," she says, as if feeling the need to explain why only three or four bird feeders wouldn't do. "Hanging out a single bird feeder just invites conflict and stress. I try to give each bird or pair of them their own food. They are much more leisurely about eating that way.

"The whole program was built on such deep resentments," she continues, "beginning with the moving of the birds from Volcano, under Win Banko's care, to Pōhakuloa. Everyone on the state's side wanted to justify the state's taking of the birds, and this meant being successful at breeding them. Well, I guess that in the end I made the state look pretty bad, and I have all the enemies I need to prove it.

"Yes, I made mistakes. My God, I had no formal training and just couldn't go it alone! When things started to go wrong, it showed just how ill-conceived the whole program was. The state looked really bad, and I became the scapegoat.

"My burial of 'Ele'ū was what broke the camel's back," she

continues. "I could not limit myself to thinking like a scientist. I had feelings! I will never forget driving up the mountain at Hualālai with 'Ele'ū in a small box on my lap, tears streaming down my face. In my lap I held one of the last broken links between a species' existence and its extinction. There was this deep voice of Hawaiian history and belief in me, telling me that to bury 'Ele'ū was the only thing to do. In the old days, warring groups hid the bones of their own for fear the enemies would dig them up and defile them by making fishhooks and other objects. To this day, no one knows where the bones of King Kamehameha are hidden — probably deep in a cave somewhere along the Kohala Coast. I didn't want the enemies of 'Ele'ū to have her bones, either, because they would defile them in their own way, leaving them in a freezer or dried on a shelf until they get thrown out. I know burying her wasn't technically the correct thing to do, but it was the right thing to do. No scientist is going to understand this issue of dignity and respect.

"I'm sorry it made the state look bad. But at the time, it seemed beside the point, especially when it was doing everything it could to make itself look bad. Ever since the beginning, when the state forced the birds from the hand of the feds, there was an undercurrent of competition, animosity, and a 'We can do it ourselves' arrogance. Of course, in the end, the state looked like a fool, and I looked like some sentimental and unstable woman gone mad. I was following a larger voice of showing respect for one of the last members of a native Hawaiian bird that will soon be no more. I guess that's as good a definition of madness as any other."

After tea, I follow Lee up a narrow staircase, the railing corner posts piled precariously high with magazines, past an overloaded bookstand, and into an attic whose walls are lined with books and photographs of the 'alalā she cared for. Tables and desks are piled high with papers, manuscripts, and magazines, and against one wall stand several shoulder-high bookshelves. It is a repository of information coming apart at the seams. For lack of organization, only the binding force of her inability to let go of the bitter past seems to hold the room together at all.

"This is where I have kept almost every word written about the 'alalā," she explains, pulling open the top drawer and lifting out a manila folder. "I have not looked in here in years, but I still remember where everything is!"

Not only does she remember where everything is; she also seems to have near perfect recollection of all the pages in the files and all the words on the pages, as if she has committed them all to memory. She quotes from memory a letter written several years before — the letter of reprimand from Ron Walker. Then she walks over to the files, plucks out the letter, and sweeps it in front of her face as if trying to wave off an offensive odor. She points to the words she has just recited as if to say, "See, I don't make things up."

She then pulls out her letter of reply. "Here's what I wrote back," she says proudly, letting the words spill from her lips as we sit in a puddle of late afternoon sunlight: "'Only the morning star knows.' That is what the Hawaiian historian Kamakau wrote of Kamehameha's bones."

Surrounded by photographs, files, and other 'alalā memorabilia, Lee spends hours leading me through documents and dozens of photographs. She opens a yellowed envelope and out tumbles a feather. "From 'Umi," she says. She hands it to me. "Keep it if you would like."

I hold it up to the light that streams through the southern window and run the soft tip along my lower lip, as if trying to savor 'Umi's presence.

Her anger seemingly overcome by the pain of an old back injury, Lee says she will spend more time with me later if I would like. As I leave, I imagine her sinking into the dark depths of a cold sea of reclusion.

What unexpected twists and turns of endangered species conservation this journey has taken, I later muse: a library in Philadelphia, wild dogs on a mountain, a ramshackle house in the Kohala hills. I once naively believed that science drove the conservation of the 'alalā. But it was turning out so far to be mostly a story of political conflict and personal anguish. Above all, the endeavor to save the 'alalā seemed more about people protecting their own turf than about preserving the birds' habitat.

chapter 13

THE BIRD CATCHER

W ITH ONLY SIX ʻALALĀ
in captivity after the calamitous five-year history at Pōhakuloa, the
state desperately needed more birds if the propagation program
was to succeed.

But there was a problem.

Adult ʻalalā in the wild had become exceedingly rare. Fledglings
suitable for the breeding program were rarer still. What's more,
federal law prohibited the unauthorized capture of any protected
species — even by state biologists — without a special permit. Violation of these laws could result in large fines and even prison time.
The Hawaiʻi Division of Fish and Game would need a federal permit to capture more fledglings. But getting the required permit
from the U.S. Fish and Wildlife Service could take months — time
that some state biologists believed the species did not have.

Fish and Game already had one federal permit from 1973. But
that permit allowed biologists to rescue only sick or injured ʻalalā
from the wild, which had been the rationale for capturing all those
that had been under Lee's care, and the propagation program
needed healthy ones. So in March 1977, Fish and Game applied to
the Service for a permit to capture healthy ʻalalā fledglings.

Some two months after this application was filed—the Service still had not issued the permit—biologist Jon Giffin captured two young 'alalā in the wild. The day after, Fish and Game chief Ronald L. Walker called Marshall Dillon of the Hawai'i office of the Service to report that, because both of the fledglings were sick or injured, they had been captured legally under the existing permit. Walker then wrote a letter "to follow up on a phoned report of the recovery of injured (disabled) endangered species provided you this day. The subjects were two young 'alalā (Hawaiian crow) nestlings recovered in an emaciated condition on Hualālai in Kona by our wildlife biologist Jon Giffin. . . . This salvage action was taken pursuant to my Endangered Species Banding and Scientific Permit Number PRT 8-103-B-C issued 9/31/73 effective that date. . . . I trust that this letter and the phoned report satisfy the conditions of the permit."

The problem was, Walker's remarks and letter to Dillon directly contradicted Giffin—as did a later note to colleagues by Walker on this very point. Indeed, Giffin's own report on the capture stated that the two birds were "removed from the population for captive breeding stock" and that "none of the fledglings . . . showed any indication of parasitism or illness."

Michio Takata, director of Fish and Game, perhaps reflecting anxiety about the lack of the required permit, wrote to Henry A. Hansen, the Hawai'i administrator of the Service: "To date, we have had no response" concerning the earlier application to capture healthy birds. "As you know, we have salvaged two fledglings under the authority of our general, endangered species salvage permit on the basis that they were 'injured' upon advice from your office, pending receipt of requisite permit specifically for the 'alalā." Although getting the required permit months after the fact would not have made the two captures legal, the proper permit would offer a fig leaf should those captures ever be publicly questioned.

In June 1977, with the fledging season drawing to a close and still without the required permit in hand, Giffin captured a third ʻalalā fledgling. When the required permit finally arrived, two months later, Fish and Game must have breathed a sigh of relief. Walker wrote to Giffin and several other colleagues: "You will note from the enclosed permit that we have been given authority to collect young ʻalalā on Hawaii for the project, but that we are limited to five (5). Meaning that we have two more to go to fill our quota." According to the terms of the new permit, while only five healthy birds could be captured, an unlimited number of injured or ill birds could still be brought into captivity.

The actions of state biologists suggest worry that even five healthy new birds would not be enough to reinvigorate the captive breeding program, and the following spring biologists captured three more ʻalalā. They were named Hiʻialo, Mana, and Imia. With the first two birds now described as having been healthy upon capture, that made a total of six healthy birds, exceeding the allowable number by one. That is, unless one of the six birds could be reclassified as "incapacitated due to broken limbs or disease"—and soon one of the birds, Imia, recorded as being healthy when captured, was recast in the files as ill or injured. According to Giffin's original handwritten report on Imia's capture, "the young bird was in excellent condition & was almost adult size." But the state report signed by Walker and Kosaka indicated that the bird was emaciated and that "the keel bone of the fledglings was prominent, especially the McCandless bird." Not only that, but records suggest that the fledgling was taken from a nest on McCandless Ranch without knowledge of the landowner—an allegation that would later fan flames of discord between the rancher and biologists.

I tried to contact Jon Giffin, now the state's chief biologist on the island. After numerous phone calls and e-mails, Giffin finally took my call. He couldn't speak to specifics, he said, because all his files were in "deep storage" and inaccessible. But after several more communications, Giffin did agree to meet face to face. And so, on March 31, 1998, I flew to Hawai'i Island, where his office was located in the small town of Waimea.

During our meeting, Giffin told me that he didn't remember the details about all the permits. When I asked about the discrepancy regarding the health of Imia, he said that to answer that question he would have to refer to his notes, which, unfortunately, he'd subsequently thrown out after they had sustained "water damage."

I showed him my copy of the report on Imia's capture, written in his own hand, describing the bird as being in excellent condition. He seemed taken aback but remarked that "the permits permitted a wide latitude for interpretation." The language in the Code of Federal Regulations concerning endangered wildlife tends to be unforgiving, however: "The authorizations . . . which set forth specific times, dates, places, methods of taking, numbers and kinds of wildlife or plants, location of activity, authorize certain circumscribed transactions, or otherwise permit a specifically limited matter, are to be strictly construed and shall not be interpreted to permit similar or related matters outside the scope of strict construction."

Giffin then told me that he "had thought they had the proper federal permits for capturing the birds. Besides, I didn't handle the permits directly."

At the time of my visit, Giffin probably had more pressing concerns than the lingering permit questions. His boss then was Michael G. Buck, head of the Division of Forestry and Wildlife (DOFAW) within the Department of Land and Natural Resources. As a forester, Buck viewed Hawai'i's forests as much as an economic resource as a conservatory of species. He also questioned the wisdom of spending so much money on a species that was all but doomed. He viewed the 'alalā quagmire as a waste of the state's time and money — an involvement that had been deepened by Giffin's capture of the birds several years before.

As if these problems were not sufficient to put Giffin on the hot seat with his boss, the biologist had earlier shot two wild sheep at Puʻuwaʻawaʻa Ranch without the lessee's permission. While shooting sheep on state land was virtually a time-honored tradition at DLNR, news of it emerged at a particularly inopportune time for Giffin, who had been under consideration for a promotion. According to Buck, someone leaked the news of Giffin's sheep shooting, and the story was all over the two Hawaiʻi Island newspapers, *West Hawaii Today* and the *Hawaii Tribune-Herald*.

In the generally politically charged atmosphere of DLNR, where one's reputation, career, or promotion potentially rode on every utterance and action, just surviving the place was a day's work well done. Reginald David, former executive director of the Hawaiʻi Audubon Society, asked regarding this environment, "Do you really think there was room for the ʻalalā's interest?" Giffin, meanwhile, weathering the political storm, was promoted to chief biologist of Hawaiʻi Island.

SCIENTISTS TO THE RESCUE

R ARE, GLAMOROUS, AND
still mysterious, with little having been published on its biology or
behavior, by the late 1970s the 'alalā had become a golden topic for
academic research. The bird's continuing descent toward extinction only increased its allure.

In the spring of 1978, Stanley A. Temple, an assistant professor in the Department of Wildlife Ecology at the University of
Wisconsin–Madison, joined C. John Ralph, a research ecologist at
the Pacific Southwest Forest and Range Experiment Station in
Honolulu, to determine why the 'alalā was suffering from such
catastrophic mortality in the wild.

Temple had received his Ph.D. degree in zoology from Cornell
University in 1973, and by 1978 he was a rising star in the field of
ornithology. Earlier in his career, as a research biologist for the
World Wildlife Fund and the International Council for Bird
Preservation studying endangered birds on Indian Ocean islands
including Mauritius, former home of the now extinct dodo bird,
Temple began to formulate an interesting theory. Some biologists

claimed that a large tree on Mauritius known to natives as the tambalacoque had not reproduced in almost three hundred years — since about the time the dodo became extinct. Temple hypothesized that the tambalacoque's tough seeds, which the dodo ate, required the crushing action of the bird's gizzard to abrade the seed wall and allow it to germinate once expelled from the bird. To test his theory, Temple fed tambalacoque seeds to domesticated turkeys, planted them after they had passed through their guts, and found that 30 percent of them germinated. His conclusions, which were published in the prestigious journal *Science* and were widely aired, including on PBS television, soon came under vigorous scientific attack. Subsequent researchers pointed out flaws in his methodology, including the citation of literature that supported his theory while ignoring previous studies that did not and failing to compare his results with those of a "control group". Today, Temple's hypothesis regarding the dodo and the tambalacoque is largely discredited.

In the spring of 1978, Temple circulated among USDA Forest Service personnel a proposal to find the "smoking gun" of what was killing the 'alalā. He proposed to set up time-lapse cameras near 'alalā nests to record nesting behavior and incursions of predators or other disruptions. For the work, Temple enlisted one of his new graduate students, David Jenkins, who had done his undergraduate honors thesis on the use of time-lapse photography at Rutgers University, in New Jersey.

By that time, only a remnant population of 'alalā resided on McCandless Ranch. Since the study would require crossing ranch land to reach the birds, C. John Ralph, Temple's collaborator, visited the ranch owner, Cynthia Salley, to secure her permission. Salley expressed reservations.

Although a few scientists came and went on ranch land, Salley's view of their work had begun to deteriorate from polite skepticism to suspicion. She complained of "all these people tramping up the mountain" in quest of "meaningless studies," each arguing why their research was crucial to the 'alalā's survival. But mostly, she worried that researchers were disturbing the 'alalā, perhaps even contributing to their decline in numbers by so doing. Nevertheless, she relented. "Sure, go study the 'alalā," she recalled telling Ralph. "But only on two conditions: Number one, no climbing trees. Number two, watch the birds from behind blinds at all times." She said she repeated herself to make sure he understood.

"Okay! okay! okay!" she recalled Ralph saying, as if to emphasize that her point had been beat into him sufficiently.

A few weeks later, Temple's eager young graduate student, David Jenkins, showed up at Salley's door to introduce himself and explain that he'd be the one doing the fieldwork as part of his master's thesis at the University of Wisconsin. Temple and Ralph would be his supervisors. Until Jenkins' appearance at her door, Salley had heard nothing of graduate student involvement. Jenkins had just traveled from the mainland to Hawai'i Island, and it was too late, Salley realized, to renege on her permission.

"This wasn't really a study for the 'alalā's sake, after all," she recalled about the encounter with the graduate student. "If you have a population that is so fragile and small, it shouldn't be somebody's degree work study. They shouldn't be learning on the job. At that point you need all the experience you can get."

Before launching the camera study, Ralph had solicited the opinions of several biologists, including Winston Banko, his son Paul, and Jon Giffin.

"There is at least some circumstantial evidence that indicates that human activity near nests prior to incubation may cause the birds to desert," the younger Banko warned. "For this reason I generally postpone fieldwork until late May, when nesting activity is well under way and some young have already fledged. I would recommend that precautions be taken in locating nests and observing preincubation behavior prior to setting up cameras."

An existing body of anecdotal evidence did suggest that human disturbance could cause 'alalā to abandon their nests. In 1964, for example, P. Quentin Tomich made one of the first detailed observations of an 'alalā nest on the lower northeastern slope of Hualālai. Closely observed for several weeks by teams of two or three researchers, who also climbed the tree, the 'alalā pair abandoned the nest.

Of the abandonment Tomich wrote, "When the birds did not return after 9 minutes I quickly climbed to the nest. A single egg remained which was heavily stained with yolk from other eggs broken and which was infertile or had otherwise failed in development. It was then obvious that the nest was a failure and that the alarmed behavior observed that morning was part of the process of voluntary abandonment of the nest." Tomich went on to claim that the 'alalā is "outstandingly tolerant of humans . . . and quickly accommodated to our presence." He proposed that "the unfortunate loss of the nest may be attributed to the softness of egg shells which could not withstand the usual pressures during the turning of the eggs and during incubation. A second possibility is that the roof rat . . . may have been a predator on the eggs." A third distinct possibility—nowhere mentioned in the paper—is that the observers' frequent startling of the 'alalā caused them to abruptly launch from the nest, breaking the eggs in the process.

In 1975, the Bankos had also warned that "at the very outset of population surveys, 'alalā were observed to be aware of and react to human activity in their proximity. Signs of curiosity were frequently replaced by those signaling anxiety during the breeding season. Increased vocal and physical activity, including use of the large bill in breaking off twigs, flaking bark, and hammering on tree limbs characterized behavior of pairs disturbed in the vicinity of nest trees. Since the effects of such agitation on nesting success are unknown . . . intensive studies of 'alalā breeding biology were postponed."

Jon Giffin also expressed concern to Temple and Ralph that "frequent disturbance of changing film or other manipulations may result in nest abandonment." Giffin was one who knew first-hand about nest abandonment. In his early studies, the birds had done just that. He wrote of one nest he had discovered in the spring of 1977: "One bird was sitting in the nest while the other stood guard in a nearby Koea . . . tree. The pair was observed for about ten minutes then left alone. When the observer returned fourteen days later, the nest was abandoned." It wasn't the last time that nests were abandoned shortly after being visited by humans. Giffin conceded that the "breeding ʻalalā became extremely agitated when a nest was approached by human intruders. They commonly made threatening dives, scolded and broke sticks with their bills. In several instances it appeared as if a pair might attack, but none ever did." Yet even he concluded at the time that "disturbances by this investigator played no part in the nest failures described because contact was so minimal." Noted ornithologist K. C. Lint had once warned Giffin that "the most critical period in the nesting cycle of common crows is the first seven days of incubation. These birds will occasionally abandon a nest if excessively disturbed during that time, but seldom abandon after incubation is well in progress."

It is impossible ever to know the exact role that up-close human observations may have played in these abandonments. What is known is that in the common mainland raven, interference or competition by fellow corvids in an area can trigger nest abandonment. Overflights and surveillance by other competitors, such as hawks, can also cause common ravens to abandon their nests and build elsewhere. This would make sense for nesting birds being eyed by a predator.

As for ʻalalā, nesting males often buzzed one another's territories or trees, harassing competitors and sometimes even enticing the female from another pair into infidelity — any of which might cause a pair to abandon one nest and build another elsewhere. As the 'alalā population dwindled, one could imagine the competition and conflict over ever rarer mates intensifying, increasing nest abandonment. All this might suggest that, even in the best of times, 'alalā commonly abandoned their nests. It also suggests that, since 'alalā were exquisitely sensitive to disruption, human disturbance probably joined natural occurrences as an additional factor in nest abandonment.

Because the vast majority of research on the 'alalā was conducted only after the bird became extremely rare, little is known of its ways or habits in happier and healthier times of greater abundance. Most information about the 'alalā was derived from a species in distress. There is little of what scientists call "baseline" information with which to compare these final hour observations.

'Alalā normally lay three to four eggs per nest. Of these, only one or two chicks usually survive—if recent observations are a measure of the bird's nesting behavior. 'Alalā at the very beginning or near the end of their reproductive years would very likely produce fewer. In theory, the nine pairs under observation should have produced more than five surviving chicks. Given that the factors responsible for this poor showing cannot be scientifically proven, circumstantial evidence, if not the best guide, was the only kind available.

Giffin listed a number of "inimical factors" to the 'alalā in the wild: reproductive failure, poor survival of young, high mortality rates of fledglings, fowl pox, avian malaria, parasites, predation, loss of habitat, and hunting. Nowhere in his 1977 field report, however, does Giffin suggest that human disturbance might also bear some responsibility.

In the spring of 1978, another state wildlife biologist, Howard F. Sakai, photographed three nests on Mauna Loa. He later set up a surveillance camera about forty-five feet away from one active nest about thirty feet high in the forked branch of an 'ōhi'a. He went to check on the camera the next day. When he returned again two weeks later, the birds were nowhere to be found. The following day Sakai found the relocated pair busily carrying blades of grass and other building material in their beaks to a new nest site. The researchers quickly moved the camera from the abandoned nest to the new one, stationing it about forty-five feet away. When they returned two weeks later, the 'alalā had again apparently deserted. That was just one example of several that he witnessed.

With such a history of abandonment, apparently in the wake of human disturbance, Ralph had received plenty of warnings in the comments he solicited on his and Temple's research proposal. He forwarded these to Temple, along with a cover letter referring to Sakai's ill-fated study, of which Ralph himself was co-investigator. Ralph told Temple that "the season in regards [to] the camera work was, I'm afraid, a bust; too much vegetation and too high up. One of the nests fledged two (!) young—one of which was taken to Pōhakuloa for their colony. The other two pairs under our observation deserted, one three times. For your information ONLY: I suspect that our disturbance early in the nesting cycle was the factor. This bodes ill, if it is true, for nest manipulations early in the cycle. Give this some thought."

Temple agreed, and in his final proposal he stated that "the cameras should be placed into position about midway through the incubation period to avoid the possibility of causing disturbance and abandonment early in the cycle." He added, "Because they need to be checked only infrequently, time-lapse cameras cause minimal disturbance while yielding an enormous amount of information."

However, David Jenkins said that it "made a pretty loud click when the camera went on." And Giffin had already warned, "The 'alalā's sense of hearing is extremely sensitive. The click of a camera shutter at close range has been known to produce a fright response."

Over the 1979 field season, Jenkins set up several cameras to study the nesting biology of seven pairs of the birds in three nests outside McCandless Ranch and four on the ranch. Of the three Hōnaunau Forest Reserve pairs, only one produced a fledgling— and that was in the only nest without a camera mounted nearby.

One of the nests had a nestling. Before the chick fledged, a camera was mounted in the tree. When researchers later returned, the chick had apparently left the nest prematurely. The researchers put it back in the nest, but the following day they found the chick dead at the foot of the tree. This raises the question of whether the noisy camera and its eyelike lens caused the chick to flee from the nest.

In another case a camera was installed in the nest tree. When one of the researchers returned four days later, the 'alalā pair was incubating three eggs. By the time researchers returned three weeks later, the pair had abandoned that nest and taken up residence in an empty nest from the year before. On June 11, researchers found the 'alalā pair incubating two eggs, and the following day they mounted a camera in an adjacent tree. When they returned to service the camera a week later, that nest, too, had been abandoned.

The four pairs under Jenkins' surveillance on McCandless Ranch fared no better. One pair came under camera surveillance on May 11, 1979, within about a week of beginning incubation of three eggs. Jenkins returned five days later to replace the film, and then again eight days later, only to find that the nest had been abandoned. The pair re-nested—only to abandon the nest shortly after another visit by researchers. The pair made yet a third nest. Although no camera was set up, the 'alalā abandoned that nest, too, a few days after researchers visited.

In 1980, Winston and Paul Banko published a paper in which they analyzed the fifty-seven nests studied by Giffin, Jenkins, Sakai, and others in the preceding years. They concluded that the earlier in the breeding cycle the nests were visited, the more often they were abandoned, in effect supporting what had long been suspected.

As the Bankos pointed out, there was no conclusive proof that human disturbance caused nesting failure. If not conclusive, the weight of evidence nevertheless suggested that human disturbance *did* cause abandonment.

Yet Temple maintained that "fears that nest abandonment and low nesting success resulted from our research activities can be allayed. In all cases, abandonment occurred after the birds had incubated their eggs for longer than the normal incubation period. No pairs abandoned nests before the normal incubation period had been completed and eggs failed to hatch. Furthermore, the unhatched eggs which we recovered were found to be infertile."

But there was no conclusive evidence that all the eggs were infertile. According to one of Temple's memos, conclusions were drawn on the basis of a field examination of the eggs in which they were held up against a bright light—a process known as candling. Stronger evidence would have come from laboratory examination of the egg contents for evidence of an embryo, such as spider veining on the inside of the shell. The conclusion drawn by the lab that later examined the broken shells was that the eggs "appeared" to be infertile—a less than certain conclusion.

Even some biologists took exception to researchers' claims that human disturbance had no significant effect upon the nesting 'alalā. In a telephone conversation of January 3, 1980, according to the phone log, U.S. Fish and Wildlife Service staffer Wayne White told Ernest Kosaka that "there was uniform concern that the time-lapse cameras may be causing nest desertion, contrary to the statement made by the two scientists."

All told, during the two years of Temple and Ralph's study, eleven pairs had been monitored for at least a portion of their nesting cycle. Some two thousand feet of film had been captured, covering 3,800 hours of nesting activity. Soon after the study was completed, Jenkins quit the graduate program without obtaining his degree, to take a job in New Jersey. According to Jenkins, the film gathered during the experiment was never completely analyzed.

With the time-lapse study completed, in June 1980 Temple gave a talk at the Third Conference in Natural Sciences at Hawai'i Volcanoes National Park, which he began by stating that "the Hawaiian Crow seems a likely candidate to be the next extinct bird on the island of Hawaii." He reiterated the familiar litany of possible causes for its decline—habitat destruction, hunting, and avian diseases. "Within the past ten years, when work on the crow has been most intensive, we have been able to document the decline in the crow population of at least two breeding pairs per year. . . . During 1978 and 1980, one of my graduate students, Jenkins, and one of C. J. Ralph's biologists, Howard Sakai, have worked intensively on the nesting crow populations. . . . We discovered that this poor rate at fledging young has some very readily identifiable causes . . . senility, diseases, and perhaps inbreeding problems are all likely candidates to explain it."

At the end of Temple's talk, a member of the audience asked, "Do you think it might be possible that all this observation and manipulation could be affecting their present reproductive problems?"

Temple replied: "Well, I've studied a lot of birds during their breeding season, and I think it's safe to say that I have not discovered a species that is quite as amenable as the Hawaiian Crow is. They are certainly sensitive to certain types of disturbance, but the type of disturbance that we have been causing as researchers doesn't appear to cause any observable problems at all."

By the time the study ended, fewer than two dozen 'alalā remained in the wild.

David Jenkins did not share his mentor's confidence that disturbance was not causing nest abandonment. To the contrary, years after the study, Jenkins would lament the potential disturbances that he had naively been party to.

Hoping to talk about the study, I met Jenkins one cold and forlorn spring evening at a restaurant in Milford, New Jersey, an old, not-quite-forgotten settlement on the Delaware River near where he lived. He was on the thin side and had the look of an outdoorsy scholar, with tortoiseshell glasses, a thick reddish brown beard, and thinning hair. He wore khaki trousers and a moss-colored shirt. Jenkins lived in nearby Frenchtown but kept a room in Ocean City near his workplace at Cape May, where he studied the rare piping plover for the state. During our conversation, he wore a disarming expression of mischievous humor—as if his lips always verged on saying something witty and unexpected. In the end, Jenkins proved to be sincere and painfully honest.

He told me that his application to the graduate program at the University of Wisconsin had originally been rejected because he had no experience in fieldwork. It was only after two other students had turned down the opportunity to work on the 'alalā project that Jenkins was accepted into the program.

"To tell you the truth, I was never sure of what I was doing in Hawaii. I was green," he said. "Stanley Temple didn't have tenure yet and had a large number of students working on a lot of his projects. I felt lost and was always asking myself, 'What am I supposed to be doing?'

"I knew nothing about crows but became fascinated with the 'alalā. I remember how an adult would give a call with its mouth full." Jenkins leaned over his beer and imitated the sound as a muffled "Rah! Rah!" "The young in the nest would hear that and give a begging response. As the adult got closer with the food, the relay of calls back and forth grew more feverish. Then the adult landed, and you could tell right off because it gave a completely different sound. And then you could tell the adult was feeding the young because there was a hungry gurgling sound.

"I remember a nest in Hōnaunau, which we thought the birds had incubated for too long. We took out the egg, analyzed it, and determined that it was probably infertile. We mounted the camera, and adults were off the nest for maybe an hour. Probably the eggs were infertile, but it left this nagging feeling. Maybe they're not. Maybe we caused them not to hatch. Quite a few eggs were thought to be infertile, but that was a mere guess. The adults may have abandoned the nests and so the embryos died. So, many of those eggs that we described as 'infertile' may have been viable eggs that were abandoned because of us." Inexperienced and lacking confidence, Jenkins was hesitant to express his growing concerns about the study at the time.

"Also, we climbed some trees when the 'alalā were getting ready to fledge and venturing out onto limbs. I would never do that now. We caused some of these birds to leave their nests. But we put the chicks back in and made sure they were in the nests when we left. But I don't know if you could return a bird that had been disturbed like that to the status quo. If a bird was exposed to a 'predator' once, wouldn't it stand to reason that the predator would be back? I can't imagine a young bird frightened out of the nest by a big predator would just go back. We couldn't just return it to the nest and say, 'It will be okay now.'

"It's true that 'alalā and other birds will make 'false starts' in building nests. They start one, then go build another somewhere else. But we don't know if the human observer is causing this behavior. Birds often try to build their nests secretly, and perhaps if they know a predator has spotted them building it, they'll start a new nest somewhere else. We once found a nest which we thought the 'alalā had already laid eggs in. We climbed the tree. And subsequently the 'alalā abandoned it, right at a critical time around egg-laying. We probably caused that.

"I remember once with Jon Giffin when we got two fledglings on Hualālai. We banded them and took blood with a needle. One of the birds went into shock. Boy, was it scary when the 'alalā started panting and its wings drooping. We put it back on the ground. It survived, because we saw it later. But the other one we never did see again.

"Then there was all our filming. We used Super 8, which made a pretty loud click when the camera went on. Some of these were only a few feet from the nests."

I told Jenkins that Temple had earlier told me, during my correspondence with him, that he didn't think the filming disturbed the nests but that the filming had happened around the time other ranching activities were occurring in the forests, including road and fence building. He was aware that something was disturbing the 'alalā, but he blamed it on ranch activities.

"After I left, there was some heavy ranching activity, and maybe Stanley got confused. It was a long time ago. The point is, we did a lot of things in our research that we should never have done."

Jenkins' insights had revealed some of the myriad contradictory and complex motives and impulses that drove people to devote years of their lives to understanding the vanishing 'alalā. But they also raised questions. What, exactly, did the raven have to offer to its would-be protectors? And what did the raven's protectors have to offer the 'alalā? To most, studying it was neither just a job nor just a passion. It was a life-consuming mission. But for better and for worse, each person, in his or her own heroic, misunderstood, or well-meaning way, was altering the fate of a species.

KAPU

Acording to Cynthia Salley, a few weeks after Stanley Temple and C. John Ralph's study was completed, David Jenkins called her at home and asked if she'd like to see the results. "When it comes to studies of the 'alalā, I'd like to see any results of any study—period!" she recalled telling him skeptically.

A few days later, Jenkins stopped by the ranch house with a portable movie viewer. As he began flicking through the frames of film, revealing scenes directly inside the 'alalā nests, Salley grew angry.

"How often did you climb the trees to change the film?" she asked, her voice trembling.

"Two or three times a week," Jenkins innocently replied.

"Nobody told you weren't supposed to climb the trees?"

"No, ma'am. What do you mean?"

"Okay, so you were not told," she said, believing that Jenkins had operated in ignorance of her restrictions.

"You go. I'll take it up with Ralph."

Salley called Ralph and, by her own admission, blasted him. "I told you no climbing of trees! Observation from blinds! Minimally invasive research! You totally ignored what I said. Researchers are no longer welcome on McCandless land!"

Ralph replied, according to Salley, that he hadn't known that climbing trees was part of the research plan and that Temple, not he, had made all the arrangements. "It was all just a misunderstanding," he said.

For Salley, it was one misunderstanding too many. In 1980 she placed a kapu—the Hawaiian word for taboo or prohibition—on McCandless Ranch. No more researchers would be allowed to set foot on the property. To the consternation of many biologists, the kapu would last for twelve long years.

Salley said that, whenever a researcher came to her door to ask for permission to enter the ranch—and there were many—she would tell them, "There are only a few dozen ʻalalā left in the world. Nine are on my ranch. You've got others to try to save. You've got one experiment trying to raise them at Pōhakuloa. And you've got other experiments to study them in the wild. Well, I've got my own experiment going on here. It's called the ʻLeave Them Alone Project.' We'll compare results in a few years. Meanwhile, stay off my ranch!"

In 1987, according to Salley, DOFAW officials formally requested that she allow state biologists onto the ranch, not only to further study the ʻalalā but also to try to capture more birds for captive breeding.

"No on both counts," she told them. Salley, amused and alarmed by the request, telephoned Libert Landgraf, a senior official at the Department of Land and Natural Resources, and told him, "When you can prove that biologists can learn to produce and care for the ʻalalā in captivity, then come back to me."

For several years, officials of the U.S. Fish and Wildlife Service had tried to gain access to the ranch by what Robert P. Smith, the then Pacific Islands administrator of the Service, called the "foreplay approach." "My predecessor or Service people would go up and sit on the porch and talk story over lemonade with the owners of the ranch, including Salley and her siblings." To no avail.

Before long, rumors of a pending lawsuit against the ranch began to circulate.

"If someone shot at the birds, we'd have had reason to go investigate," continued Smith. "But in this case we had people who ostensibly cared about birds and who felt that the best policy was to leave them alone. That the last birds were there was a historical accident in my opinion, not because of anything the ranch was doing. I definitely felt that as a biologist and from a commonsense point of view that intervention was needed. The threat of a suit resulted from tremendous frustration."

In 1989, William Paty, chair of DLNR's Board of Land and Natural Resources, had written to the state's deputy attorney general inquiring "what authority we have to enter private property to conduct such programs." The reply: "We do not feel DLNR can enter onto McCandless Ranch property, without the landowner's permission, to capture the ʻalalā."

In May 1989, an increasingly frustrated National Audubon Society, which was seriously contemplating a suit to force open the ranch gates, sent an "Alert" to its Hawaiʻi members. The Society accused the U.S. Fish and Wildlife Service, by not forcing access, of kowtowing to Salley, out of fear of "alienating" large landowners.

Hoping to head off a suit, in December 1989 U.S. representative Patricia Saiki from Hawaiʻi wrote to John Turner, director of the Service, asking "what steps the Fish and Wildlife Service can or will take." Turner reiterated the response to the earlier National Audubon Society request: "The Department of the Interior's Solicitor General has concluded that the Endangered Species Act . . . does not empower the Service to enter private lands unilaterally for purposes of implementing recovery actions."

The Audubon Alert, meanwhile, had inflamed opinions on both

sides. Barbara Lee, for several years secluded in her jungle home in Hawai'i but now finding it hard to stay out of the fray, wrote to Harold E. Woodsum Jr., then chair of Audubon's national board of directors, criticizing the recently appointed head of the Hawai'i Audubon Society:

> The hasty and ill-advised actions of your inexperienced and newly appointed representative in Hawaii, Miss Dana Kokubun, regarding the Hawaiian Crow, 'alalā, have been a disservice to the Society and to the cause of Conservation. . . .
>
> Miss Kokubun . . . has not only placed an endangered species in jeopardy during breeding seasons. She has severely disrupted delicate and tenuous relations between public sector agencies and private landowners who manage protected habitat on the island of Hawaii. Her confrontational . . . tactics have drawn battle lines even between Audubon Society members. She has widened the gap between the environmental and scientific communities and the various species they profess to protect.

Salley and Lee, like Hawai'i Audubon, engaged friends and surrogates in the frenzied letter-writing campaign. Wrote Suzanne Haight of Kamuela to Peter Berle, president of the National Audubon Society:

> I don't like the new ideas of experimental manipulations in producing birds as if they were chickens on an assembly line. . . . That kind of mentality should not be dealing with any birds, let alone endangered and highly sensitive species. . . .
>
> McCandless Ranch is doing an excellent job of protecting the crows living there, as well as protecting their lands and business. Mrs. Salley, the ranch owner, is being hassled by biologists out of pure curiosity and pique, since she refuses to allow researchers on the ranch. Frankly, I think Audubon owes her a vote of thanks and appreciation. She could have said, "Take those birds, they are a nuisance," and had far less trouble.

Scientists also joined in the heated debate—most condemning Salley's refusal to allow biologists back on the ranch. Sheila Conant, an associate professor at the University of Hawai'i, for example, claimed in a letter to Paty that "entry to the Waiea Tract to accomplish capture of crows should be an action where the State, not the McCandless Ranch, calls the shots."

Alan A. Lieberman, curator of ornithology at the Zoological Society of San Diego, argued that "to delay in establishing as many unrelated breeding pairs [as possible] would be genetic suicide for the species. . . . To ignore this biological reality is folly. I am in total support of the Hawai'i Audubon Society's resolution supporting the captive rearing of the 'alalā, which includes the capture of additional wild birds." And Stuart L. Pimm, professor of ecology at the University of Tennessee, Knoxville, and his research associate went right to the top and wrote to John Waihee, governor of Hawai'i: "If the 'alalā is to be saved from extinction, biologists need to remove the wild colony from its current habitat and incorporate it into the state's breeding program. . . . Wild birds must be brought into captivity and brought into captivity now."

In November 1989, *Audubon* magazine published a staff-written editorial in which Kokubun was quoted: "The ranch is using the 'alalā as a smokescreen. . . . There is a lot of logging going on there. The owners are afraid that if biologists get in and find the 'alalā's almost gone, they'll invoke the Endangered Species Act to stop logging in their habitat." And Berle, Audubon's president, there accuses the state of Hawai'i of allowing "personal opinion and petty politics to intrude into the realm of scientific fact, giving an individual landowner the power to dictate public policy."

Salley, fearing a suit was just around the corner, attempted to head it off by opening her gates just a crack—and then to a select few. Governor Waihee, Paty, and several federal officials managed to convince Salley to allow them to make a two-day fact-finding visit to McCandless Ranch. The National Audubon Society claimed credit for this coup. The *Maui News* praised Berle for being "willing to flex a little muscle locally in the 'alalās' behalf." Despite the solicitor general's earlier conclusion that the "Endangered Species Act . . . does not empower the Service to enter private lands unilaterally for purposes of implementing recovery actions," Berle was quoted in the *News* as saying, "We believe that the legal tools are available to allow entry onto the McCandless property."

By the summer of 1990, Governor Waihee, unable to defuse the conflict and feeling political heat from the vocal conservation community, all but begged Salley to open the ranch gates to biologists:

> I am writing to request your permission to allow the State of Hawaii and the U.S. Fish and Wildlife Service to enter the McCandless Ranch. . . . We must have access to the crow's range that coincides with the lands of your ranch to determine the number, age and sex of the remaining wild crows. . . . I ask, also, that you allow the most qualified experts to study the wild 'alalā. I have been assured that any scientists or other personnel allowed onto the ranch to study the 'alalā will conduct themselves in a professional manner and be respectful of your property.

If he expected empathy from Salley, none was forthcoming. She wrote back:

> No research done over the past 20 years by State and Federal employees has accomplished the goals set forth in your letter. . . . I cannot believe that you would have the 'alalā's best interest at heart by encouraging more disturbance. The arrogance implied, through you, by the wildlife biologists, that their approach is the only salvation of the 'alalā, is repugnant and in error. . . .
>
> Our experiences concerning the honesty and professionalism of the State and Federal agencies and wildlife biologists have been less

than satisfactory. . . . FEDE, SED CUI VIDE—Trust, but take care whom you trust. . . .

Lastly, it is difficult to believe that there are those who would think that our integrity would allow us to answer you, any differently than we would answer the low man on the Bureaucratic totem pole. We feel that our arguments stand rationally against other viewpoints and singly, on their own.

In February 1991, with biologists no closer to getting through the gates, the National Audubon Society began soliciting funds for its war chest in order to take legal action.

In 1990, Sierra Club Legal Defense Fund attorneys representing the National Audubon Society and Hawai'i Audubon wrote to Manuel Lujan Jr., secretary of the interior under President George H. W. Bush, threatening a suit while offering a primer on the Endangered Species Act, which Lujan, in the view of many conservationists, sorely needed:

> The Service has a legal obligation to enter the McCandless Ranch immediately to take the actions necessary to save the species from extinction . . . if you do not take immediate action, we will file a lawsuit to compel you to do so.
>
> The Service has failed in its management and recovery duties for the 'alalā because it has timidly bowed to the objections of the landowner . . . the Service has taken the position that it is powerless to gain access to the Ranch without the owners' express permission. . . . To the contrary, the Service has the clear right, and indeed the obligation, to take . . . immediate actions.

According to plaintiffs, federal law provided several justifications for the Service to enter the ranch. For one, the Endangered Species Act required the Service to use "all methods and procedures" necessary to save an endangered species. "Although the ESA does not expressly grant authority to enter private property over the objection of the landowner for purposes of conserving listed species," the letter read, "such authority must necessarily be implied by the express statutory duties to conserve endangered species. . . . The crows themselves, of course, do not belong to the McCandless Ranch owners . . . they are a public resource under the stewardship of the Service and the state DLNR. Because of this status, the McCandless Ranch owners cannot exercise authority over them."

Second, according to the plaintiffs, the Endangered Species Act also required the Service to "develop and implement a recovery plan for this species." In fact, the Service had approved a recovery plan for the ʻalalā back in 1982. The letter to Lujan argued that "simply preparing a Recovery Plan is not enough, however. The ESA also required the Service to 'implement' that plan." And that, according to the letter, would mean storming the gates of McCandless Ranch.

Peter Simmons, the manager of McCandless Ranch at the time, didn't care much for lawyers or researchers and expressed Salley's own view when he told one reporter, "We really have a lot of aloha for the birds, but we don't give a hang for scientific research."

chapter 16

YAHOO!

I N THE WAKE OF BARBARA LEE'S
and Fay Steele's stormy departures from Pōhakuloa in 1979, the
program remained leaderless for four years, surviving on a shoe-
string budget. During this time the birds, held captive without
apparent purpose, occasionally laid eggs but never reared young,
and endured days extinguished by boredom, with some maladjusted individuals whirling in circles and attacking their own feet.
Such was the state's reply to the plight of the suffering 'alalā.

Despite the lengthening shadows of the failing program, hopes
soared with the hiring of a new director in 1984. Fern Duvall had
been trained as an animal behaviorist in the tradition of Nikolaas
Tinbergen and Konrad Lorenz. Duvall grew up in Michigan and
studied for a time at the University of Michigan, Ann Arbor. He
then traveled to Germany, where he attended Freie Universität
Berlin and the Albert-Ludwigs-Universität in Freiburg and Breis-
gau. He eventually obtained the equivalent of a Ph.D. degree in
zoology, with a focus on the behavior of the hooded crow and the
rook.

Duvall arrived at Pōhakuloa just after the 1984 breeding season, during which time the birds had laid twelve eggs—once again, without a single chick surviving. A confident Duvall was determined to solve "the majority of the problems facing the propagation project" by the following breeding season.

In 1985, the nine 'alalā under his care laid five eggs. No chicks survived. A bitterly disappointed Duvall wrote to Susumu Ono, chair of the Board of Land and Natural Resources:

> I must report to you, with great discontent, that the State's captive 'alalā produced *zero* offspring, quite in spite of all of the efforts made on my part. . . . The reasoning for this failure is due to, in part, external causal factors, and in part flock-inherent factors. Of the former category the most important factors are certainly comprised of military disturbances, the (wrong) biogeographical-altitudinal location of the captive breeding facility, and inadequate housing of the 'alalā. Problems stemming from such external factors are further compounded by inherent problem factors, apparent in the captive flock, such as mis-imprinting, and permanent physiological and/or physical damages and defects in the individual 'alalā.
>
> The external causes which negatively act and interact with the State's captive flock can and must be addressed and changed. . . . I most highly recommend and do urge that the State do what it can to assure that the 'alalā captive flock be moved in a timely fashion to another permanent location, sufficient to the needs of not only the 'alalā but also of the entire Captive Breeding Program. . . .
>
> To circumvent the inherent factors I can only recommend that the State obtain new 'alalā for the purposes of captive propagation—if indeed this can be done. I urge the state at its highest levels to inquire into the claims that "indeed there are many 'alalā" on certain private lands—towards the ends that some (few or even one) might be added to the captive flock, since even one addition would be an immeasurable aid to saving the species.

Military activity had been disturbing the 'alalā at Pōhakuloa from the beginning. Now the failing captive birds would have to endure another year of artillery barrages, nighttime flares, detonations that rocked the facilities, drones, helicopters, machine-gun fire, and explosions that acted much like the "effect of a strong earthquake in shaking" the facility. The 'alalā periodically rose up in fright, so stressed that the males sometimes pulled out their mates' feathers, while the females plucked out and ate their own.

Nor did the 1986 breeding season produce any chicks.

Still, Duvall took heart, writing in the annual state report that "unlike any previous year at Pōhakuloa all nine individuals were reproductively active and built nests." The pair consisting of Hi'ialo and Kalani built a nest on the ground inside the aviary and produced two eggs. 'Umi and his mate, Lu'ukia, also nested and produced two eggs, which Duvall immediately collected and placed in an incubator—to no avail.

With a gift for conveying to reporters and readers his own passion for the 'alalā, Duvall soon emerged as one of the raven's most eloquent spokespersons. "They make a tremendous noise before the sun rises," he told a reporter for the *Maui News* in 1986. "They scream. They groan. They make noises like a big cat, and they scream like someone being stabbed by a knife."

That same year, after eight years of life and death on the edge of the bombing range, the nine 'alalā were finally relocated from Hawai'i Island to Maui and into a more spacious home on the slopes of the volcano Haleakalā. Duvall's wife, Renate Gassmann-Duvall, a veterinarian, would provide medical services for the feathered inmates. The facility once had been an honor prison camp called Olinda, informally known as the Maui Jail. Duvall was elated to be rid of the cold, dank, dilapidated facility at Pōhakuloa. As he told a reporter for the *Maui News*, "What they have here is a thousandfold better for them."

Hopes were high indeed for the 1987 breeding season. A few months before it began, William Paty, Chair of DLNR's Board of Land and Natural Resources, bragged that "much of the recent success of this program can be attributed to studies, care, and planning by Dr. Fern Duvall, Jr., contract aviculturist for the project. Dr. Duvall's extensive experience in the research and propagation of other species of crows has proved invaluable to this project . . . we are now well prepared to breed 'alalā."

It wasn't at all clear what Paty meant by "success of this program." There were still no new 'alalā. Nor would there be any that year, 1987, their first year in Maui, when a mere two eggs were laid. An article in the *Honolulu Star-Bulletin* on May 17, 1987, based largely upon an interview with Duvall, blamed the low egg production and lack of chicks on "a big rainstorm." He also blamed "situational circumstances at Olinda before the reproductive season began full force"—the pairs had not yet become "confident" enough to breed in their new aviaries at Maui, he suggested, and had been damaged by their "fundamentally boring environment" at Pōhakuloa, as compared with their better and "more complex environment" at Olinda.

Duvall chastised Barbara Lee for having hand-raised several of the birds, leading them to become imprinted on her. This left them behavioral misfits, unable to successfully mate with other 'alalā, he said. Duvall had also accused Lee of taking all the bird-keeping records from Pōhakuloa and hiding them in her basement to conceal his contention that no eggs had hatched under her care—contrary to Lee's own claim.

In a letter to Paty on May 27, Lee angrily dismissed Duvall's criticisms: "Duvall's desire to justify his own hypotheses and methods is understandable, but he has only damaged his own credibility . . . by attacking my competency and character." She cc'd the letter to Duvall.

Less than a week later, on June 3, Duvall wrote to Lee:

I found it quite presumptuous for you to believe that statements I made about 'alalā during my tenure were specifically related, directly or indirectly, to your person or tenure at Pōhakuloa Endangered

Species Facility. . . . Perhaps you have never realized that when I arrived . . . *only 3* ʻalalā, about which you take up arguments with me, had ever been under your care . . . you had lost the ʻalalā Hina, Kekau, ʻEleʻū, Ulu during your tenure.

Eight days later, there was another loss, this time at Olinda: Hiʻialo, who had once been under Lee's care. According to Duvall, he had entered the pen on June 10 to feed Hiʻialo and her mate, Kalani. As usual, Hiʻialo attacked him, and Kalani joined in. Somewhere in the fray, Kalani ended up with a badly bleeding broken toenail. Duvall noted that Hiʻialo, "slightly hunched . . . on the highest perch above the nest," didn't seem her usual self. Duvall said he suspected that an egg had lodged in the bird's reproductive tract because of "no egg-production coupled to the now apparent sluggish non-normal behavior."

That afternoon, Duvall wrote, "Status much poorer. Bird not alert." He hand-caught Hiʻialo and placed her in the intensive care cage. Growing increasingly worried, late that night Duvall called his veterinarian-wife, who was visiting the Big Island at the time. Early the next morning, Duvall concluded that the bird's "status [was] very serious."

Over the next twenty-four hours, Duvall delivered a grueling series of treatments in an attempt to save Hiʻialo's life, including internally probing the distressed bird, once with a small glass rod, and later, "dilation with thermometer and simultaneous abdominal pressure."

Shortly after seven in the morning on June 11, Duvall wrote that Hiʻialo "weakens and stumbles from perch for first time." At about a quarter to eight he wrote, "Three powerful heaves and bird arrests breathing." Hiʻialo was dead.

The pathology report concluded that Hiʻialo had died from infection after an egg got lodged in her oviduct. But not everyone was satisfied with the accounts of the events surrounding the bird's death. Some believed that Duvall should not have undertaken the measures without the supervision of a veterinarian or other medical expert. (His wife was away at the time.) Ernie Kosaka later wrote of Duvall's notes, "Being a Fed, I am always skeptical of outward appearances and would like a second opinion. . . . It is possible that although the report may be accurate, it may not be complete."

Whatever lingering questions remained about Hi'ialo's death, the breeding program had suffered another devastating blow. The death of Hi'ialo, who was apparently of a different bloodline from the other captives, shrunk an already limited gene pool. As the *Honolulu Advertiser* reported weeks later, the death left only "eight others in the state's captive propagation program and perhaps another eight individuals left in the wild."

Apparently still unaware of Hi'ialo's death, Barbara Lee responded a week later to Duvall's chastising letter of June 3: "Either get your facts nailed down, or keep quiet in public," she wrote, enclosing documents to prove her claim that at least one chick had, in fact, hatched during her tenure and offering detailed rebuttals on five of Duvall's points.

She went on to say:

It is my belief that time ran out for the species Corvus hawaiiensis long before you or I arrived on the scene. . . . I shall mourn their passing, and feel shame that fellow human beings helped accelerate their extinction. I also mourn the passing of intellectual honesty, moral responsibility, human compassion, and plain hard work. These qualities are also rare and vanishing.

William Paty, growing impatient with the feud, wrote to Lee, "I would prefer that Dr. Duvall enter into a dialogue with you in the hope that you can resolve your differences of opinion." For his part, Duvall, no doubt humbled by Hi'ialo's recent death, replied to Lee in a conciliatory tone, thanking her for her lengthy letter and supporting documents and conceding, "I now feel comfortable that there was one nestling ʻalalā that hatched during your tenure."

The clouds of failure seemed to momentarily break in 1988, when Duvall reported that the breeding season had been "dramatic and successful. The highlight of the season was the hatching of Hoʻoku, the first chick produced by the captive crows since 1981." The thirteen eggs produced that year, he said, were "by far the [most] ever produced by the captive flock."

The *Honolulu Advertiser* reported, "Duvall now believes that he has found the proper incubation time and temperature to hatch more eggs. 'Any fertile egg we get from now on should hatch,' he said yesterday. 'That's why everybody has been yelling "Yahoo, we saved another endangered species."'"

DLNR's description of Hoʻoku's hatching was only slightly less giddy:

> A welcomed event in the State's captive propagation program for this species was reached with the hatching on June 11, 1988 of a single egg which has since developed into a healthy fledgling ʻalalā. It was named "Hoʻoku," meaning in the Hawaiian language "to continue" as in the perpetuation of a lineage.

The hatching of Hoʻoku brought the number of captive ʻalalā back to nine—the same number as when Duvall arrived in 1984. But the birds had continued to age, and the genetically valuable Hiʻialo had died.

The 1989 breeding season also began with promise: Luʻukia, who was paired with Kalani, laid eight eggs. But "for a variety of reasons," Duvall wrote, "all but one failed to hatch." The successful egg gave rise to Hoikeikapono, the newest member of the captive flock. Encouraged by a new chick two years in a row, Duvall echoed his claim of the year before when he told a reporter, "We're not at the stage where we're producing them like poultry, but we think we've got it figured out."

Then, in 1990, with the successful hatching of Kinohi, DLNR began to embrace the language of victory. But few beyond the small circle of giddiness believed that the species had been saved. The noted ornithologist Andrew Berger had written shortly before, "I have now been studying Hawaiian birds for a little more than 25 years. I suspect that for the crow, it is too little and much too late."

However good the Maui Jail looked next to Pōhakuloa, Berger, who earlier had seen a television report on the aviary, was incredulous that the state would relegate one of the world's rarest species to such a facility. "I was shocked to see what looked like cement prisons for the crows. I don't know whether these cages were used because they already were there or whether someone designed them anew. If the latter was the case, the designer didn't know much about endangered birds, and especially passerine birds. . . . Nor have I yet met Fern Duvall. I begin to doubt that he knows very much about passerine birds, and especially endangered species."

While the limited successes may have been a tourniquet on DLNR's hemorrhaging public image, the false hope they raised may have done more harm than good: it may have led many state officials to believe that the flaws in the program had actually been fixed. In fact, during the prior six years, two 'alalā had died and only three had hatched—a net gain of a single bird. And even the three hatchings proved to be Pyrrhic victories.

The gregarious 'alalā, raised without other birds its age, grew up to be abnormal. Because each of the three new 'alalā was hatched in a different year, each was raised without the benefit of nest mates or the company of similarly aged birds. As a chick, Ho'oku had spent 459 days alone in a cage. More troublesome yet, the three chicks had been raised in aviaries next to adult 'alalā who reacted aggressively to the youngsters. The ill-fated combination of unnatural forces would ultimately doom the chicks to becoming social misfits. Indeed, later in life, Ho'oku and Kinohi developed such bizarre behaviors that they risked smashing their own eggs or disrupting nests. During her egg laying and incubation, Ho'oku often suffered outbursts in which she violently pounded a stick or other object with her beak while frantically flopping her body from one side to another. During breeding season, Hoikei would flop on his side on the nest platform and viciously bite at his own feet, as if he were suffering violent hallucinations. The intensity of the foot biting increased as breeding season progressed. His mate, Wa'alani, trying to nest, would eventually drive the disruptive and maladjusted Hoikei away.

As an adult, Kinohi, the third bird hatched and raised under Duvall's stewardship, had violent fits of flopping on his side and biting his legs and wings whenever the keepers entered the aviary. This was the stuff of freak shows, not of a successful breeding program.

At the end of the 1991 breeding season, a discouraged Duvall wrote to Susumu Ono, this time citing the small gene pool as the main problem: "As in the past seasons this [failure of new chicks] is due to inherent very likely genetic-lethal factors related to the specifics of the current captive flock composition." The only way around this, he argued, was to bring in more birds from the wild.

And the 'alalā in the wild were not faring well, either. Given their deteriorating, disease-ridden habitat, even a surplus of birds in captivity would have been to no avail if there was no safe place to release them. Even in the best habitat available—presumably McCandless Ranch and environs—the wild 'alalā were still declining. Not only was it overrun with predators, but also much of its protective understory was damaged or gone. To be suitable for the 'alalā, the land would first have to be restored, and that would be enormously expensive. DLNR wasn't about to deepen its involvement by offering up state land. If anything, the state wanted to pull the plug on the captive breeding efforts. As Michael G. Buck, administrator of the Division of Forestry and Wildlife, diplomatically put it, "it is a very difficult task to recover a species already on extinction's doorstep."

By the end of the 1991 breeding season, fewer than a dozen 'alalā remained in the wild—all on McCandless Ranch and beyond the eager reach of biologists. Or so it seemed.

chapter 17

HELICOPTER
DREAMS

NOT ALL OF THE
60,000-acre McCandless Ranch belonged outright to Salley and
her siblings. For years the ranch had leased from the state a 1,258-
acre parcel known as the Waiea tract. Several years earlier, Waiea's
long-term lease had run out and the deal had quietly morphed into
a month-to-month arrangement.

As it so happened, the remaining 'alalā frequented this state-
owned tract. And since it was being leased month to month, the
state could have terminated the lease on short notice. When this
potential Achilles' heel for Cynthia Salley dawned on Fern Duvall,
who wanted nothing more than to get his hands on more birds for
captive breeding, it must have come with the force of a religious
vision.

Recognizing that she, in fact, could *not* keep biologists off this
tract of state land, Salley proposed a compromise: she would
permit a limited number of biologists to use the road across
McCandless property to reach the Waiea tract. But with certain

rules: "No one, I mean no one, can step off the road and put a foot on ranch land, or, for that matter, even travel up the road to the Waiea tract without my prior permission."

Two biologists soon showed up at her door. They wanted permission to use her road to reach the Waiea tract. And those two biologists were Fern Duvall and Jon Giffin, whom Salley had dubbed "Crow Enemies Number One and Two." She suspected Duvall of masterminding the Waiea strategy—that is, using her month-to-month lease on that tract, which the state could revoke at any time, to force her to allow access. This was something Duvall didn't deny and was delighted to take credit for. Salley's anger toward Giffin had been cemented long ago, in 1978, when he had captured the fledgling on her land. Here they were, nemeses one and two, standing at her door, asking her to make good on her agreement.

After gaining Salley's reluctant approval, Duvall and Giffin proceeded up the road to the Waiea tract, where they planned to camp for several days. They had even brought along a part-time cook. On the evening of April 13, 1989, Salley happened to pass the cook along the road as he was driving home for the day.

In a friendly sort of way, Salley asked, "How things going up at Waiea?"

"Okay," he said, unaware of the tension. "Today they're just playing some crow recordings to try to get the crows to come."

"They are *what*?"

"Oh, yes, ma'am. The crows are calling back," the cook said.

Technically, nothing in the agreement prevented the playing of 'alalā recordings to attract the birds—nothing, she reckoned, except integrity. Salley was even more furious.

A short while later, Salley confronted Giffin as he drove down the ranch road. "You playing recordings up there?" she asked.

"Yeah, we are," he said.

"Why?" Salley asked.

"We're trying to count the birds."

She suspected that they were trying to lure the birds in order to capture them. "That's really crummy," she muttered, angrily driving off in a cloud of gravel and dust.

Duvall and Giffin, meanwhile, were ecstatic about their trip up to the Waiea tract. On April 18, Duvall wrote to Ronald Walker, who had by then become acting administrator of the Division of Forestry and Wildlife, telling of their having seen three ʻalalā on the Waiea tract five days earlier. "These detections . . . thrilled me," Duvall wrote, explaining that the birds were calling back to the taped sounds and could therefore be located and captured. "I urge you to initiate all actions necessary to have a team in the field attempting capture by May 1, 1989." Knowing that Salley would refuse access along her road for this purpose, Duvall wrote, "It is only feasible to employ helicopter access to the State's tract."

Duvall laid out his proposed mission with military precision:

1. Arrive with helicopter and establish basecamp at Hooper's Junction. Staff on-site 8 persons (see list). Set-up and man mist-nets at site(s) where detections were made, call-in birds with amplified vocalizations of ʻOlinda' birds, ʻalalā distress calls, and/or ʻIo calls. Decoys of crows (have available) and/ or owl (needed) will be placed at nets for capture. . . .

He elaborated on several more steps before concluding the operation: "Helicopter out. Reconvene, only if evidence of necessity for additional capture(s) is given." He signed the memo, "Sincerely and Urgently. Dr. Fern P. Duvall, II, Aviculturist."

Giffin called Salley to inform her of the planned capture. As Salley put it, "I went into orbit!" After screaming at him, she hung up and called William Paty, reminding him that it was breeding season. "Why didn't you fly the helicopter over the cages at Olinda to see what kind of effect it had on the birds there, since they were laying eggs?" Convinced that the scheme was harebrained after all, Paty called off the raid.

The *Honolulu Advertiser* described the fiasco several days later: "The State has abandoned a planned helicopter assault on a South Kona forest to capture members of the last wild 'alalā population. . . . Scientists proposed a helicopter drop on state land leased to the ranch, hanging of huge mist nets in the forest, and luring crows over from the McCandless property. The ranch staunchly opposed the collecting. In the face of that opposition, Paty canceled the state plans—to the dismay of the National Audubon Society."

Paty is quoted in the article: "[Salley] points out in, effect, 'you want to raid my flock and you don't have a successful program of your own.' Very honestly, it (canceling the collection) was a judgment call on my part, hoping for cooperation in the future." At the same time, Paty acknowledged that new blood at the Olinda breeding facility on Maui was critical. Since none of the captive 'alalā were related to the McCandless birds, as best the biologists could figure, the ranch flock represented the much-needed new blood for the breeding program.

The proposed helicopter assault had taken the situation, in Salley's view, from the bizarre to the surreal. "Force-pair the birds, build new facilities, move the facilities, take the eggs, artificially incubate them, candle them, and break them open! Call in the state, call in the Sierra Club and the Hawai'i Audubon. Bring in the helicopters! What are these people doing? Let the 'alalā be!" she fumed.

Michael Buck, head of the Division of Forestry and Wildlife (DOFAW), a division of DLNR, had already concluded that trying to pull the 'alalā from the brink of extinction was futile. With the helicopter fiasco only adding to his woes, he wanted more than ever to shift the task of recovering the 'alalā back to the U.S. Fish and Wildlife Service. But the state would have to live with fifteen years of 'alalā recovery squandered—a decade and a half under state care during which dozens of eggs had been laid in captivity, with only three new 'alalā to show for it; a time during which the captive crop had grown from young birds in their reproductive prime to old and mostly barren ravens, with little hope for a future.

But how to get rid of the birds without appearing to abandon a species in need? There were many hurdles, not least of all DOFAW's own employees, many of whom had by now developed deep personal loyalties to and professional interests in the 'alalā.

In 1989, Buck had invited Cyndi Kuehler, one of the world's recognized authorities on the breeding of birds and an esteemed member of the Zoological Society of San Diego's professional staff, to come to Hawai'i and evaluate the propagation program at Olinda. A credible independent report—and it was all but a foregone conclusion that it would be critical, given the failure of the captive breeding—could be the first step in justifying the need for new management.

Kuehler's 1990 report was tactful in appearance and blunt between the lines. Buck agreed with most of her recommendations. Duvall's response was gracious, at least on the surface. "I think that the review and recommendations made by colleague Cynthia Kuehler were excellent," he wrote, before going on to minimize their importance. "It must be realized at the outset that much of what was offered . . . constitute[s] a last ditch attempt to increase productivity using the whims of 'well it would not likely hurt—so why not try,'" he wrote.

In his annual performance report for fiscal year 1990–1991, Duvall further downplayed her recommendations, saying that they focused on "new trial experimentation with aspects of egg-handling, incubation procedures, and radiographing of late term 'alalā eggs to determine embryo positioning, etc."

In fact, the report recommended implementing several standard husbandry practices at Olinda. While Duvall customarily took eggs from the nests as soon as possible after they were laid and put them in incubators, Kuehler wrote that "experienced parent birds of any species are the best incubators," and one should "allow females to incubate for five to seven days before the eggs are removed." Duvall claimed that doing so "could jeopardize production likelihood."

Kuehler also suggested that Olinda could "not only improve hatchability but decrease the incidence of egg predation and breakage" by removing the males from the enclosures. Duvall, on the other hand, had been allowing males to remain as co-parents. He argued that the males were needed to help the females with family responsibilities and that removing them, therefore, could "risk harming eggs." And so Duvall's point-by-point rebuttal went.

In 1991, the year following the report, no new 'alalā successfully fledged. Worse yet, Mana died. Duvall tried to spin the 1991 results the best he could: "In summary . . . the 'alalā have shown unprecedented nesting activity. . . . Three of four adult pairs have nested and produced eggs. Egg normality and hatchability however has been very poor."

A press release by the Department of Land and Natural Resources also put the best face on the 1991 season: "We're optimistic that next year our 'alalā production will be better. We have a three-year-old subadult female that likely will start breeding next year. We are looking forward to good production from an eight-year-old female that has just started laying eggs."

But Buck, unmoved by the public relations efforts flowing from Olinda or even from within DLNR, bluntly stated that his division was "reviewing its priorities" concerning the 'alalā.

Fern Duvall, meanwhile, believing that new captive blood would be the species' salvation, was still determined to get hold of the wild birds.

chapter 18

ALI'I NEO

PLAINTIFF HAWAIIAN CROW, otherwise known by its Hawaiian name of 'alalā ... has suffered a precipitous decline in population during this century and is now poised on the brink of extinction. As few as ten crows now survive in the wild, and only another eleven crows survive in a captive breeding population. . . . Plaintiff Hawaiian Crow has no voice of its own, and it therefore brings this action by its next friends.

On April 4, 1991, the National Audubon Society and the Hawai'i Audubon Society, represented by the Sierra Club Legal Defense Fund, sued McCandless Ranch and the U.S. Department of the Interior in order to gain access to the ranch and the remaining wild birds. The Sierra Club argued that the U.S. Fish and Wildlife Service's duty to implement recommendations of the 'alalā recovery plan — a version that had been approved by the Service in 1982 — trumped a private landowner's right to deny access to the birds across his or her private property. Specifically, the Sierra Club argued that the Service was required to capture some of the wild 'alalā as laid out in the recovery plan. For its part, the Service argued that it was not required by law to implement every provision of a recovery plan.

As to who was really the 'alalā's best "next friend," that was a matter of fierce debate. Cynthia Salley said that she was not only its best friend but also its most long-standing. "We were protecting that bird long before those who brought the lawsuit were born!" she said. Opponents argued that the ranch always had been and always would be managed only for profit—whatever the cost to the 'alalā. The last birds happened to be there purely by historical accident or good luck—luck that wouldn't last forever.

In truth, almost all parties sincerely believed themselves to be the 'alalā's best friend and to be acting in its best interest, even those on bitterly opposing sides.

But in Salley's eyes, gaining access to her private land was an issue much larger than the 'alalā. The birds aside, she owned the land. She was the ali'i. Large landowners were indeed the modern-day chiefs. And, like the chiefs of old, many landowners believed that the power of kapu—the power to prohibit occurrences on their lands—could be made absolute by their word and their word alone. To Salley, the suit was an attempt to deprive her of her legal rights. Indeed, to her and many large landholders, the Fifth Amendment might as well have been the Eleventh Commandment: Thou shalt not take private property "for public use, without just compensation." More than a matter of constitutional law, it was a matter of religion. And as Robert P. Smith, administrator for the Service's Pacific Region, put it, "they tended to live in constant fear or paranoia of the government."

Salley viewed the Endangered Species Act as "morally flawed." "Law had been separated from justice," she said; it was time for "introducing justice in the Endangered Species Act." She barnstormed her message across Hawai'i, speaking to business groups and at forestry conferences. "Protecting endangered species has become a political ploy for those who wish to dictate use and control over private land," Salley told one of her audiences. There is "no benefit at present for private landowners who are unfortunate enough to have endangered species on their property. The answer is: incentives, incentives, incentives!" By incentives, she meant economic rewards. "Conservation is something that happens after we pay the bills."

In February 1992, *Hawaiian Crow ('alalā) v. Lujan* came before Judge David Alan Ezra in the United States District Court, District of Hawai'i. If either party was looking for a clear win, such hopes were quickly dashed. Present was Robert Smith, who took the judge's introductory remarks as a lesson against ever thinking that one's case is above reproach, especially when it comes to endangered species.

Smith described the proceedings as follows:

> Judge Ezra sat in his lofty perch with his glasses on his nose. The environmental community sat on one side—to the right, ironically. The government and McCandless folks were sitting on the left looking very uncomfortable. The federal government was represented by Charles R. Shockey, of the U.S. Department of Justice, Environment and Natural Resources Division, in Sacramento, California.
>
> Judge Ezra kind of gazed over at the McCandless-government side and there was this uneasy distance, maybe a chair or two, between Shockey and McCandless' attorney. One of the first things Judge Ezra said, was to Mr. Shockey, "Aren't you representing government in this matter?" Shockey nodded. And the judge said, "Then please move to the center, sir!" When Ezra had finished rearranging the room, he had Shockey right off his nose, McCandless on the left and the environmental community on his right. Then he uttered, "Now we got the government in the middle, which is where it should be." Judge Ezra realized that suing the ranch owners and government as co-defendants was bogus, and that they were very unlikely to team up and fight this.
>
> Then Ezra gave his lectures—first, to the National Audubon Society: "If you think I'm going to rule and hit you guys a home run and that the Endangered Species Act gives you the right to get on private land to carry out a recovery plan, you're wrong." Well, at that point, my eyes almost popped out. I thought he had just ruled on a matter he hadn't heard yet!

Then he turned to the McCandless folks and scolded, "And don't think for a moment you have won! *You* people do not own *those* birds! They belong to the people of the United States, and those birds are in trouble. There is an affirmative obligation that people get together and help."

Then the judge turned to Mr. Shockey and said, "It's my recommendation that this matter be subject to a settlement. I'm assigning one of my senior judges to mediate this matter."

All three parties went to meet U.S. District Judge Martin Pence that very day.

At eighty-seven, Pence, who had been on the federal court bench for nearly thirty-five years, was the first permanent federal judge confirmed in Hawai'i after statehood. Before that, he had been a county attorney and a territorial judge on Hawai'i Island. With Pence presiding, the protracted negotiations began — negotiations that would stretch over nearly two years. By referring the case to settlement, Ezra had left the underlying legal point — whether the government could trespass upon private land to implement a recovery plan — unresolved.

But with opinions differing on just about everything, what was there to agree to? Even the basic question of what course of action would most benefit the 'alalā seemed beyond agreement. Should the last ravens be removed from the wild, or should they be allowed to remain free to serve one day as the core of a reconstituted population? With little scientific support to be had for either side, it was virtually all opinion.

About the time that the suit was filed, Robert Smith had contacted the National Research Council (NRC), a well-respected independent scientific body in Washington, D.C., asking it to form a scientific committee to determine the best course of action. Specifically, the committee was to "review all the available information on the 'alalā to determine the steps that would be appropriate to ensure the survival of the species."

When Salley heard that her old nemesis Stanley "Time Lapse"

Temple, as she called him, had been recommended for the committee, she protested to the NRC and presented evidence of bias — not least of all that he had been a strong advocate of bringing the birds in from the wild. Temple did not become part of the committee. Salley, in turn, recommended an old family friend, the noted ornithologist Andrew Berger. But Berger's close personal connections with ranchers doomed his candidacy. Another logical candidate for the committee was Cyndi Kuehler, who had evaluated Olinda — except that, several years earlier, she had written a negative letter to the governor of Hawai'i about what she considered to be intransigence on the part of McCandless Ranch. She would not serve on the committee either. (Several years later, Kuehler apologized for her outspokenness, and Salley frequently praised her stalwart efforts on behalf of the 'alalā.)

Despite initial disagreements, the NRC committee ultimately included many respected ornithologists and biologists, including Tom J. Cade, founder and chief executive officer of The Peregrine Fund; Hampton L. Carson of the University of Hawai'i at Mānoa; Scott R. Derrickson, deputy associate director for conservation of the Smithsonian Institution's National Zoological Park; John W. Fitzpatrick, executive director of the Archbold Biological Station in Lake Placid, Florida; and Frances C. James of Florida State University, an authority on the ecology and conservation of birds. The committee was chaired by W. Donald Duckworth, president and director of the Bishop Museum in Honolulu.

In the end, Kuehler, as one of the world's authorities on the captive breeding of birds, joined the NRC team as a special advisor. Her views on the captive breeding program would constitute one of the most important recommendations in the final report.

At one point during the preparation of the report, the committee visited Salley at her ranch. Impressed by the group's intelligence and objectivity, she asked that the court settlement be delayed until the final report was published, in a few months' time.

The report's recommendations, she believed, might offer common ground for an agreement. When her opponents refused to delay a settlement, Salley's attorney postponed it by legal maneuvers. The report was thus published before the sides settled.

The Scientific Bases for the Preservation of the Hawaiian Crow, published in 1992, was by almost all accounts a feat of clearheaded scientific synthesis and analysis. Most of the recommendations were not only practical but succinct. And they were politically doable. What's more, all sides could claim a measure of victory from the findings.

The report persuasively argued that the captive population had to be genetically reinvigorated, meaning that genes from the wild birds were needed—precisely what Fern Duvall, Jon Giffin, and others backing the lawsuit had vociferously argued all along. But rather than capture the remaining birds and breed them in captivity, as the pro-capture camp argued should be done, the report suggested that the eggs of the wild birds' first nesting each season be taken from nests. The wild birds would go on to lay replacement clutches. Nothing lost, something gained. The confiscated eggs would be hatched in captivity, and some of the chicks would remain in captivity to supplement the captive gene pool.

The remaining birds would be raised until old enough to be released to support the sagging wild population. In fact, the report stated that "addition of new wild-caught adult birds to the captive stock should have a very low priority until the wild population had increased, because this action is not likely to provide a genetic advantage." That statement largely supported Salley's central argument that the wild birds should not be captured. As Kuehler summed it up, the recommendation was a win-win situation: taking wild eggs "allows for simultaneous augmentation of the captive and wild populations without removing adult birds from the wild or seriously compromising the wild population's social organization or productivity."

The report also addressed the situation at Olinda, stating that "the husbandry and management of the captive 'alalā . . . are inadequate." The report faulted the lack of flexible or adaptive management. "There is a strong tendency to become locked into invariable patterns when working with endangered species, and there is always room for experimentation," it read. "The old adage 'nothing ventured, nothing gained' applies in aviculture as in other vocations, and creativity and experimentation should always be encouraged."

The report reiterated a number of suggestions from Kuehler's 1990 critique of Olinda. For one thing, it noted that captive 'alalā broke a lot of their eggs — an occurrence that could be minimized if workers "simply removed the males from the breeding enclosure as soon as the first eggs of the clutch [were] laid." The report also restated the importance of allowing the birds to sit on their eggs for a week or so before putting the eggs in the incubator.

In addition to old criticisms, the NRC report added a new one — one that would seem counterintuitive. Duvall had been going to great lengths to minimize incidental human contact with the birds at Olinda. For example, an article in the *Honolulu Star-Bulletin* on May 20, 1989, described how, under Duvall's management, "during 'alalā-mating season, the small band of workers are so obsessive about not disturbing the homely crows that they drive clear around the operation's 46-acre spread . . . and avoid the two-minute walk that would pass — and disturb — the crows. Because even the sight of a human sets the birds off on a din." In the article, Duvall is quoted as saying, "All human contact is kept to a minimum to avoid 'imprinting' on the birds when possible." But the NRC report argued that it was vital to "condition them to the human presence and in the long-run . . . [that will] make unexpected periods of contact much less stressful." What's more, a freer visitation policy would allow workers to clean the aviaries more often, and "sanitation in the enclosure would also be improved substantially."

The report recommended that "a full-time director . . . knowledgeable about both aviculture and ornithology and . . . up to date on avicultural techniques" be hired. In short, the NRC report offered a strong rationale for all but sweeping away the current Olinda program and rebuilding anew.

With most parties claiming that the report vindicated their positions in one way or another—that is, all parties except for those at Olinda—the NRC recommendations indeed established terms upon which opponents could agree. The agreement was signed in July 1993. The McCandless kapu had been broken. But while Salley would open the ranch gates under the settlement, she imposed strict conditions on who could pass through them—as she had earlier in limiting access to the state-owned Waiea tract. U.S. Fish and Wildlife Service personnel, members of the 'Alalā Recovery Team (ART), and several other biologists would have access, provided they gave Salley a written list of who would be on her property. Duvall and Giffin would be prohibited from ever setting foot on the ranch. The gates were open, but Salley was still standing guard.

Despite feeling vindicated by the report, Salley remained angered by the years of battle and sometimes vented her frustrations through the mighty pen. Not long after the suit was settled, she wrote a parable called "The Rose and the Dragon," which she never published: "Once upon a time, many years ago (eighty-two to be exact), a gentleman named Lincoln Loy McCandless, began purchasing land in South Kona . . . eventually amassing 30,000 Acres. That, combined with the leased land made the total acreage for the Ranch 60,000 Acres." Cowboys and cows came and went, and all the while the crows were there. In time, scientists appeared, including one who "knocked on the Ranch's door and said let me in, but the Ranch said not by the wisps on your chinny chin chin. He said, well, I'll huff and I'll puff and I'll call Audubon and they will blow your gates down. And that is what came to pass."

In the wake of the battle over the birds on McCandless Ranch, many questions about the raven still loomed for native Hawaiians. To them, the fate of the ʻalalā and other vanishing island species was about more than biology, endangered species law, or other scientific quantification. The decline represented the fading of cultural identity.

chapter 19

GUARDIAN SPIRITS

W HEN I ASKED HAWAIIAN elder Aunty Pele Hanoa, who lives in a coconut grove at the edge of a beach in the district of Ka'ū, why it would matter if the 'alalā, but one guardian spirit in a land of many guardian sprits, were lost, she could not initially find the words to answer. After a few moments, with her usually bright and cheery face seeming to turn momentarily despondent, she said, "You have many relatives, no? So if one of your aunts or uncles dies, it really doesn't matter because you have more?" Relieved that she had managed, after a little consternation, to crystallize her feelings in so few words, she then said, "Come visit me at Punalu'u. I will show you."

Aunty Pele's home sits on the edge of the black sand beach made famous by tourist brochures. It is located about twenty-five miles southwest of Mauna Loa and nearly three miles beneath the volcano's frigid summit — and about forty-five minutes' drive from McCandless Ranch. It is a crescent beach combed by a warm surf rich with red seaweed sought by sea turtles. The fine, glassy black sand of the beach intermingles with various-sized pebbles, each pitted with numerous tiny dimples.

Aunty Pele—her family name comes from the volcano goddess
—bends down to the receding surf and lifts a palmful of pitted
black nuggets. She selects a single stone. She rotates it between her
fingers. "This a mother stone," she says, comparing the stone, the
size of a lima bean, with the hundreds of tiny speck-sized stones at
her feet. She rotates the stone again. "All those tiny holes in the
stones—those are birth pits that gave birth to the baby stones.
That's why all the larger stones have tiny holes in them, and that's
why every day there are more stones on the beach. The tiniest
babies, they are the sand." In some of the larger stones, dimples
still hold the tiny stones, which will one day be dislodged.

As seawater washes over our feet and ankles, Aunty Pele bends
over and gently gives the stones back to a receding wave, as a fisher-
man might release his catch.

Small streams of water bubble up from the sand around our
feet. She dips one finger lightly in a tiny freshet and places the
clinging drop on the tip of her tongue. "Freshwater. Taste it. It
comes from springs below the sand.

"Rain from the high forests many miles away seeps through
Mauna Loa's porous rock and trickles for miles inside the mountain until it bubbles up here. You can feel the cold water springs
touch your legs when you wade out. This fresh spring water is what
makes the red seaweed grow. The seaweed brings the turtles. This
bay is a salad bowl for them.

"Soon the buses will be here. We should go."

We turn and walk toward the public parking lot at one end of
the beach. At the edge of the lot, surrounded by a roughly built
wall of volcanic stones, lies an exposed face of smooth stone
inscribed with petroglyphs. Aunty Pele bends down and traces a
finger over the barely discernible sticklike figures. Their exact age
is unknown. She puts them at five hundred to a thousand years old.

We walk along the shore and then turn up the beach toward her
house. She pauses to point to a sign: "Removal of Sand Prohibited

—Hawaiian County Code CH 15 Sec. 15-6." She taps my shoulder to point out a young woman in sunglasses scooping sand into a small plastic bag, which she closes and places in a larger blue and white nylon beach bag carried over her right arm.

"Need signs in Japanese. Let's go. The buses are starting to come."

As we cross the beach access road, two large buses harrumph over the hill toward us. They pass the parking lot and rumble noisily over the road, finally pausing, engines left running, near two small concessions at the far end of the beach. A line of eager tourists, many in white tennis shirts and Bermuda shorts, stream from the hatchways, move onto the beach, and gradually fan out across the sand. Beyond the settling dust, at the curve of black shore, a child with his parents heartily rubs the back of an escaping sea turtle.

"People have collected so much sand from the beach to sell as souvenirs that the turtles have almost no place left to nest. One night not long ago I watched a hawksbill come up from the water and go back thirteen times. She kept digging, but all she hit was rocks. She finally went back and we didn't see her again. She is my 'aumakua. She protects me and my family. But she has no place here anymore."

We arrive at Aunty Pele's home, a comfortable open-air affair beneath a large plastic tarp suspended from palms at one end. A cupboard with a gas stove stands beneath one end of the tarp. We sit in the warm shade as the trade winds comb our hair. "It will be warm tonight. Sometimes we sleep on the beach under the stars." Aunty Pele, her daughter, Keolalani, and I sit and chat until tangerine light bathes the top of the coconut palms. They tell me about all the other 'aumākua of Hawaiian families—or those that remain—along the coasts. The honu (turtle), 'io, shark, lizard, and owl are just a few among the great family of protective spirits from which they draw. Among them, the 'alalā has now all but vanished as an 'aumakua. The 'alalā's story, I know, is just one among many similar ones — stories not just of dwindling Hawaiian species but also of beloved ancestors lost one by one, and with each threatened passing, a loss of reassurance, at least for some native Hawaiians, of what lies beyond this life and into the next.

As we sit beneath the palms swaying in the trade winds, Aunty Pele tells me of her namesake, the volcano goddess Pele; of Pele's sisters, Laka and Hiʻiaka, patrons of the hula; and of the goddess Hina and the 'ōhiʻa tree. Aunty and her daughter speak of the forests they share with the 'alalā — the cloud forests high above and miles distant from where we sit in evening light. They tell me of the four maile sisters and the story of how the 'ieʻie vine came to be. They tell me what it is like to see the raven through native Hawaiian eyes. They tell me what it is like to be an 'alalā.

Returning to my small hotel just before dark, I gather up my pillow and blanket, and, an hour later, return to Punaluʻu, walking the length of the beach in darkness and bedding down beneath the coconut palms. The surf whispers and the trades comb steadily through the palms, the world lit by the watery lights of the universe.

As I lie there beneath the soft blanket in the twilight before sleep, the stories of Aunty Pele and Keola seem to crystallize into a momentary vision of how they might have experienced the 'alalā and its cloud forest world, so different from the analytic framework in which my own views of the bird are embedded.

PART III

LAST
LIGHT

chapter 20

HOPE—AT LAST

To THE STATE OF HAWAI'I,
the National Research Council's report was far more than just a set
of scientific recommendations. It offered political cover, justifying
relinquishing control of the 'alalā to the federal government. The
state was not the only preordained beneficiary. As the report was
being written, The Peregrine Fund (TPF), a nonprofit bird conservation organization based in Boise, Idaho, was positioning itself
to lead the renewed 'alalā breeding effort. Indeed, TPF's founder
and chief executive officer, Tom J. Cade, would help to write the
report. Working in Hawai'i—a hotbed of vanishing species—
could only enhance the organization's profile and income, or so he
believed. But he had been warned: Hawai'i was a gorgeous land
beset by ugly politics, especially when it came to conservation.

The U.S. Fish and Wildlife Service, the federal agency with final
oversight and jurisdiction over the 'alalā project and its subcon-
tractors, had successfully collaborated with TPF on a number of
conservation projects, including the captive breeding and release
of the rare California condor. Although TPF had limited experience with perching birds such as the 'alalā, Cade thought that, by

179

joining forces with avicultural experts from the Zoological Society of San Diego, his organization would succeed where the state had failed.

What's more, the San Diego Zoo already knew the 'alalā breeding program through Cyndi Kuehler, who had done the earlier evaluation of Olinda. In fact, her 1990 visit at the behest of the state was a deliberately laid stepping-stone to eventual transfer of the program. She was one of the world's foremost bird-breeding experts, and her husband, Alan Lieberman, had managerial experience. As the scientific report was being written, enterprising individuals in the background were shaping a new organizational blueprint for the 'alalā program. The Service would fund most of the effort; TPF and the Zoological Society would manage it. Several other collaborators—including Kamehameha Schools Bernice Pauahi Bishop Estate (KSBE) and the Biological Resources Division of the U.S. Geological Survey—would fill in the remaining political and cultural gaps. The Service and TPF would thereby gain the wherewithal to implement the NRC's forthcoming recommendations, especially the most crucial: hatching eggs from the wild birds.

The state, meanwhile, would manage the Olinda facility—at least for the time being. When the time was right, the state would wash its hands of that. Winston Banko's 1971 prophecy that a state effort would "prove to be . . . inadequate" had come true, and here was a golden opportunity to pick up the pieces and start afresh with the federal government—where he believed the program should always have been.

With the multi-party collaborative agreement signed, in 1993 the Zoological Society's Kuehler and Lieberman and colleagues, working on contract with TPF, began collecting wild 'alalā eggs and hatching them in captivity. At the time, the husband-wife team was running the program out of an "egg house"—a small rented dwelling in South Kona—where the couple also lived. There they hatched wild eggs and, as the chicks matured, sent them to aviaries on McCandless Ranch, where the birds were acclimated for release. In 1993, that first year of TPF's involvement, seven chicks were thus hatched. Given that the birds in the wild at the time were raising none, TPF's success was phenomenal by any available measure. Indeed, although the normal success rate of wild ʻalalā in the past, before their numbers had dwindled, was unknown, TPF's success rate may have been higher than Mother Nature's.

In addition to taking wild eggs, NRC recommended replacing the management at Olinda. To achieve this, the state hired Peter Shannon, curator of birds at New Orleans' Audubon Zoo, to be Fern Duvall's boss. Months afterward, Shannon expressed some confusion as to who was actually in charge. Nevertheless, he made several fundamental changes, including the birds' diet. Most important, Shannon allowed the birds to incubate their own eggs for the first week or two rather than immediately putting the eggs in artificial incubators—a recommendation that Kuehler had made in a report four years earlier but that Duvall had rejected as unsound.

In 1994, less than a year after Shannon's arrival, the Olinda captive flock produced four ʻalalā, the largest single crop in the captive flock's history. Several birds who had never before produced young were suddenly parents. In June of that year, four ʻalalā—a combination of birds from Olinda on Maui and the egg house on Hawaiʻi Island—were released to the wild. It was a breathtaking milestone for a program that had languished for more than a decade.

"I believe that allowing natural incubation was the single biggest factor in our success," Shannon said. Putting newly laid eggs in an incubator can lead to more problems than if the eggs are left in the nest. Leaving the eggs alone minimized the need for "breaking out"—a risky technique used for chicks that are having difficulty hatching. In the years before Shannon arrived, breaking out had become a common practice at Olinda. More than once, the procedure had failed.

"I didn't really consider hatching crows a big accomplishment," Shannon told me. Many corvid species were routinely hatched elsewhere in captivity. "I had never worked with large corvids before coming to Hawai'i, so it certainly wasn't the result of my specific knowledge of 'alalā husbandry. I just used what I considered to be standard practice at mainland zoos at the time. Success had more to do with what I didn't do than what I did. A curator of birds at most any zoo could have done it. Mother birds are better aviculturists than humans. It's better to play to a bird's strengths than to a human's weaknesses. One of the keys to success is to listen to what the birds are telling you. They will let you know if you are following the right course. You must always be prepared to adapt your techniques and strategies to achieve the desired result."

While the captive flock at Olinda produced more chicks than ever before, production from collected wild eggs also skyrocketed. In 1994, eggs from the Kalāhiki and Keālia pairs produced five chicks. During the first two years of TPF's management, the wild birds contributed twelve new chicks, while the captive flock added another four. The 'alalā seemed to be making a miraculous comeback. Kuehler and Lieberman seemed to have the golden touch, and in 1994 the Service invited TPF to design a new, state-of-the-art breeding facility. A short time later, Congress appropriated $1.5 million to begin construction. Stepchildren of the state no longer, the 'alalā were rich and famous among endangered species.

But 1995 delivered a new dose of reality. Not a single wild egg hatched. Kuehler feared that the wild pairs, most over ten years old, were passing reproductive age. That same year, but a single chick was produced at Olinda. "We have brought some of the much needed genes of the wild birds into the captive population," Lieberman said, focusing on the positive.

Olinda, meanwhile, was still under state jurisdiction. That

began to end in 1996, when Michael Buck, head of the Division of Forestry and Wildlife, asked TPF—"begged us," in Lieberman's words—to assume the day-to-day operations. It would be the state's last significant hand in the propagation program. The transition did not go smoothly, especially when Lieberman announced, apparently to the total surprise of people there, that the current state employees would be transferred elsewhere.

According to Lieberman, he was met there with "snide comments and thumbed-up noses." No wonder. "Peter and Greg are good, competent people," Lieberman said. "We've never recovered politically from letting them go. Shannon was one of my favorite curators to work with. Now he can't stand us. Greg Massey, the veterinarian there, has never forgiven us. We didn't hire him because we felt we didn't need a full-time veterinarian."

The Olinda staff would remain on the job for another four months while Lieberman and the TPF team settled into Olinda—a time that Lieberman called "hell in paradise." As he settled in, Lieberman was "horrified" by what he found at the chronically underfunded facility, including a plugged plumbing system. According to Lieberman, he telephoned the state agency responsible for maintaining Olinda's physical operations. "Come unstop these!" he said. "TPF doesn't pull hairballs out of the drain for anybody!" So much debris—from obsolete cages to discarded shower stalls—had accumulated at Olinda that during his first week Lieberman filled rental dumpsters with "four tons of junk." In time, the Olinda facility was remade and renamed the Maui Bird Conservation Center (MBCC).

Despite the tumult of the 1996 takeover, TPF managed to raise five chicks there that year and another chick from a wild egg. In addition, early that year the new state-of-the-art breeding facility, the Keauhou Bird Conservation Center, had been opened on a 155-acre tract outside the town of Volcano, near Kīlauea, no more than a two-hour drive from McCandless Ranch. In time, the

facility became home to not only the ʻalalā but also other struggling forest bird species, including the palila; the Hawaiʻi ʻākepa;
the Hawaiʻi creeper, or ʻākohekohe; the rare puaiohi, also known
as the small Kauaʻi thrush; and the Maui parrotbill, of which only a
few hundred remained.

For the most part, the news was good. In 1997, seven ʻalalā were
raised at Olinda, in addition to two at the new Volcano facility, for
a total of nine—a new season record for captive ʻalalā. These
included Uila, ʻEleʻele, Makani, and Kona Kū. I had had an opportunity to see all of them that year when I visited with Peter Harrity.
Forever an optimist, Harrity told me he had high hopes for the
ʻalalā. And now the species seemed, indeed, about to be reborn.

chapter 21

A CRUEL KINDNESS

IN AUGUST 1997, HILU,
who I remembered from my first trip up Mauna Loa the year
before, was found dead. I sadly dug up my notes from my visit that
spring: "Hilu . . . Quiet One . . . backlit by sun . . . and slipping
into the shadow."

"Hilu was seen early last week associating with Noe and Nanu
and she looked healthy and vigorous," Donna Ball wrote. "We have
heard and seen several 'io's between 4,000–4,300 feet in Ho'o-
kena, including a juvenile flying and begging from its parent. We
will be watching."

So were the Hawaiian hawks. A few days later Ball wrote again:
"The remains of HiwaHiwa were recovered near the south
boundary of Kai Malino. Her transmitter was located six feet off
the ground in an uluhe. . . . Shortly after the carcass was discovered a juvenile 'io flew into the area with its parents."

And one of the wild Ho'okena birds had gone missing. Now,
both, into the shadows for good.

Despite these two deaths, the number of 'alalā in the wild soon grew again when, in September of that year, four more—Hiapo, Makoa, Puanani, and Kahuli—were released.

But the increase was not to last. The release of the four was quickly followed by the death of Nānū. The following month, Uila's carcass was found in a burrow under the exposed root of a large koa tree. She had apparently died from an infection. Add to these the deaths of Paniolo, Hōkū, and Mahoa in the months preceding and the dark realities of trying to release birds back into the wild were laid bare. By the end of October 1997, ten of the twenty released 'alalā had died.

"Nature must be cruel to be kind," Kuehler commented when I asked for her thoughts. "The death of the weak will permit the strong individuals—and therefore the species—to survive over the long run." Maybe, she seemed to suggest, young 'alalā naturally suffer very high death rates in the wild. Or maybe, she said, the population would again need to reach a critical number so that flocks could help individuals by serving as sentinels against the 'ios. "I don't have the answer. All I know is we've got to keep pumping 'em out as long as there are enough birds to do it. That's the only way we'll ever save the species in the wild. Do or die is nature's way. It must also be ours."

Some members of the 'Alalā Recovery Team (ART), however, had begun to doubt the do-or-die strategy, among them John M. Marzluff, an associate professor of ecosystem studies at the University of Washington. He argued that release was a suicide mission for the young 'alalā, and he began lobbying other members of the recovery team to recommend against releasing any new birds, at least until the cause of the 'alalā deaths could be determined.

Kuehler and Lieberman felt that they knew what the problem was—poorly managed habitat. They argued that only a continual release of new birds would offer the species any hope of survival, if nothing else, by forcing the Service into a game of chicken. That is, "Buy these birds some habitat or they will die!" And die they did.

Nevertheless, Lieberman dismissed Marzluff's opposition to the release as an attempt to settle an old score he had with The Peregrine Fund. According to Lieberman, the sore feelings had originated several years earlier, when TPF had contracted Greenfalk Consultants, an organization Marzluff worked for, to study the reproductive behavior of mainland crows. This knowledge of a common related species might help biologists to better understand the 'alalā. But by the early 1990s, TPF's president, Bill Burnham, had concluded that Marzluff's surrogate work had contributed about all it could. According to Burnham, he recommended that the U.S. Fish and Wildlife Service terminate Marzluff's funding.

The head of the ART was Scott Derrickson, who had done some of the earliest work on breeding of Hawaiian forest birds at the National Zoo in Washington, D.C., and who had also helped to design the new Hawai'i forest bird conservation program. This would have made him a natural candidate to lead it. But when TPF moved in, Lieberman, not Derrickson, got the job. "Derrickson had some feelings about that," Lieberman said. "He and Marzluff were two votes against The Peregrine Fund from the beginning, no matter the issue."

Derrickson agreed that "there was so much history and bad blood," but as for wanting to run the 'alalā program, "I wasn't trying to drum up business," he told me. "I already had a job."

Bad blood—or perceived bad blood—was only part of the ART's complicated interpersonal dynamics. Recovery teams established to save rare species often bring inherent conflicts of interest. Any recommendation a team makes to the Service can potentially steer funding away from one project and to another. For example, Marzluff's recommendation that no more 'alalā be released could have been interpreted—or misinterpreted—as suggesting instead that more money be spent on surrogate work, which happened to be his line of work. By voting in tacit alliances, recovery team members could thereby slant their recommendations to financially benefit the research of various team members. "This potential conflict of interest," Derrickson pointed out, "is almost impossible to avoid because recovery teams require people with expertise about that species, and they're probably all going to be involved in some aspect of research about it."

When Marzluff recommended to the Service that releases to the wild be stopped, another ART member, John W. Fitzpatrick, director of the Cornell Laboratory of Ornithology, wrote a letter in TPF's defense:

> The biological purpose of the captive rearing and soft-release exercise in which the Peregrine Fund personnel are engaged is straight forward, and it should not be compromised. Their biological purpose is to increase *to the maximum extent possible the effective birth rate of the wild population.* Period. Full stop. In my estimation, they are doing an extremely good job at this, and should be allowed to continue at what they do best. . . . Natural selection and experiential learning must continue to operate among the free-living population. Our most important role in this recovery operation is to "pump out new 'alalā" in order to allow all the natural factors to operate on real birds, flying around and learning in the single best example of real Kona forest left on the Big Island.

Kuehler and Lieberman also wrote to the Service in their own defense:

> We believe this action will be viewed as a general step backwards for the conservation of endangered species in Hawaii. . . . We are concerned that halting releases brings into question the efforts of the land-owners, biologists and administrators who have worked diligently over the past several years. . . . By delaying the release of birds for an undetermined period of time, we are sending the message that we are giving up on the wild flock and not following through with our commitment.

As a clincher, TPF warned that "if the release program does not continue, we will be forced to re-designate breeding aviaries as holding pens or discontinue breeding more 'alalā"—a warning that TPF could bring the captive breeding program to a screeching halt. If the release program were stopped, they let it be known, they would quit the project and say aloha to Hawai'i.

Cynthia Salley also enthusiastically endorsed the continued release of birds. She was concerned about the 'alalā as well as the ecotourism business she had going at McCandless Ranch. Without 'alalā for the visitors to see or hear, an increasingly important source of income for the ranch would dry up. To this day, the extent of koa logging as a source of ranch income remains, as Salley often reminds people, her and her family's business and no one else's. Keith Unger did tell me that, at the time he was trying to get the ecotours running, koa logging accounted for $25,000 to $30,000 per year. But Salley and Unger believed that having the birds pay their way—that is, financially justify their existence—would amount to sustainable conservation.

With the 'alalā all but gone from the ranch, ecotourism offered little hope for future income, however. And recognizing that the current harvest of koa was unsustainable, Salley began erecting fences around certain areas to keep out cattle and other animals in order to let the forests—especially the valuable koa—regenerate. "Our hope is to have koa growing on a sustainable basis," she said. "We are working with the Service in trying to sell conservation easements . . . it's a long process. But these are mostly plans, not history."

Plans, indeed. But the 'alalā needed suitable habitat now. Although Lieberman and Kuehler never said it publicly at the time, they were growing deeply pessimistic about the 'alalā's chance of survival. Neither the state nor the U.S. Fish and Wildlife Service had set aside any protected land for the bird. As for the recovery team, its draft 'Alalā Recovery Plan remained, according to

Lieberman, "a confusing jumble of half-baked recommendations." And Kuehler had already concluded that "we are spinning
our wheels in Hawaii."

The Service, meanwhile, sent a copy of Lieberman's and
Kuehler's pro-release letter to Marzluff for comments. He vented
his frustration with their arguments in an e-mail to Karen Rosa, a
Service higher-up in Honolulu: "To me this is simply a knee-jerk
response to a perceived threat to authority. In my opinion, Cyndi
and Al are just troubled by the fact that the recovery team is recommending something other than what they recommend. Every time
this happens they get defensive, say we're wrong and unreason-
able, and threaten to stop breeding birds if we don't do it their way.
I for one am sick of their threats."

It took no time for a copy of his e-mail to wind up in the hands of
Cynthia Salley, who fired back:

> Dear John:
>   In Hawaii we refer to our experienced and wise elders as Kupuna
> and it is in that custom that I write. Although I am neither a member of
> the 'Alalā Recovery Team, nor an addressee of your response to the
> Kuehler/Lieberman letter, I nonetheless feel compelled to respond
> with sadness and dismay. John, I felt that your letter was inappropriate
> and totally out of line. It came across as a personal attack on the
> Peregrine Fund and their personnel. Regardless of your position on
> their stand, a personal attack was unseemly and unbefitting a person
> of your stature. Your personal grievances need to be addressed in a pri-
> vate arena, not a public forum. You are too nice a person John, to allow
> your anger to compromise your credibility.
>   Aloha from your Kupuna,
>   Cynnie.

On December 23, 1997, the Service rejected the 'Alalā Recovery
Team's recommendation to stop the release of captive-hatched
birds. Less than two weeks later, on January 8, 1998, four of 'Umi's
great-grandchildren were sent into the wild. These were Ao, Hulu,

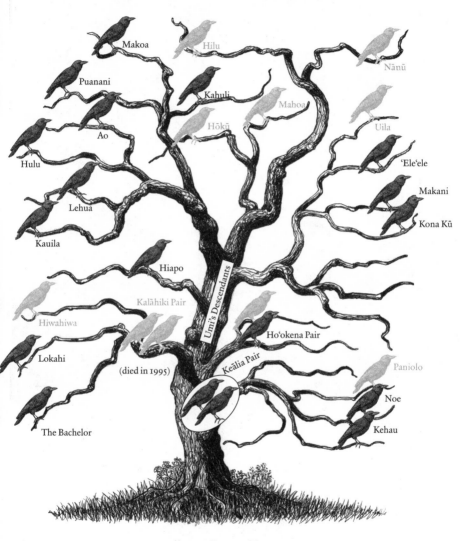

ʻALALĀ FAMILY TREE
Early January 1998

Lehua, and Kauila, referred to by one biologist as the "Desperate Four." This brought the total number of 'alalā in the forest at the time, including the four remaining wild ones, to eighteen. Although it was the largest population in the wild in at least a decade, everyone waited for the next hawk to drop from the sky.

chapter 22

DEAD RAVENS
FLYING

I N JANUARY 1998, Kahuli's remains were found at the base of a tree. Her wings, pelvis, and legs had been "picked clean." Several weeks later, a project volunteer discovered one of the earlier releases, Hiapo, lying on his side by a log, near death, at Waiea. Hiapo, the first hatch of 'alalā at the new facility, the Keauhou Bird Conservation Center in Volcano, succumbed several hours later.

Then, in late June, the carcass of Hulu was discovered. Disease may have originally weakened the bird, making her easy prey. A short time later, Lehua's body was discovered in a small burrow under a clump of ferns. The calling card scat of a small cat or mongoose had been left at the entrance of a nearby den. Of the four most recent releases, only Ao remained—and that bird would soon be recaptured for its own safety. In early July 1998, Noe, one of the most experienced of the releases, was killed. Her numbered leg bands were found in a clump of her feathers on the forest floor.

Kahuli, Hiapo, Hulu, Noe, and Lehua—all gone within a mere

seven months. The branches of the ʻalalā family tree now seemed nearly bare.

In September came more deaths — those of Makani and his two nestmates, ʻEleʻele and Kona Kū — at least two of them caused by ʻio. By the end of 1998, all four of ʻUmi's great-great-grandchildren had been lost. That same year, the great patriarch ʻUmi himself, who had outlived most of his descendants, died of a heart attack.

The remaining released birds would be captured for their own safety. "Many of us are in agreement that our mortality rate is too high for us to continue with business as usual," Donna Ball said.

On September 3, 1998, TPF, the Service, and the Hawaiʻi Department of Land and Natural Resources issued a joint press release saying as much. Robert P. Smith, Pacific Islands manager for the Service, was quoted: "Since the ʻalalā recovery project began in 1992, 24 ʻalalā have been raised in captivity and released into the wild. Seven other ʻalalā raised in captivity remain . . . to broaden the genetic diversity of the breeding pairs." The release went on to point out that when the recovery program began, in 1992, a mere twelve ʻalalā had existed in the wild. Eight of these birds had died since that time. After years of valiant effort, the release program had come to an end.

But Alan Lieberman and Cyndi Kuehler argued that, given the limited space available for housing ʻalalā, any birds that were already genetically represented by the captive flock should be released. Despite the terrible setbacks, genetically redundant captive birds should be released to make way for new offspring. The show must go on. In January 1999, Alakaʻi, Alahou, and Kilakila were sent into the wild. Alakaʻi quickly disappeared. Alahou, who grew ill, was recaptured but died shortly after. Meanwhile, Makoa had also passed away.

To make matters worse, the Bachelor had vanished. That left only three wild ʻalalā in the forest: one from the Hoʻokena pair and the Keālia pair. The release program had been disaster:

twenty-seven released since 1993, the year of renewed hope for the
'alalā; twenty-two now dead. The rash of deaths had turned John
Fitzpatrick from a TPF-believer into a skeptic. He accused
Kuehler and Lieberman of "flying by the seat of their pants."

For the first time in years, *extinction* began to be uttered, even by
Kuehler and Lieberman, who could hardly bear to consider the
possibility. They continued to fault the Service: "We cannot win a
numbers game without effective control of the threats in the habitat," Kuehler said. That herculean task would have required reduc-
ing the number of cats, rats, mongooses, pigs, and cattle in the
forests—not to mention controlling mosquitoes. Nor was there
an easy answer for the hawks, which seemed to return to their
native territories even after trapping and relocation. Giving them
"aversion training" so they would leave the 'alalā alone, while rea-
sonable to some, seemed beyond the pale to others. If the 'alalā
were to survive, they would need a safe place in the wild to live.
This wasn't science; it was common sense.

In February 1999, Kuehler announced that The Peregrine Fund
would be leaving Hawai'i. "The 'alalā program continues to be a
disaster," she said.

The game of chicken had ended. So had the lives of many 'alalā.

chapter 23

THE 'ALALĀ
FROM HELL

So MANY DEATHS WITHIN
so short a time had rendered the all-or-nothing approach obsolete.
John Marzluff and his backers on the 'Alalā Recovery Team had
apparently been vindicated. But now several team members, including Marzluff, demanded to know exactly *why* so many of the
released 'alalā had died.

"It's painfully obvious," Alan Lieberman reiterated. "There's no
safe habitat!" Lieberman was also quick to point out that during
the ART's six years in existence it had done little. It had not come
up with a final recovery plan; had not made any specific recommendations to the state or to the Service for creating release sites
free of cats, rats, mongooses, pigs, or mosquitoes; had not proposed an effective plan for managing the 'io, which was delivering
a final blow to the wild birds; had not developed meaningful part-
nerships with private landowners; and had not come up with a
plan for managing the several-thousand-acre 'alalā reserve that the

Service was hoping to purchase. Who was the ART to point a finger at TPF, asked Lieberman?

But, keeping the spotlight on TPF, several ART members again demanded to know why so many young 'alalā had died in the wild.

Responsibility for securing suitable habitat was not, in fact, TPF's; it belonged to the Service and its advisory body, the ART. As Cyndi Kuehler put it, "Cleaning up the habitat is way beyond TPF's role. We're a husbandry operation. We raise birds and release them. Shortly after that, the birds become the Service's responsibility." TPF was responsible for breeding the birds and for keeping them safe within a certain window of time after their release. Once outside this, the birds came under the jurisdiction of the Service—and, by association, the ART. All the 'alalā had died outside the range of TPF's responsibility. Technically, they had died on the Service's watch. This made it difficult—but not impossible—to place blame directly on TPF for their deaths.

Suspecting that TPF's management of the young birds was to blame, the ART demanded that Kuehler and Lieberman surrender their data on the released birds—diet, weights, and any health or other problems. Kuehler and Lieberman immediately suspected that Marzluff and other team members were on a fishing expedition. Indeed, some team members apparently believed that transforming the release program into a retroactive study of the factors causing the deaths of the released 'alalā would reveal incriminating evidence against TPF's management.

In response to the request, Kuehler said that "lack of data on exactly why the released birds succumbed to these threats is certainly a valid and understandable criticism from a scientific group like the ART. But that should be leveled at the Service, which hired TPF to raise and release 'alalā, not do scientific research. That's not what we do, and that's not what our funding was for. To be angry at us for not conducting research is silly. The ART's eleventh hour call for us to become a research organization is an attempt to save its own skin. How could we ever trust that the information we did collect would be interpreted non-politically and not used against us?" The ART, on the other hand, interpreted resistance to yield the data as prima facie evidence of guilt.

Running parallel to the efforts of the ART was the work of an informal group of ranchers, federal biologists, and other concerned individuals known as the 'Alalā Partnership. The Partnership was to be, in theory, an open and apolitical venue for discussing problems, differences, and ideas, thereby defusing political tension surrounding the 'alalā. According to Cynthia Salley, who was a mainstay of the Partnership, the group "was meant to be an open forum for honest discussion, and so it some-times became a guts-on-the-table discussion. During Partnership meetings, feelings could be directly vented, unlike in the ART, where grudges and anger consequently sometimes became mani-fested in hidden agendas." While the Partnership had no official decision-making power, it had plenty of goodwill.

On May 4, 1998, the Partnership met and spoke, among other things, about the deaths of the released birds. TPF's Lieberman was at that meeting, as well as his colleague, the soft-spoken Peter Harrity. During the discussion, Harrity mentioned that Scott Derrickson, director of the 'Alalā Recovery Team, had earlier asked him for the measurements and weights of all the captive-raised birds. Harrity, who tended to give others the benefit of the doubt, had told Derrickson he'd look into the request. The Partnership meeting was the first time Lieberman had heard about the request.

Derrickson and the ART, meanwhile, who had been confident that Harrity would get the data for them, had already contracted with veterinarian Thierry Work, who had necropsied some of the ill-fated birds, to analyze the weights and other information that he felt—wrongly—would be forthcoming. Work would "provide his interpretation of the morbidity and mortality patterns of 'alalā released to date." But when Harrity told him about the request at the Partnership meeting, Lieberman, suspecting that the jig was up, said that TPF would not release the data until he could be assured that it would be used fairly. Lieberman's hesitance infuriated the ART when members heard about it. Work, meanwhile, decided to get the information through another channel, and this meant the Service field team, which possessed some of TPF's data. It was upon this information that Work based his subsequent analysis.

At the ART meeting in November 1998, Work presented his findings in a "good-faith attempt to stimulate discussion and improve the reintroduction program." He told the ART that the weight data suggested that TPF had prematurely released some of the 'alalā and that their low weights may have contributed to their untimely deaths. It was an explosive allegation—all the more so because Work had not yet run his conclusions by either Lieberman or Kuehler.

At the meeting Harrity objected, suggesting that Work's analysis amounted to scapegoating. "It makes it sound like the Peregrine Fund is doing a bad job" and "puts out bad birds!" But other team members were impressed by Work's initial findings and asked him to get even more data to analyze. Marzluff suggested that a virtual dossier be compiled on every bird from birth to death, with duplicate records of weight, diet, and other aspects sent to the ART and other interested parties. The smoking gun, some ART members believed, had been found, and Lieberman and Kuehler had gunpowder on their hands.

"I taught Marzluff how to raise crows for his own research," Kuehler bitterly complained one rainy afternoon at TPF's bird conservation center in Volcano. "Now he's become the expert on how to raise crows and is looking for flaws in our program." Several days after the meeting, when Kuehler and Lieberman saw

Work's analysis for the first time, Lieberman said he nearly "spontaneously combusted." Kuehler, meanwhile, analyzed Work's data herself. She then sent her critique to the Service, indicating that Work's analysis was a circus of errors. She pointed out, for example, that Work had analyzed only a portion of the relevant data. He had also, she said, made inaccurate comparisons between birds that invalidated his conclusions. Work's information was "inaccurate, incomplete and incorrectly analyzed. We . . . request that in the future when information relating to a TPF program is presented . . . that we have the opportunity to review the information and correct any errors prior to distribution," she wrote.

When Work got a copy of the letter, he blamed the Service field team for giving him bad data. Later he admitted that his analysis "may depict a misleading picture."

Cynthia Salley, who dubbed the fiasco "Datagate," chastised the ART for attempting to "pursue an agenda against other members" and accused Marzloff, Fitzpatrick, Derrickson, and Dave Ledig, another Service employee, of teaming up against TPF to deflect blame for the collapsing propagation program. As Salley explained it, Work "had not checked his sources or the accuracy of the data he received," leading to the erroneous conclusion that 'alalā were being released underweight.

Undeterred by Work's bungled analysis or Salley's reproach, the ART still called for more TPF data. When the Service, acting at the behest of the ART, wrote a letter requesting it, Kuehler and Lieberman responded that they were, understandably, "hesitant" to share it with "individuals who have misrepresented our information in the past."

Datagate, meanwhile, had distracted almost everyone's attention from the 'alalā program's real failure—the lack of safe habitat for young 'alalā. "Truly depressing," Kuehler said. "We can breed, hatch and raise them but the habitat cannot support them. It doesn't seem to matter how many captive-reared birds you throw out there, they are not going to survive with rats, cats, mongoose, toxoplasmosis, avian malaria, 'io, avian pox and degraded forest." Without an outright purchase of a large tract of land by the federal or state government, Kuehler believed, and without money to restore that habitat, the 'alalā was lost.

Meanwhile, the well-intended Partnership meetings continued. At one of them, a Service biologist presented the results of a computer prediction of what would happen to the population if the 'alalā continued to die at the present rate—that is, assuming that releases continued. In response, Keith Unger quipped: "We don't need a computer analysis of the obvious. If they keep dying like this, there won't be any left." As for Salley, she was completely fed up. On May 25, 1999, she delivered to the Partnership what would become known as "The Sermon":

> This is going to really sound weird, coming from me, but . . . in order to look at ourselves holistically, we need to probe a lot deeper and take a good look at and in—our souls. . . . If we are not in touch with our souls, we won't be in touch with or experience love in its deepest sense. If we are not in touch with our souls, we won't be in touch with our code of honor or our ability to accept responsibility for our actions or inactions. . . .
>
> A lot of time has passed and a lot of water has gone over the dam. . . . Emails have whizzed around in cyberspace, chatting and chatting have gone on over the clotheslines (or more accurately the phone line), perceptible attempts have been made to discredit a variety of people, so many fingers have been pointed in so many different directions that it is impossible to follow them (thank goodness!), behind-the-scenes politicking and manipulation is rampant, rudeness and anger have been in the forefront. A little maturity has prevailed recently, but it's all about to hit the fan anew and I hope that, once again, selfish motives are not the force pushing the behind-the-scenes attempt to discredit. What a shame. If only all of that energy could go into positive open and constructive dialog; something that will help the 'alalā instead of pursuing personal agendas.

The Peregrine Fund is the greatest thing that has happened to the 'alalā captive breeding program, since its inception. If their success rate for hatching, rearing and hacking had only been minusculely met over the past two decades, the 'alalā wouldn't be in the position we find them in today. When the chips are down it's only natural to react, blame and find a scapegoat. You need to look somewhere else; The Peregrine Fund has done an exemplary job.

Then, in a single enlightened moment, Salley seemed to sum up Datagate with the question "Are we having a problem over data that we don't even need to collect?"

chapter 24

REGRETS

O N THE EVENING OF December 2, 1999, I met Alan Lieberman and Cyndi Kuehler for dinner at Kilauea Lodge, nestled at the edge of the cloud forest in Ka'ū at 3,500 feet. Between sips of red wine and the intermittent clinking of silver on china, they expressed regrets and, at times, bitterness.

The Peregrine Fund's participation in the project would end the next month, in January 2000, when the Zoological Society of San Diego would assume responsibility for the 'alalā, they said. Kuehler and Lieberman, however, planned to remain in Hawai'i after all and work for the program. They put the best spin they could on the transfer. The San Diego Zoo's entry onto the scene would "take the program to the next level," and "the 'alalā work was getting too big for our size organization." All of which was true. But not the whole truth.

Back in Boise, Idaho, TPF leadership was tired of the organization's being the lightning rod for bad press and all the problems of working on environmental issues in Hawai'i. As TPF's president, Bill Burnham, said, "Even if you do good work you get beat up there."

It all added up to TPF now wanting out of the program no less than the Division of Forestry and Wildlife's Michael Buck had wanted out years earlier. He'd gotten the state out by getting TPF in. Now it was TPF's turn to get out—by getting the Zoological Society in. It was musical lightning rods.

Most important, TPF needed to cut its political losses. "At this point, there is a real question about the 'alalā's ability to survive," Kuehler told me at dinner that night. "I doubt it will ever be reestablished in the wild. I think there is a real question of whether the 'alalā can be maintained even in captivity. It is so inbred that it may just die out from attrition. The efforts may have come too late. We are realizing now that a lot of our problems in captivity are behavioral, like incompatibility of breeding pairs and nest attentiveness—the result of the isolated rearing of 'alalā in the early years. It's a problem that can't be fixed.

"We're also going to lose our two best breeders over the next few years because they are very old. All the money in the world cannot make them younger. We're very worried about it. The 'alalā is probably not going to go extinct from the earth anytime soon, but we'll probably never see them in the wild again."

Lieberman kept an ear to the conversation as he put a triangular bite of sirloin into his mouth and beads of light rain struck the restaurant windowpane. "In retrospect, we were being used," Kuehler continued. "The state wanted us here because they knew that raising the 'alalā in captivity would give the appearance of doing all that could be done. But then the state didn't make the commitment to give us places to release them. The state had it both ways—good publicity, but no responsibility for the 'alalā. We fell into that trap.

"Our instincts said no. We failed to face the fact that the state asked us to be there not for the 'alalā but as a face-saving measure for their failures. Once the publicity turned toward the success of captive breeding, even if this would not save the 'alalā, the state was

Makoa
Hilu
Nānū
Puanani*
Kahuli
Mahoa
Ao*
Hōkū
Uila
Hulu
'Ele'ele
Lehua
Makani
Kauila
Kona Kū
Hiapo
Alaka'i
Alahou
Kalāhiki Pair
Umi's Descendants
Kilakila*
Hiwahiwa
Ho'okena Pair
Lokahi*
(died in 1995)
Keālia Pair
Paniolo
Noe
The Bachelor
Kehau*

* Returned to captivity

'ALALĀ FAMILY TREE
January 2000

free to leave without being seen as abandoning the 'alalā. Captive breeding without improved habitat would not save the 'alalā. We felt that putting birds into the wild would force the state to manage habitat for them. The state refused because it had already achieved its goal: to escape from the 'alalā debacle it had created.

"In retrospect, we should have been a lot more vocal and ornery about the state's failure to manage habitat, explaining that the released 'alalā were dying as a result. We also would have taken a harder stand against the Service's failures to secure habitat for the 'alalā."

After we said good-bye that evening, I sat on a bench beneath the restaurant's porch light and opened my journal to the 'alalā family tree. Virtually all its leaves had fallen. If things continued this way, they would not return next spring. The 'alalā family tree was dying.

chapter 25

HEART OF KOA

O N   A   H U M I D   A F T E R N O O N
in 2000, I joined Cynthia Salley at McCandless Ranch. She had
just returned from an 'Alalā Partnership meeting, held in her adjacent office building. Exasperation still showed on her face. We
strolled onto the lanai, bordered by red geraniums, and Salley lowered her tired body into a koa wood chair.

Salley's silver Mercedes, a fixture at the ranch, was parked in the
carport. The ranch house is of gray stained wood with a corrugated
metal roof that must sound magical under rain. The gentility of its
occupants is evinced by manicured gardens with azaleas, other
shrubs, and many blooming flowers surrounding the house. A
Romanesque blue-tiled pool, graced by a nearby white arbor laced
with a vine bearing small, fragrant, creamy white five-petaled
blossoms, stands between the ranch house and separate guest
quarters, often rented as a bed-and-breakfast, across the drive.
Antherium and other broad-leaved and blossoming plants sprout
from earthen urns of various contours and sizes on the long,
sweeping lanai. Visitors are greeted by a large, shiny koa wood
front door framed by elaborate crystalline leaded glass windows
with beveled edges and a floral motif.

Salley gazed at the tangerine sky above the blue sea a mile away and a thousand feet below us. She clasped her hands behind her head, arched her neck back like a stretching cat, and then drew a deep breath, released her hands, and lowered her head. She was looking back into the earliest days of her family's life in Hawai'i.

"In the 1860s, the McCandless brothers, well drillers from Indiana, Pennsylvania, were hired to come to Hawai'i to drill artesian wells. My grandfather, Lincoln Loy McCandless, was one of those four brothers. He worked hard drilling wells and began to secure land. He also learned to speak Hawaiian fluently and became a politician. He started this ranch in 1915, when he leased thirty thousand acres from the Bishop Estate. Over the next twenty-five years, he added to it with parcels he bought outright. By the time he was done, the ranch had sixty thousand acres.

"For the first thirty years, the ranch was managed as a wild cattle operation. There weren't any roads, pastures, or fences to speak of. The cattle just roamed through the forests at will, and when it was time to sell them, cowboys on horseback lassoed one animal at a time and tied it to a tree until it quit struggling. Next day, they'd lead it to the nearest corral. Once enough cattle had been amassed, they'd be yoked and tied together two by two to form a line, and a few yoked-pin oxen would lead the seven-hour procession down the mountain. By today's standards, it was an impossible task.

"I grew up in Honolulu, and I was only three years old the first time I came up to the ranch. The ranch was run by a manager, and we visited there off and on during the summers. From as early as I can remember, the 'alalā were always part of it. We used to see them all over when we rode horses up the mountain to the cabin. We never stopped to say, 'Oh, look, an 'alalā,' any more than we said, 'Oh, look, a tree.' They were both just a natural part of our lives here. If you didn't see them, you'd hear 'alalā all the time. Then a flock would take off from the trees and fly overhead. They'd come to see you and perch nearby. They were very curious."

As Salley wandered through memories of her past, her words

came out in a soft, almost reflective tone—no longer the words of a warrior. "After World War II, lots of surplus military equipment flooded the market—jeeps, bulldozers, horses, you name it. The availability of these vehicles and equipment led to the building of the first roads up Mauna Loa. It also meant that the cattle could be easily moved down the mountain. More pastures were developed, and the wild cattle began to be eliminated and replaced by herds. There are still a few of those wild cattle that roam the forests to this day.

"When I got married, in 1960, my husband and I moved to the ranch permanently. I remember going up the mountain with him on a number of occasions, and I thought there weren't as many 'alalā around as during the summers when I was growing up. You could still hear the birds and see them, but they weren't an everyday sight. I once commented to my husband, 'What's become of the 'alalā?' We just shook our heads.

"In all those years since that we've lived here, they were still around but not exactly common. Sometimes a few would come to feast on the carrion of a dead cow. You'd hear stories from the hunters way back when; when they shot the gun, the 'alalā would show up expecting a meal. We'd hear their distant calls occasionally, especially in the morning. I guess all this time their numbers were decreasing but so gradually that we didn't even notice just how few there were.

"In the 1970s and 1980s, all those scientists began showing up to study the 'alalā. The ranch, as it turned out, was one of the few places where any were left. In the early days, ranches had an open-gate policy, and people who wanted to study the 'alalā could come and go. For a long time, biologists came to study and count them in the spring, when they were nesting, and were supposedly helping the birds. All the while, there were fewer and fewer 'alalā. It was in 1992 that it dawned on me that the 'alalā were for all intents and purposes gone. I never heard or saw them anymore.

"We were always very tuned in to the plants and animals on the

ranch. Joseph Rock, the father of Hawaiian botany, was a close
friend of my parents, Loy and Lester Marks. Rock lived with them
for many years and is even buried in the McCandless family cemetery in Honolulu. Rock—we called him Pōhaku, Hawaiian for
'rock'—named several plants after my parents."

Salley couldn't remember the details, but after some research in
the botanical literature, I learned that Rock had named *Clermontia
loyana* "in honor of Mrs. A. Lester (Loy) Marks of Honolulu,
Hawaii, an ardent lover and grower of plants, who is especially
interested in the preservation of Hawaiian plants." Rock named
the "beautiful species" *Cyanea marksii* in honor of Cynthia Salley's
father, A. Lester Marks, "to whom I am indebted for many courte-
sies and for hospitality."

"My father inspired my mother to build the world's finest and
most extensive tropical botanical library, and he first conceived of
the idea for a tropical botanical garden, which eventually resulted
in the National Tropical Botanical Garden on Kaua'i. The library is
in a climate-controlled warehouse while we figure out what to do
with it. My mother mentioned something in her will about the
Bishop Museum, and even though their botanical department
folded and they have big financial problems, the museum is fighting us for my mother's valuable collection. My mother would have
wanted the collection to go to the National Tropical Botanical
Gardens in Kaua'i, and she set up a foundation to support the collection. But we have not endowed this yet. The Bishop Museum
has not sued us for the collection—yet.

"So it's not like conservation is some sudden interest for the
family. We have a history of conservation on the ranch, and as
proof, we still have the best prototype forests on the islands. Then
these environmentalists come in and think they can do it better.

"There used to be a lot of money in ranching, but there's little in
cattle anymore," she said. "We need to cut koa to keep the ranch
going. We also offer tours of the ranch—oh, well, you know that—

you were on one of the first tours with Keith, almost four years ago. You saw a bunch of 'alalā back then, didn't you?"

"Twelve, to be exact," I said. "Three wild and nine released."

"Who would have imagined it would come to this?" she asked, before suddenly answering the question herself. "I predicted the outcome once biologists started messing with the birds and the bureaucrats took over."

In 1999, the U.S. Fish and Wildlife Service had asked Salley whether she was interested in selling her land. She was — until she heard the offer, which was well below what she thought was market value of the ranch. "About half!" she told me with some consternation. She paused as her adrenaline receded.

Then she handed me a copy of her speech to the Governors' Forest Conference the year before. "We have separated law from justice," she told the group.

How then, does this pertain to me, a private landowner? The most important example I can cite is the Endangered Species Act. . . . As a law, it is full of punishments for what you do and for what you don't do. Punishments both monetary and condemnatory, of assets and person. Who does it affect and who runs the risk of facing these dire punishments, advertently or inadvertently? Me, a private landowner whose family, multi-generationally, have been good stewards of the land they owned and managed and consequently have a prototype native forest with an abundance of endemic and indigenous flora and fauna. . . . I should be rewarded, not punished. Where is the justice in this? There is none.

"I guess this 'alalā debacle has turned me into a crusader for the rights of private ownership," she confessed, meaning that measures such as the Endangered Species Act of 1973 had come to symbolize, in her view, the dangerous power of the federal government over the lives of individuals.

In fact, the Endangered Species Act, while one of the most

powerful U.S. laws ever enacted to protect vanishing plants and animals, gave few directives when it came to the intersection of endangered species and private land. Among numerous other provisions, the act requires the secretary of the interior to develop a recovery plan for all species that are determined to be in danger of extinction. In addition, the secretary "shall develop and implement" these plans. But it doesn't explicitly state that all provisions of the recovery plan must be implemented, nor does it give the Service the express right to enter private land in order to implement the recovery recommendations. Because the McCandless suit was settled through mediation rather than a ruling, that area of the law remained as gray before the lawsuit as afterward. But it had allowed a breath of new life to enter the captive breeding program through the eggs of wild birds.

I excused myself, and Salley directed me through a white sliding screened door, saying, "Through the room and to your right." I was amazed by the house's interior, especially the warmth and beauty of the solid koa wood walls and ceiling. It was as if the house itself had been hewn from the heart of a massive koa. The rich reddish brown wood gleamed with swirling honey and cream-colored grain. The walls radiated a warmth so intense as to seem aflame.

We spoke a bit more, and Salley began to bring up the current problems with the ranch. She explained that her grandfather, Lincoln Loy McCandless—L. L., or Link, as he was known—had died just before World War II. After Salley's own parents died, Lincoln's three grandchildren—Cynthia and her two siblings, Lester Marks and Elizabeth Stack—inherited the ranch. "That's a whole other mess, having to divide the place up," she said. "We can talk about that tomorrow."

Curious about how it would be to spend a night on the ranch, taking in its smells and getting a sense of the place, my wife and I had decided to rent—for a considerable fee—the cottage behind the ranch house for the night. "We'll see you early," Salley said. "Keith and the biologists said they'd drop by to get you at seven."

Two o'clock in the morning. A single light shines in the main ranch house, across the tiled pool. Mauna Loa smells like cold stone. I step outside the bungalow beneath a sky of crushed diamonds. Starlight gleams through pinpoint holes in the black canvas of the universe. The star Hōkū-hoʻokele-waʻa—better known as Sirius— wheels brightly over Polynesia, and low on the horizon lies the constellation Makaliʻi—Little Eyes, or the Pleiades. Behind me, in darkness, Mauna Loa is an old, hunched woman with a heavy rag coat over her sagging shoulders.

As I stand beneath the stars, I think of Earth's immense age. Volcanoes grow, age, and die—and the one on which I stand is young. Planets come and go. I ask myself, as I have done many times before, Does the ʻalalā's passing matter? Somewhere on the quiet slopes, among the somber winter ʻōhiʻa, the last ʻalalā, perched black and mute in the shadows of starlight, sleep.

When I return to the cottage an hour later, the stars have perceptibly shifted, Hawaiʻi has crawled a fraction of an inch to the northwest along its tectonic path, and my wife is curled like a cat exactly where I left her.

chapter 26

KAHUNA ʻALALĀ

OLYNESIANS HAD BEEN
farming or gathering on the land now known as McCandless
Ranch for more than a thousand years when Lincoln McCandless
was born. Traces of those early inhabitants might seem scarce on
the ranch today, but if one walks carefully, the vestiges of numerous ground burials, trails, rights-of-way, old house sites, temples,
and boundary walls are still to be found. The land is still dotted by
the cavernous mouths of ancient lava tubes, created when molten
earth drained beneath the cooling and hardening surface of fresh
flows, leaving tunnels behind. Customary burial places of Hawaiians, many of these tubes still contain the relics and bones of
ancient chiefs—and of the ancestors of some Hawaiians living in
the area today.

Nor have the souls of these early dwellers departed. One senses
them at the edge of darkness, lingering near the mouth of a lava
tube and beneath boughs of druid ʻōhiʻa weeping in fog. Souls
linger across the landscape like wandering shadows. At least, that
is how Jimmy and Clarence Medeiros view the forested slopes of
what is now McCandless Land and Cattle Company. Here, they
say, the souls of their departed ancestors still live.

Some of the many old Hawaiian land divisions, or ahupua'a, that McCandless Ranch encompasses are Kalāhiki, Ho'okena, and Keālia—namesakes of the wild 'alalā—as well as Honokua and Waiea. The thousands of Hawaiians who once lived on these ahupua'a have long since perished, and their descendants have been displaced. By the early 1800s, many of the original inhabitants had been swept away by the diseases bestowed by Europeans, diseases that may have claimed the lives of half the Hawaiians within a century of Captain James Cook's arrival. Many of those who survived to occupy their original lands were disenfranchised by the so-called Great Mahele, or privatization of land, in 1848. In its wake, much of the former communal land was sold to foreigners. When foreigners secured title to land, they often found these remnant Hawaiian families still living on their old ahupua'a. Many Hawaiians became occupants with the right to gather on the land that was left. The new landowners sometimes viewed these Hawaiians as illegal squatters.

Among those to linger on the ahupua'a of Honokua was the family of John Mokuohai Puhalahua, who was born in 1850. His middle name came from his birthplace, near the battlefield known as Moku'ōhai, where the warrior Ke'eaumoku cut the throat of Kamehameha the Great's main rival, Kīwala'ō, with a shark-tooth knife, thus helping Kamehameha gain control over the districts of Kona, Kohala, and Hāmākua on Hawai'i Island.

Puhalahua was a builder of fishing canoes, a craft that had been passed down through many generations and that has since been passed down his family line. He was affectionately known as Kahuna 'Alalā because the birds were once common in the highland forests where he sought koa trees for his canoes. Kahuna 'Alalā spent many of his working days in the koa forests among 'alalā and within the ahupua'a of Honokua, Waiea, Keālia, and Kalāhiki and elsewhere—tracts that would one day be encompassed in the sprawling McCandless Ranch.

Puhalahua's grandson, Charles Mokuohai Parker, took up his

grandfather's craft of constructing the six-man fishing canoe, and by the 1930s he had become one of Hawai'i's most famous canoe builders. As a canoe builder, Parker also spent many of his days in the koa forests among 'alalā on the land now making up much of the ranch. His descendants tell of a time when the 'alalā would follow him down the mountain and, as they had with his grandfather, join him for lunch.

With the traditional fishing canoe rapidly falling into obsolescence, Parker adapted the skills his grandfather had taught him to design and build racing canoes, streamlined versions of the fishing canoe. A master builder and hewer of these magnificent koa vessels, Parker is also credited with being one of the early designers and builders of the canoes. The Outrigger Canoe Club, in Honolulu, possesses a particularly fine one; its hewn-out hull gleams like a fiery womb of koa wood.

Stories about the life of Kahuna 'Alalā and his descendants — and their struggle to reclaim land from McCandless Ranch — are still frequently told by living family members, including two of Kahuna 'Alalā's great-great-grandsons, Clarence A. Medeiros Sr. and his younger brother by nine years, Jimmy Medeiros Sr.

"The 'alalā is one of our family's 'aumākua, or protective spirits, through my mother's side," Jimmy Sr. told me one afternoon. We were standing under a corrugated tin roof on which he and his wife dried coffee beans harvested from bushes his father had planted years before. He explained that the family also had other 'aumākua, including the 'io and the owl. "What I know of Kahuna 'Alalā comes through the stories my father told me. He spent much of his time in the koa forests among the 'alalā as he looked for trees suitable for canoes. It could take a long time to select the right tree. One way to determine a good tree was to watch the 'alalā. If the 'alalā pecked at it or peeled off the bark, it was looking for insects, and the tree had rotten spots. When a tree was finally selected and cut, it had to be snaked by horse all the way down the mountain.

The ʻalalā would caw and cackle and make conversation as they followed my father and his helpers all the way back to his house, where they would gather for a while before returning to the forests. My great-great-grandfather was so closely associated with the birds, that's how he got the name Kahuna ʻAlalā.

"It made sense that the ʻalalā would be our ʻaumakua, and it passed down through the generations to my own family," Jimmy Sr. continued. "But there are many other ways to come by an ʻaumakua. An ʻaumakua may present itself as an unexpected helping voice or physical presence, especially when you're in trouble, maybe lost in a forest or in personal trouble. Or you can discover a guardian spirit in a dream. In our case, it goes way back because our family built canoes further back than anyone can remember, before history."

I asked Jimmy what would happen if the ʻalalā were to go extinct. "That is an issue," he replied, stopping to think about it. "When the ʻalalā goes, we will no longer have its protection. Luckily, through my other grandfather's side we inherited the pueo, or owl, as ʻaumakua too. Families have several ʻaumākua. But how long will the pueo be safe?" he asked, wondering aloud whether it would be around for his great-grandchildren.

"There is a planned housing development not far from here that would destroy an ancient nesting area of the pueo. What happens when we have no more ʻalalā, no more pueo, no more ʻaumākua? The loss of land took away our traditional diet of taro and sweet potatoes, and it's taking away the animals. That is how the destruction of land destroys culture, health, and self-identity. In the end, it's always about land. The land is about who we are— or once were. It's really the same as with the ʻalalā. Its land was taken away, too."

By the 1970s, one of Kahuna ʻAlalā's other great-great-grandsons, Jimmy Sr.'s brother Clarence Sr., and his family were among the last Hawaiians remaining on the old family ahupuaʻa.

Cynthia Salley and McCandless Ranch obtained clear title to most of their original land, but at least one tract of some 1,600 acres was entangled with numerous competing claims of Hawaiian ownership. At times, the disputes sank to the level of Wild West threats.

One day in mid-October 1988, Clarence Jr. went up the mountain to tend his vegetable garden and encountered a group of wild pigs digging up the plants around the macadamia trees. His dog gave chase. After killing a pig with his knife, Clarence, who was accompanied by his son Jacob and three of Jacob's young friends, awaited more barking from the dogs. Instead of the sound of dogs, suddenly, from about 150 feet away, "a bullet 'zinged' by in our general direction," Clarence Jr. said, "and I knew that we were in danger. So I immediately picked up the pig and instructed the boys to run back down the trail and go back to the truck." As a Vietnam War veteran—he had received spinal injuries when the five-ton truck he was riding in near Fire Base Vandergrift received nearly a direct rocket hit, throwing him twenty or thirty yards—Clarence Jr. considered himself experienced in firefights. "So I know what the sound of a gun being fired is and I know the sound of a bullet and its proximity." Six months later, according to Clarence Jr., the McCandless Ranch manager, Peter Simmons, "confessed that he was the one that fired the gunshot."

Clarence Jr.'s father, Clarence A. Medeiros Sr., who died in 2000, had hunted, gathered, and tended taro on the family's old ahupua'a of Honokua, Kalāhiki, Ho'okena, and elsewhere as a child. He was a master carver of canoes and tiki, or totemlike idols, many of which still stand in the proximity of Pu'uhonua o Hōnaunau, or City of Refuge, a place where Hawaiians who had broken a taboo could find safe harbor. One day in June 1988, despite an agreement with McCandless, Clarence plowed a road through a disputed section of the ranch in order to reach some 'ōhi'a trees. He planned to cut the trees and drag them along the road to his shed, where he would carve them into idols.

Cynthia Salley filed a complaint against him for trespassing. A bitter twelve-year legal battle—or, rather, a war with many different battles—broke out. Clarence Sr. and Clarence Jr. argued that part of the tract belonged to them because many pieces of land had been conveyed to McCandless Ranch as if these tracts had a single owner. "But records clearly show that many people had fractional interests in these tracts, including my recent ancestors," Clarence Jr. maintained.

As part of the lawsuit, Clarence Sr. and his son painstakingly reconstructed family genealogies going back many generations and relating to family occupancy of the land, which they say support their claims of ownership. In the process, they reconstructed the history of how some of these old ahupuaʻa, including parts of Honokua, had become part of McCandless Ranch.

After the Great Mahele of 1848, the 7,000-acre ahupuaʻa Honokua—most of which would eventually wind up with the ranch—went to Victoria Kamamalu, an heir of Kamehameha the Great. This land was handed down to Princess Pauahi Bishop, who willed her land to her husband, Charles, and to S. Damon. They eventually sold the land to Clarence Jr.'s great-great-granduncle, Lapawila. Lapawila, in turn, sold it in equal parcels to twenty friends and family members, according to Clarence Jr. One of those "twentieth" owners was Kelii O kahaloa, whose 340 acres were inherited by his two sons. One of them married Kahuna ʻAlalā's sister Kauhewa, who ended up with 77 acres. Three of her heirs inherited her interests in Honokua: her second husband, Gideona Maele, and her two brothers, Samuel Kanamu Puhalahua and John Mokuohai Puhalahua. They all conveyed their interests to Samuel's daughter Emily Kanamu Puhalahua Atkins in 1914. On the same day, Emily conveyed her interest back to Gideona, and then, in January 1928, Gideona conveyed his interest in Honokua to his wife, Mary Maele. However, in May of that year, Emily conveyed the interest she had already given to Gideona to Edward Hea, her sister Mary's son. (Mary was married to Samuel Puhalahua.) That same month, Edward Hea and his wife conveyed their interests to McCandless.

And so it was, after the Great Mahele, that land flowed, often in confusion, from common to private ownership: first as a deluge, then a flood, then a dribble, a drab. Then, drop by drop, it ended up as McCandless Ranch.

And this complex chain of land transactions represented only one-twentieth of the seven-thousand-acre ahupua'a Honokua that Victoria Kamamalu came to own after the Great Mahele. How most of the other nineteen-twentieths of the ahupua'a came to be part of McCandless is not nearly as clear. Nor is the ranch's acquisition of part of the ahupua'a of Waiea and Ho'okena. The Medeiros family believes that at least parts of ahupua'a Honokua, as well as of neighboring Kalāhiki and Ho'okena, are still rightfully theirs. This was also, they believe, how 'alalā habitat often came to be broken, divided, and sometimes torn asunder, leaving the 'alalā populations as fragmented and displaced as native Hawaiians.

In the end, McCandless dropped the trespassing lawsuit against Clarence Sr., suspecting that no matter who "won," the other side would appeal, stretching out the costly legal battle until the next big meteor strike, if necessary. McCandless then filed a new suit against the 52 Medieros claimants.

That action was settled when the ranch agreed to forfeit 160 acres to them. The recipeint families were also granted traditional gathering rights to much of their old ahupua'a that were still part of the ranch, where they could camp, gather wild plants, and hunt.

By then there were few 'alalā to be seen, unlike the situation in the 1950s and early 1960s, when Clarence Jr. accompanied his father into the mountains to gather and hunt:

> For over 6 generations, my family have seen the 'alalā in Honokua, and in the ahupua'a to the north—Waiea, Kalāhiki, Ho'okena, and in the ahupua'a to the south. . . . I have seen the 'alalā as far back as the

1950s and 1960s when their numbers were plentiful. The mountain was our store where we would go to hunt for wild game to eat, to gather maile for special occasions, pick watercress, hoʻio, kakuma to eat, gather plants for medicine purposes, [and] cut wood to make utensils to clean taro and fish. On our way down from the mountain, the 'alalā would follow us, flitting from tree to tree, making loud, crowing calls. The 'alalā would follow us down to about the 2000 foot elevation and then they would disappear. They never came any lower than that. But in the 1990s, one 'alalā would frequent one of my kuleana in Honokua which was at the 1500 foot elevation. It would be crowing in the mango tree at about 6:30–7:30 in the morning. This lasted for only an hour's time. The 'alalā did this for about 9 months, then I never heard it again.

In the 1960s, Clarence Jr. and Clarence Sr. hunted feral cattle and wild pigs in these higher reaches of their family's traditional ahupuaʻa. "Even then, 'alalā were fairly common," Clarence Jr. told me. He said that large wooden water tanks were built at about the 4,500-foot level on Mauna Loa. This water was then piped to troughs for cattle lower down in the dry pastureland. There was a gap of several inches between the flat roof and the tank itself. "We almost always saw the 'alalā gathered on the tops of the towers," he said. "When my father and I got thirsty, we'd climb up the side to dip water to drink. We'd almost always find a few 'alalā floating inside. I think they tried to drink the water and fell in. Maybe they thought it was shallow and just jumped in, or maybe when they leaned over in the narrow opening they fell. Many of them drowned, and we saw them floating.

"So my father and I went out and cut two-foot sections of hau wood. Hau floats and was used for the outriggers on Hawaiian canoes. We fastened three pieces together like a raft and put these in all the water towers so when the 'alalā fell in they'd have something to grab and maybe not drown. We figured if we did this they'd find a way to save themselves and fly out. I know the cutting of forests had a lot to do with the bird disappearing. I think a lot of them also drowned in water tanks, which were built right in some of the areas where the birds were most common back then."

Still embittered by the suit and its aftermath, Clarence Jr. and his wife alone had spent $238,000 in pursuing the claims for the benefit of the entire family. As of yet, they had no clear title to any of the land to show for it. The remains or burial plots of many ancestors remained painfully close to their hearts but just beyond their grasp: Clarence Jr.'s great-great-grandfather Kahuna ʻAlalā, buried in his old taro patch next to a sweet guava tree on a hillside above the Salley home; along the beautiful cliffs of Palianihi, which run over a mile long through the ahupuaʻa of Waiea, Kalāhiki, Kauhakō, and Hoʻokena, his fifth-great-grandfather, his fourth-great-grandparents, and his fourth-great-grandaunts; and buried along the Waiea-Kalāhiki boundary a quarter mile from the shoreline, on a plateau where his ancestor Palea resided and grew pineapples in the 1800s, more bones of his ancestors.

The Medeiroses believed themselves to be related to the land not only through this history of ownership and occupation but also, much more fundamentally, through genealogy, which for Hawaiians is the web of meaning that ties them to nearly every facet of existence. For the Medeiroses, their genealogy, while appearing impossibly complex to most outsiders, provided a path not only to human ancestors but also to the ʻalalā. Their genealogy includes even a great Hawaiian king, the namesake of the patriarchal ʻalalā ʻUmi. It was Liloa and Akahi-a-Kuleana who begat Umi-a-liloa; and Umi-a-liloa and Kapukini-a-Liloa who begat Kealiia-kaloa; and down through the generations into the more recent territory of their familiars.

And that was only a beginning of the genealogical web of which Clarence Jr. considered himself a part, for through the ʻUmi line his family was also woven into the vast genealogy of the great Hawaiian creation story, the Kumulipo.

Over the past few decades, the Medeiroses had not been the

only ones with eyes, in large part through the genealogies of ownership, on parts of McCandless Ranch. The state, too, had begun making noises about rezoning parts of the ranch from agricultural to conservation land. Making the land more valuable for the 'alalā, however, would have dramatically cut the land's market value, thereby making it far less financially valuable to Cynthia Salley. So when she heard rumors of rezoning, she immediately hired an engineer and surveyors to subdivide the property—at least on paper. She knew that once subdivision of land had begun, the state would not be able to rezone it. As she put it, "I was preserving the 'highest and best' use of the property."

The logical areas for the ultimate refuge included not only Kalāhiki and Ho'okena but also Waiea and, most significantly as far as Salley was concerned, Honokua. That was where, after the partition, the bulk of her land now lay. And the Medeiroses' long oral record of seeing an abundance of 'alalā there made her uneasy. The National Audubon Society and the Hawai'i Audubon Society —not to mention her Hawaiian neighbors—could potentially use that knowledge against her, strengthening their case for opening up the ranch for 'alalā conservation.

This bitter history of animosity between the ranchers and the native Hawaiians was long. Clarence Medeiros Sr. said that in 1953 or 1954 he witnessed a McCandless Ranch hand evict native Hawaiian Agnes (Akaneki) Kalama from her home on contested land. "While she was sitting in her house I saw one of the McCandless Ranch cowboys put a cable around the post of her house and [pull] it with a truck bringing the house down," he recalled. "She barely made it out of her house alive. . . . McCandless Ranch later burned the house down."

And so into this tangled web of history, myth, truth, fate, law, genealogy, geology, and ecology the Medeiroses, the owners of McCandless Ranch, and the 'alalā had all been cast. They were all related now, in one happy or unhappy way, by shared history.

chapter 27

BROKEN HOME

F OR YEARS, CYNTHIA SALLEY, her sister, Elizabeth "Tita" Stack, and her brother, Les Marks, owned in common the almost mythic sixty-thousand-acre Mc-Candless Ranch—half outright, half leased from the Bishop Estate. It was a mostly magnificent tract of forest and pasture reaching from South Kona to Kaʻū, from ocean shore to the alpine zones of leeward Mauna Loa—and, for the family, a place of mostly pleasant memories going back just about as far as anyone could remember.

But common were the scars of human habitation: roads old and new, fence lines, and areas of cut forest, most of the natural lowland trees and cover having been cultivated out of existence a thousand years ago. And, like the rest of Hawaiʻi, it was a land continually besieged by foreign species, including feral pigs and cattle.

When Cynthia and Tita's brother, Les, died in 1989, it became necessary to partition the ranch so that his share could be given to his three daughters. By the mid-1990s, the contentious partitioning process, driven largely by Cynthia Salley, was well under way. Throughout it, all eyes were on the ʻalalā because whichever piece of property ended up with the most birds would also end up with the most biologists and other "damn federal bureaucrats," as the ranchers often called them.

In the end, Cynthia Salley claimed the southernmost section of the original ranch, which retained the McCandless Ranch name. Tita Stack settled for the northernmost section of the original ranch, known as Keālia Ranch. Les' three daughters, who operated as the Les Marks Trust, inherited the center portion of the original ranch. They called their ranch Kai Malino. Each party also received a parcel of coastal land.

That all overlapped 'alalā habitat was only one potential complication of the partition. Inheritance and other taxes were another. In inheriting their father's land, Les' three daughters were hit with a large inheritance tax. They decided to sell part of Kai Malino to pay it.

In the 1996 federal budget, Congress earmarked funds to buy 5,300 acres of Kai Malino. The Service had only to await the final appropriation. In the interim, an American conservation organization that specializes in transactions of conservation land worldwide, The Nature Conservancy (TNC), negotiated an option to buy the Kai Malino property for $7 million so that the three sisters could pay their taxes and move on with their lives and the property would not be at risk for development or other sale while the Service awaited the money. Once the congressional appropriation was approved, TNC would sell the land to the Service, adding a modest fee for serving as middleman. If all went according to plan, everyone would live happily ever after — maybe even the 'alalā.

Over the next three years, TNC paid the owners nearly a third of a million dollars to maintain the option while the Service waited for the money. When Congress severely cut back on funds for conservation, the final appropriation became stalled. TNC, fearing that the money for Kai Malino would not be forthcoming, allowed the option on the property to expire. To the three sisters, still stuck with a large, interest-accruing tax bill, the broken deal only proved what they had already long assumed: that dealing with federal bureaucrats—even through a middleman such as TNC—was a waste of time.

After the purchase stalled, a front-page article in the *Honolulu Advertiser* stated, "Owners of the last habitat for the endangered Hawaiian crow—frustrated with government delays to buy their land—plan to begin logging rare koa there." That, the sisters argued, would provide the money they needed to pay their taxes. They also believed that it was sure to light a fire under the Service.

But the article quoted Robert P. Smith as saying that he still couldn't guarantee that Congress would authorize the expenditure anytime soon: "We've been negotiating in good faith for 18 months or so. Recently one of the owners said they were going to engage in a logging program. I didn't have any money, so I wished them luck." The article also quoted Nohea Santimer, one of the sisters: "We've given up our lives for the last three years to make this plan work, and it really hasn't come to fruition. I would really have liked the Fish and Wildlife Service to have bought it, but the Fish and Wildlife Service doesn't have the money."

The ranchers' intentions for Kai Malino were laid out in a "forest restoration plan" written by a forester and family friend, Bill Rosehill, whose reputation in the environmental community preceded him. In the 1980s he had overseen logging on a portion of the Bishop Estate's Keauhou Ranch in Ka'ū, where, according to *Environment Hawai'i*, he was "remembered for clear-cutting the area in the name of restoring a 'decadent' koa forest."

Not long after the plan for Kai Malino became public, the Sierra Club Legal Defense Fund sued the ranch to prevent the cutting of trees in 'alalā habitat.

The 'alalā "faces a new, deadly threat," the suit read.

The owners of the Kai Malino Ranch . . . home to the last 14 'alalā known to exist in the wild, are poised to commence logging operations that will destroy the native forest habitat on which these last wild 'alalā depend for their continued survival. This habitat is so vital to the 'alalā that the United States Fish and Wildlife Service ("Service") has identified Kai Malino as its single highest priority for habitat acquisition in the United States. Without it, the 'alalā face almost certain extinction.

Even Michael Buck, head of the Division of Forestry and Wildlife and a forester's friend if ever there was one, said that while South Kona needed a responsible forestry plan, cutting shouldn't start in the middle of the 'alalā habitat.

While the Service continued to wait for Congress to appropriate the money, the sisters refused to allow biologists on the would-be refuge. Rosehill said that the government had bungled the deal by not dealing fairly with the owners of Kai Malino. Access would be denied until the land was actually paid for. Anyone who trespassed would be arrested.

Cynthia Salley, meanwhile, had been quietly cutting koa on McCandless Ranch. Fearing a similar suit, she stopped. The ranch continued to make up some of the shortfall with ecotours, inviting birders to come and see the 'alalā, which had become a holy grail for birders. As long as there were 'alalā, the tours proved popular, sometimes attracting a dozen or more people in a day—at $200 each.

The owners of Kai Malino, meanwhile, abandoned their logging plan two months after the lawsuit was filed. Finally, about $7 million in federal money became available, and the Service began negotiations to buy the property. They were contentious from the start. As Robert Smith later characterized the situation, "every other word out of those ranchers' mouths was 'damn federal bureaucrats this, damn federal bureaucrats that.' It would be hard to overestimate just how much they hated any government interference in their affairs."

Rather than buy the land outright, it was agreed that the Service would initiate a friendly condemnation, meaning that it would take possession at an agreed price through the law of eminent domain. This course was taken because the three sisters did not have clear title to all their land. In fact, down the mountain, the Medeiroses, whose ancestors had historically used the area, considered making a legal claim to part of it. For the sisters, having the Medeiroses involved at Kai Malino would have been worse than meeting the Minotaur in the Labyrinth. By condemning the land, the government could preempt complicating claims of landownership.

In December 1997, the Service finally took possession of the 5,300 acres of Kai Malino for about $7.8 million. The news only got better when the California-based David and Lucile Packard Foundation promised the Service $1.1 million to build a pig-proof fence around the entire refuge. At last the ʻalalā would have a place to call its own.

While many were relieved by the purchase, the Sierra Club Legal Defense Fund was eager to drive home its original point: "Without vigorous citizen enforcement under the ESA [Endangered Species Act], there might not have been a forest worth purchasing or any ʻalalā left in the wild." Linda Paul, president of Hawaiʻi Audubon, was about as gracious: "Our lawsuit demonstrates the important role citizens play under the federal Endangered Species Act in conserving critically endangered species like the ʻalalā."

These claims of credit rankled McCandless Ranch manager Keith Unger, who had always believed that the ranchers, paradoxically, had protected habitat for the ʻalalā. He fired off a letter to the editor of *West Hawaii Today*:

> There is something missing here. It appears that the USFWS has mobilized and is swooping in to save the forest and all that is in it. From whom? The previous landowners? This area is rich and botanically diverse due to the private landowners stewardship for the past 80

years. . . . Rather than implying that the feds are performing an emergency rescue, wouldn't it be more appropriate to give credit where it is due and thank the present landowners of Kai Malino for their history of good stewardship without which there would be no forest to save?

Not long after the purchase, Bill Rosehill, the three sisters, and Georgia Shirilla, a senior realty specialist from the Service's Division of Realty in Portland, Oregon, who had done most of the negotiating, gathered at Kai Malino. It wasn't long before Shirilla got the distinct feeling that her work was not yet done. "The surveyors and engineers walked up the hill with Rosehill," she said. "When they came back down we knew there was a disagreement."

'Alalā, we've got a problem.

Because the new refuge was an island of federal land amid a raging sea of private property, the purchase agreement identified various rights-of-way through the properties for both the ranchers and the Service. According to Shirilla, one clause stipulated that the Service would pay to build a half-mile connector road from the main highway up to an existing ranch road that led to one corner of the refuge, a mile farther on. Service employees would use this mile-and-a-half stretch—located on ranch property—to reach the new refuge.

But Rosehill and the sisters maintained that the agreement guaranteed no such access along the sisters' existing mile-long road. Rather, they insisted that the Service build not only the half-mile connector road but also an additional mile of new road along the refuge's northern boundary. Shirilla called their conditions for gaining access to the refuge "outrageous."

But the access disagreement was just the beginning. Along with the purchase agreement, the Service, as a federal agency, was required to help the sellers pay for moving certain personal items from the property. The list of personal property that the ranch sent to the Service included customary items—vehicles and cattle, for example—and a lot more, including wildlife: 2,500 turkeys; 8,000 Kalij pheasants; and 300 Erkel's francolins, African game birds related to partridges. The ranch also demanded compensation for "all contents within all lava tubes (caves) including but not limited to: all living organisms, bones, remains of any kinds, artifacts, petroglyphs, etc." Clarence Medeiros Jr. and his wife, Nellie, who believed that many of their ancestors were buried in some of the caves, called the claim a "declaration of war."

"We offered what we felt was a fair price for legitimate claims," said Shirilla. "The sellers rejected our offer and took us to court."

As if the problems on Kai Malino were not enough, soon trouble began brewing next door at Keālia Ranch.

Tita Stack, Salley's sister and the owner of Keālia Ranch, had recently received from the U.S. Department of Agriculture's Natural Resources Conservation Service (NRCS) a grant for pasture improvement. But Service officials worried that the "improvements" were occurring in 'alalā habitat, and this was a serious problem because, by law, government officials from any federally funded project that might harm an endangered species have to "consult" with the Service. And the regional NRCS office in Kona had not consulted with the Service about the project on Keālia Ranch.

One day in the spring of 2001, biologist John Klavitter returned to Keālia Ranch to monitor the last remaining 'alalā in the wild. It was then that he discovered that a bulldozer had knocked down trees and displaced large rocks to clear the way for the new NRCS-funded fence. Klavitter immediately told the refuge manager, Dave Ledig, and supervisory wildlife biologist, Jeff Burgett. They drove up the mountain in their four-wheel-drive vehicle to survey the damage. Ledig told me that he then called Tita Stack and warned, "Your activities may have been in violation of the Endangered Species Act."

Stack said she was surprised and felt "censured" but took the call in stride. "Using a bulldozer to clear a fence line had been standard practice for the ranch for decades," she said. "We didn't give it a second thought. That's how all the roads were made, including the one that the biologists routinely used to reach the ranch." Still, Stack knew that running afoul of the Endangered Species Act, even inadvertently, was not a matter to be taken lightly. If she needed an attorney, she had one in her husband, but rather than risk entanglement with the government, she withdrew the grant application. The ranch paid for putting in the new fence. But the matter was not over.

When Salley got word of the episode, she angrily called an emergency meeting of the all-but-defunct 'Alalā Partnership, which woke up like a dead man. At the meeting were Ledig and Burgett. Paul Henson, field supervisor for the Service's Pacific Islands office in Honolulu, joined by conference call. New to paradise and new to the job, Henson had never met Salley. But even his experience with the controversial northern spotted owl controversy would not have prepared him for this first meeting with her. Nor was Salley fully prepared for him.

At the meeting, Salley railed that reporting the bulldozer incident broke the spirit of the so-called partnership. Anyone who had a problem, she said, should tell the involved parties directly, not run to the authorities. And "if reporting the bulldozer incident was an attempt to teach the NRCS a lesson for not consulting with the Service, Keālia Ranch should not be the 'sacrificial lamb.'"

Salley then reminded Ledig, Burgett, and Henson that, until the Kai Malino access fiasco was resolved, the only access to the new refuge was over McCandless land. The bulldozer incident, she said, was sorely tempting her to eliminate that.

As it stood, the court-negotiated settlement that, several years earlier, had broken the McCandless kapu was still in effect, and the Service was paying Salley $30,000 each year to help maintain the gravel road it used. Salley emphasized that the earlier informal conditions — conditions that had been accepted by Robert Smith — set for individuals to cross her property remained even though Smith had retired.

Depending upon who you talked to, Salley's list of "Thou Shalt Nots" was nearly as long as Hammurabi's, and the punishment for breaking them seemingly as severe. Some of the rules were based on what Smith called the ranchers' "paranoia of the federal government," while others were built on Salley's own hard experience.

One time, Salley's husband, Ray, who made fine wood furniture, had gone up the mountain to salvage a koa tree that had fallen across the road. After his bulldozer — koa log in tow — passed the Hula Dome, one of the field technicians stepped out of the forest and snapped his picture, apparently unaware that the dozer had rearview mirrors. Ray feared that the photograph was just the kind of "evidence" that could stir up trouble. The technician was promptly fired. When Cynthia met with him on his way out that night, she confiscated his film and had it developed. She discovered that the technician had also photographed survey lines — long, straight corridors that had been plowed through the forests as a necessary part of the partitioning process. "This is what he called 'habitat destruction,'" she said. 'Alalā researchers were henceforth prohibited from bringing cameras onto the ranch.

Researchers were also prohibited from taking notes about anything other than 'alalā and 'io, from deviating from any path except in direct fulfillment of their 'alalā duties, and, of course, from otherwise recording or reporting on any activities that might be construed as a violation of the Endangered Species Act.

Despite the bulldozer incident and "out of the kindness of our hearts," Salley said, she would continue to allow passage through McCandless Ranch to the new refuge until the Kai Malino mess, now in litigation, was sorted out. And she still insisted that anyone who came onto her property take the McCandless oath of allegiance by promising not to gather any evidence "to build a case or another lawsuit against us."

Then there was the steep access fee Salley had imposed, which in December 1999 — less than a year before the bulldozing incident — had been increased from $30,000 to $100,000, according to several Service biologists. Unger called the increased fee a matter of "prudent business." Ledig interpreted it as a brazen attempt to raid part of the Packard Foundation grant, which had been awarded to the Service but not yet spent. The fee also rankled Ledig because most of the access to the refuge was across the Waiea tract, land that the ranch leased from the state; only a short stretch was across McCandless property. Whatever the reasons for the increased fee, Salley said that it would be needed to maintain the road after it was "torn up by Service people who didn't know how to drive their 4-wheel drive vehicles."

Whereas Smith might have been comfortable with these previous handshake agreements, Henson, Burgett, and Ledig were not — at least not with the new price tag. Henson thought that Salley, knowing how desperate the government was to reach the refuge, was trying to take advantage of the situation. Ledig had also come to deeply resent the "humiliation" that all government biologists — would-be visitors of the ranch — had to suffer. "Cynnie or Keith would sit us down and give us the third degree about what we could and could not do," he said. "They were interrogations. I don't know what else to call them."

When Ledig accused Salley of "jeopardizing our jobs by asking us not to report illegal activities," the emergency meeting of the 'Alalā Partnership grew more heated. "You want us to continue to turn a blind eye toward the degradation of 'alalā habitat on the ranch," he said.

"You're telling us we can't come on your land unless we promise not to report or notice or see anything potentially illegal," Burgett chimed in, reasoning that this could have potentially meant "a dead body on the side of the road." He continued, "In the past, we turned a blind eye. We can't operate like that any more. At Keālia we saw something that we thought was potentially illegal, and we were obliged to report it."

Salley shot back: "Our family has been managing this land for eighty years with 'alalā. We know good stewardship!"

"Bulldozers and crows just don't mix!" Ledig defiantly replied. "We can't be bulldozing next to crows' nests and expect them to survive!"

When Salley sailed into Ledig with her choicest invectives, reserved for Service employees and other federal bureaucrats, Henson retorted: "I'm completely taken aback by the disrespect you show to someone you hardly know! I'll tell you right now, I respect what Dave's trying to do. He's worked successfully on the California condor with just about every kind of person—ranchers and cattlemen and everyone else!"

Fearing the worst, several Service employees at the meeting made silent mock slashes at their throats with the sides of their hands—futile gestures, since Henson was on a speakerphone. Henson continued. "You have a hostile view of anyone with a Fish and Wildlife patch on his shoulder. Dave is extremely dedicated and energetic and respectful of private landowners. He's just the kind of guy you want to be working on a project. We aren't here to hunt for crimes. We're here to work with everyone we need to, to help this bird. We're here to work with you if you'd let us!"

Surprised that the Service would not agree to her conditions for access, Salley no longer felt obligated to allow its employees on her land, since no crows were left on McCandless. And she knew that barring them from her land would eliminate the only road access to the new refuge. "Fine! You can no longer enter my ranch. Take a helicopter to the new refuge," she huffed. The Kai Malino refuge had become Kai Limbo.

The emergency Partnership meeting still wasn't over. Rosehill accused Henson — or, rather, the Service — of being a serial "wife-beater." It had beat up Salley to gain access to McCandless, it had beat up the three sisters in the process of buying part of Kai Malino, and now it was beating up Tita Stack for her activities on Keālia Ranch. And each time the Service beat up on someone, Rosehill continued, it would come back the next day profusely apologizing, begging for forgiveness, and promising never to do it again. Henson was infuriated by the comparison. Even Salley, who wasn't one to mince words, admitted that Rosehill's analogy was extreme.

At one point during the meeting, Rosehill was leaning over angrily, on the verge of "losing it," as one Service employee put it. At that point, John Klavitter interceded.

"Bill, if we're going to work this out, you're going to have to calm down."

"Don't tell me to quiet down!" Rosehill retorted.

Henson then effectively banned Rosehill from further Partnership meetings. That is, if Rosehill showed up, no one from the service would.

After the explosive emergency meeting, Henson said that he called Tita Stack to "make up" for the bulldozing debacle. According to Henson, he told her, "We have no problem with the work you're doing." He explained that, under the law, the NRCS had to consult with the Service, which it had failed to do. "If they don't, and some group like Hawai'i Audubon wanted to stop the work, they could file suit and the work would stop in a minute." (Stack recalled no such conversation.) Henson subsequently wrote a letter to the NRCS "reminding them" of their obligation to consult with the Service. "We exchanged letters with them. The consultation requirement was met," Henson said. But not without a black eye for the NRCS and bruises for nearly everyone involved.

An intensely private person, Stack later said that the bulldozer incident was "a little thing that got blown out of proportion." Through it all—and to the admiration of all—she continued to allow biologists to monitor the last wild 'alalā on her land. "I invited biologists on the ranch because it was a natural extension of the work they were doing. Having the last two birds arrive here, I allowed the biologists to follow them," Stack told me. "Make no mistake: I minded the biologists' being on the ranch. But allowing them on was the right thing to do."

"On one hand, I can't blame the ranchers for being a little suspicious of the 'government is here to help' approach," Henson said. "We don't want to create any bad blood with any private landowners because it makes our job a lot harder or even impossible," he explained, referring to the fact that most endangered species are found on private land. "But we're renting Salley's son-in-law's house on the ranch as refuge headquarters and the Service is pumping money into the area, and she's denying us access across the same land. You can't take advantage of the federal government. And there was a lot of that going on."

"It was phenomenal," Ledig recalled. "I spent twelve years on the California condor, whose politics were amazing, but I had never seen anything at the level of the 'alalā. It was extremely frustrating to deal with someone who tried to control what activities occurred on a national wildlife refuge, based on her personal attitudes, by controlling access to that refuge. There were some very well qualified restoration ecologists she refused to allow to cross her land because she was afraid they might spot something. This really hindered the elimination of wild pigs and other exotics on the refuge. It really set the program backward. McCandless Ranch activities and attitudes were not beneficial for the 'alalā."

Through the fog of personal invectives, realities about the new refuge were setting in. Soon the sound of whirling helicopter blades throbbed above Kai Malino. Because there was still no fence, wild cattle and pigs continued uprooting understory plants. Without road access to bring in fencing materials, the Packard Foundation finally withdrew its grant. All this was costing the last wild pair of ravens precious time that they did not have to lose.

As Henson summed it up, "At Kai Malino the Service got shafted. The poor 'alalā was in the middle."

chapter 28

QUAGMIRE

AUGUST 3, 2000, seven in the morning. I am eating breakfast with Keith Unger and Cynthia Salley at McCandless Ranch. The ʻalalā have not been seen for five weeks, Salley says. The manager of Keālia Ranch recently heard at least two of them, Unger adds. Soon we are joined by Glenn Klingler, the U.S. Fish and Wildlife Service biologist, and refuge manager Dave Ledig. Klingler, with a week-old beard covering his slender face, thinning light brown hair combed back, and a small silver earring in his left ear, wears a warm, broad smile. Ledig has dark hair and deep-set eyes that give a serious look to his otherwise lighthearted manner. He is direct, letting his words fall where they may. After breakfast, Unger, Klingler, Ledig, and I drive up the mountain to the first aviary, where I first met Peter Harrity several years before. There is no sign of the ʻalalā. We drive higher up the road and across the mountain toward the new refuge. Still no ʻalalā. Keith pulls over into a pastured roadside clearing adjacent to a pasture. We get out and stand around. Keith points to some ʻōhiʻa and a few towering gray koa at the forest's edge. "That's where the Kalāhiki pair had their nest," he begins, as a muffled bang rings out in the distance.

"Well, there's a gunshot," Klingler says, as if it wasn't the first time he has heard one.

"And on the refuge," Ledig adds.

"Gunshot?" I ask. "By who? For what?"

"Or for whom?" Unger adds lightly.

"Hard to say," Ledig replies.

"It may be the Kai Malino people shooting cattle or pigs."

"On the refuge? Do they have permission?" I ask.

"Not exactly," Ledig says, a little strain showing in his voice at this unplanned interlude of apparent lawlessness on his refuge. "It can be a problem. If we catch them with firearms in their truck, they deny they were hunting." The fact of the matter is that while the Service owns the refuge, the sellers still insist on controlling it —at least insofar as they still control access to it. In any case, they believe they have a right to use the land.

"I got shot over my head not long ago," Klingler says as we lean against the hood of the big blue Suburban. "I was wigged! It was in the middle of the night. I was on McCandless property, at the edge of the refuge in the field camp about a hundred yards from the aviary. I could hear a truck and the door being slammed and could hear voices, but I couldn't see anything. It's pitch-black up there on the mountain. Then the shot rang out, like a high-powered rifle! I think it was folks from Kai Malino. I'm guessing they were out poaching and said, 'Let's scare these guys.' It worked. Did I get out of there or what?"

The beeper on Unger's belt keeps going off. He picks it up, but again there's no number. "I'm going to drop this damn thing in a cow pie," he says, climbing back in the driver's seat.

We follow the road up until it reaches the Waiea tract; then we drive toward the refuge. As we approach a fence and cleared line in the forest, Ledig shouts from the backseat as if fearing for his life. "Stop! We can't go any farther. That's the Kai Malino ranch line!" Here is a voice of genuine fear. He and Klingler aren't the only Service employees who sometimes fear for their physical safety. They genuinely worry that if someone were to put a rifle in the hands of a mentally unstable ranch employee—of which there are rumored to be a few—and then goad him with enough anger, somebody could get "accidentally" shot. Some locals who are firm believers in what the Service is trying to do for the 'alalā have also warned Service personnel that the forests of the hula goddess could be a dangerous place. For some people, the mallard duck flapping across the shoulder patches of a Service employee might be a tempting target.

Keith pulls to a stop and we get out again, the memory of the gunshot still fresh.

We stand for a few moments. Still no 'alalā. Incoming fog cloaks the druid trees. Ragged, scudding drifts move through, turning a vivacious green into a world of gray.

"Could the gunshots be a warning?" I ask.

"You just never know," Unger says, resigned to the implausibility of our situation. "With everything still getting worked out, people are tense and bitter."

He scratches his neck and pauses to take a breath. Ledig peers over Unger's shoulder while Klingler stands on the edge of the road and gazes into the cloud-banked forest, scanning for either 'alalā, which are nowhere to be seen, or rifle toters.

"The plan was to fence in all five thousand acres of the refuge and exterminate the pigs and cattle," Ledig says, shaking his head. "The people taking the heat for this snafu are in the realty division in Portland, Oregon. Their attorneys wrote up the deal, and the solicitor general was supposed to have studied it in detail. But this one got past them," he says, referring to the complications in the refuge purchase—the result, he thought, of the purchase agreement's failure to adequately cover all the eventualities that can come up when working with angry and disenchanted sellers.

"So how's this going to play out?" I ask.

No one answers.

We fall into silence. We see no ʻalalā—no surprise, given that only three wild birds now remain: the surviving Hoʻokena bird and the Keālia pair.

Klingler speaks for the first time in a while. "It's been hard to watch what's happening. I moved from Washington State several years ago to be with the ʻalalā. Things were going so well, and suddenly it reversed course. It's been hard emotionally. I remember most of all the Hoʻokena bird, how after it lost its mate it cried out for weeks. I'd wake up every morning and hear the mourning—a terribly high-pitched sound, like an inconsolable moaning, from the top of an ʻōhiʻa. First it would be here, and then a moment of silence, and then it would be there. The sound just went straight through my heart."

He says that the Hoʻokena bird is now so lonely that it searches the forest over and over again, sometimes wailing without end. "It's so lonely now that the bird has taken to disturbing the Keālia pair. The Hoʻokena bird is so obviously looking for company, but none is to be found—nowhere. And now it has to watch the Keālia birds, the last pair. You just don't know what goes on in the lonely bird's mind, but it must be something akin to fear or loneliness. I'm anthropomorphizing, and scientists aren't supposed to do that. But how else can I describe it? I can't remove myself from the emotional content of what is happening, what I've witnessed, and how I've come to know these birds. I'm sorry, but I can't."

On the way back down the mountain, we speak of everything but Michelangelo. I ask how many stone walls remain from the ancient Hawaiians' croplands. "We've come across a few," Unger says with some bitterness. "You know, some Hawaiians still think they own this land. There's a law that says Hawaiians can visit and

LAST LIGHT

gather on their ancestral lands, and there's no land in Hawai'i that isn't ancestral. What does 'gathering rights' mean? Does it mean to just visit and leave, or drive up in a jeep and set up a trailer? Does it mean them hauling their fat Hawaiian asses up the mountain to tend their marijuana patches?"

At the last gate at road's end, a scrawled sign reads, "If you are caught on this land you will be shot." We pass through it. I do not wonder for whom those words are meant.

c h a p t e r 29

LAST LIGHT

SUMMER, 2000. I LEAVE THE
smoking, sulfuric rim of Kīlauea at daybreak in a silken drizzle. As
daylight burns off the mist, Mauna Loa's winter white summit
appears. Behind the alpine summit's horizon lies its slumbering
caldera, Mokuʻāweoweo.

Hawaiʻi, the land of happiness and sunshine, stirs sadness.
Another ʻalalā—the Hoʻokena bird—has disappeared. With but
two individuals now remaining in the wild, I know that the raven's
ten-thousand-year story on the land could end this very day. I have
made many trips up the mountain, but the ʻalalā's hour is late, and
most likely I will not see them alive again.

As I drive along the highway down the southwestern rift, I gaze
up into the hills of ʻĀinapō—Land of Darkness. The drizzle continues. I turn off the main highway and down the narrow blacktop
road to the Leaping Place at Ka Lae. Mauna Loa's summit has vanished in the mist.

So much love for the ʻalalā. What has driven these years of effort
on its behalf? So many people have struggled in so many imperfect
ways for the sake of a raven. Millions of dollars spent, lives and

careers devoted and sometimes broken, all for a bird. What drives this love? And how, having been pursued so hard for so long, has the object of affection slipped away? Was it not loved in time? Was it loved to death?

Hours pass.

I flip through my journal and find the section in which, years earlier, I wrote of the Hawaiian belief in the Leaping Place here: "In the Hawaiian kingdom of Ka'ū, on a black volcanic seacliff at the foot of Mauna Loa, there is said to grow an old kukui tree from whose green boughs the souls of the departed leap into the afterlife." It is now the 'alalā that seems to be the departing soul. Who, I wonder, will accompany it?

Inexplicably I am drawn back to the mountain, and I drive again toward the very place I left only a few hours earlier. It is nearly dark when I reach the Māmalahoa Highway. I pull over, stand beside the road, and gaze up the mountainside into the distant curtain of darkening 'ōhi'a. The night air is cool, and soon the moon appears above the mountain. Although light illuminates only a sliver, the entire orb is faintly apparent—dark, round, and blue as a cannonball. Do ravens dream by moonlight? I imagine the last two 'alalā nestled together, feathers ruffled against the chill, bodies pressed side to side on the 'ōhi'a bough, heads buried in feathery warmth, the sound of beating hearts. In that way, night after night—for a day or a year, until those hearts stop—they will pass their last dark Mauna Loa nights. A wisp of fog trails a crepe paper streamer across the moon's edge, which momentarily reappears in silvery brightness before being swallowed again by mist, along with the mountain's profile. I stand there seemingly without end, hoping that the moon will reappear. It doesn't. I take this not as an omen but merely as a metaphor for what the dark side of my heart already knows.

EPILOGUE

On June 14, 2002, federal wildlife biologist Jeff Burgett drove up to Keālia Ranch as usual. It was one of those warm Mauna Loa mornings when the forests release their ferny perfume and ʻapapane and ʻiʻiwi sing between sunlight and shadow.

"The Keālia pair were right in the same place they always hung out," Burgett reported afterward of the only remaining wild ʻalalā. "They had finished their breeding attempt for the year, which hadn't been successful in a long time and still wasn't. They were molting and looked pretty shaggy. The female slept a lot and appeared very tired. The male was feeding her a couple of fruits. He tried to prod her, but she seemed unresponsive."

It was the last time an ʻalalā would be seen in the wild.

"I don't know how long after that one of them died," he later said. "If I were to guess, the female died first, because she looked so tired and was probably the older bird." After one died, the other bird probably saw no reason to show up at the nest site. "We came to expect that the ʻalalā would disappear for a while but would come back. They never did."

For many, sorrow rushed in to fill the absence. "The ʻalalā, as I knew them, will never be back," Cynthia Salley lamented. "The captive birds' teachers are gone, and along with them, their lore and wisdom. The death of the ʻalalā has left a hole in our hearts and in the heart of our forest."

"To me, the forest will always be quieter and lonely without the ʻalalā," Donna Ball grieved. "There is a feeling I carry daily about how we all failed. Symbolically, its plight represents what is happening everywhere on planet Earth."

Sadly, the raven is one among innumerable species fading from the planet, in an epoch in which other species, unable to contend with massive human disruption of their homes, are in a mass exodus from Earth. During the decades in which people struggled to save the ʻalalā, thousands of other species have perished. In many cases, their passing has brought the extinction of human experience.

For biologists who knew the raven, the emotional turmoil surrounding the last wild birds' disappearance gave way to practical considerations of what to do next. Although the ʻalalā was extinct in the wild, some forty birds remained in captivity, in aviaries on Maui and Hawaiʻi Island. And they were breeding. By 2006, there were fifty—more ʻalalā than there had been in many years, the optimist would point out. The pessimist would reply that the birds were gone from the wild, probably never to reappear in their former numbers—with all the dark complexities attendant to their predicament.

When the poet W. S. Merwin wrote, "When we hold a bird what is in our hands / is not the bird any more and . . . when we look at birds / we see only a little of them," he breathed poetry into science. A bird raised in captivity may never have the knowledge or develop the skills required to survive in the wild. What may look the same to a human observer is a profoundly changed bird.

"Unfortunately, we no longer have wild ʻalalā to learn from," said Ball, mourning the loss of the experiential knowledge that wild adult 'alalā once taught their young. This traditional knowledge, passed down through generations of 'alalā, may have included skills ranging from foraging and identifying suitable foods to executing coordinated scouting strategies against potential predators such as hawks. Without these skills, will captive-bred ravens ever survive in the wild?

And then, biologists caution, there are the long-term implications of preserving a species in captivity. Successive generations of 'alalā will be selected for the genetic traits best suited for surviving and reproducing in captivity, not in the wild. Generation by generation, gene by gene, the original wild species may be left behind.

Like the 'alalā, most species have been driven toward extinction by habitat loss. That is, the ecological fabric on which they depend is torn from beneath them. It has long been appreciated that because many different plants and animals share the same habitat, species often disappear not singly but in great assemblages; not as a book stolen but as a library burned.

Why, then, was so much effort directed at saving the 'alalā and so little at preserving its habitat, along with the raven's myriad cast of ecological kindred characters? Partly because saving habitat takes time—time the 'alalā did not have. Efforts came too late, and preventive medicine is infeasible once the patient is critically ill.

But the story of the 'alalā is singular in that the pivotal time for its salvation was identified more than three decades ago, in 1972, when Win Banko warned that it would immediately require "a comprehensive program built around the sanctuary concept, captive breeding projects, and beefed-up conservation and research manpower. . . . Midnight for the Hawaiian crow, at least, is not far off. History is not kind to those who misjudge priorities."

That subsequent history is one of belated efforts ending in failures. And what should rightfully have been a quiet space for recovery of the 'alalā became instead a stage for human sound and fury.

Yet the intentions and daily motivations of most of those involved were marked by exhaustive toil, personal sacrifice, and even nobility. Perhaps the most encouraging of belated success is that although the ʻalalā is extinct in the wild, in 2005 the bird got its first protected land when the U.S. Fish and Wildlife Service finally gained clear access through Kai Malino to the new five-thousand-acre preserve.

"While the refuge may be twenty to thirty years away from what it needs to be in terms of high-quality ʻalalā habitat," Ball said, "this is where we have to start. We don't have time to grieve for every species. Time is precious. While I will always mourn losing the wild birds, they have taught me important lessons about what needs to be done for what still remains of Hawaii's native ecosystems."

Once the new refuge is fenced in and the grazing cattle and marauding pigs are removed, a semblance of a protective understory will return. But the refuge will always be porous, and keeping out feral cats, rats, and mongooses while minimizing the omnipresent disease-carrying mosquitoes will require constant vigilance and trapping — the endless bailing of a leaky boat. Birds released anytime soon will require the ecological equivalent of life support.

Despite the daunting challenges, according to The Peregrine Fund's Alan Lieberman, "the plan is to keep breeding the ʻalalā in captivity. When the population reaches approximately seventy-five, in three to five years, birds will be selected for release."

And a new chapter — uplifted by rising hope or cruelly brief — in the epic to save the species will begin. While the ʻalalā have lost the experience of their forebears, one can hope that biologists and others will not forget the lessons of theirs: that the road toward extinction is paved with the best intentions.

To Salley, the issue of reintroduction is moot. "It matters not to me how they go about trying to reintroduce the captive ʻalalā into the wild, as long as it is not on our property. We're exhausted, and the captive birds are strangers in disguise. The 'alalā, as I knew them, will never be back."

As for me, I now realize that my quest to know the raven, begun on the volcano's slopes many springs ago, will never end. I still can hear the 'alalā singing in their wilderness wasteland, their keening and howls emanating and fading through morning light. I see Hilu, Noe, and Paniolo in afternoon's glow, moving among the 'ōhi'a blooming bright and scarlet across the volcano. I hear koa leaves rustle in the high mountain breeze. I hear the ancient echo of the ax as Kahuna 'Alalā moves with spirit ancestors through the highland groves in search of the perfect canoe. But now, for me and for those who devoted their lives and hearts to the 'alalā, all is just memory and imagination.

Someday, if my heart can bear it, I will return to listen to the cloud-forest stillness of the vanquished 'alalā. Someday, perhaps after my soul has traveled to the Leaping Place at Ka Lae, may my children return to the highland forests I have traveled and hear the ravens' incantations anew.

ACKNOWLEDGMENTS

Although most of the words in this book may belong to me, much of the knowledge belongs to others. To those who have shared insights about Hawai'i over the years, thank you: William Akau, Bud Pomaik'i Cook, Ma'ulili Dickson, Eric Enos, Karen Eoff, Samuel M. 'Ohukani'ōhi'a Gon III, Aunty Pele Hanoa and Keolalani Hanoa, Takiora Ingram, Mel Kalāhiki Sr., Māhealani Kamau'u, Kekuhi Kanahale, Pualani Kanaka'ole Kanahele, Daniel Kawaiaea, John Keolamaka'āinana Lake, Tom Layton, Clarence Medeiros Jr., Jimmy Medeiros Sr., Nellie Medeiros, Maile Meyer, Manu Aluli Meyer, Pi'ikea Miller, Luana Neff, Susan O'Conner, Angel Pilago, Chipper Wichman, and Carol Wilcox.

Many others informed this book in extended interviews (in some cases, over the course of years) or in brief but helpful exchanges: David Agro, Donna L. Ball, Paul C. Banko, Winston E. Banko, Michael G. Buck, Jeff Burgett, Bill Burnham, Tom Cade, Reginald E. David, Scott Derrickson, Fern Duvall, John W. Fitzpatrick, Joanna Gaspar, Jon Giffin, Peter Harrity, Paul Henson, David Jenkins, John Klavitter, Glenn Klingler, Ernest Kosaka, Cyndi Kuehler, Dave Ledig, Ah Fat Lee, Barbara Lee, Alan Lieberman, John Marzluff, Greg Massey, Joan Mattox, Bruce Rideout, Bill Rosehill, Cynthia Salley, Georgia Shirilla, Robert P. Smith, Elizabeth Stack, Stanley Temple, Elsie Thompson, Patricia Tummons, and Keith Unger.

To friends and colleagues at the University of South Florida and within the Department of Journalism and Media Studies, thank you for your company, confidence, and support. A special thanks to Christopher D'Elia, V. Mark Durand, Deni Elliott, Gary Mormino, and Karen A. White for their encouragement.

David Abram, Edwin Burnbaum, Peter Forbes, Marion Gilliam, Jeff Golliher, Laurie Lane-Zucker, Margot McLean, Diana Rose, Jonathan Rose, Andrew Rowan, Mary Evelyn Tucker, and Ken Wilson have offered many valuable insights on culture, values, and our vanishing animal kin. My deep gratitude to James Hillman for many enchanting conversations and discussions. You taught me much about animals: to receive them in a way that I, the scientist, might never have; to see them, in my writing and my dreams, such that "they may come and tell us about themselves."

My appreciation to the Nathan Cummings Foundation's board of trustees, especially Adam Cummings, for the time during which the foundation worked valiantly to preserve the culture and vanishing natural landscapes of Hawai'i. The foundation's former executive director, Charles Halpern, and my colleague there, Henry Ng, encouraged my writing of this book during the years that I directed the foundation's Hawai'i program.

To those at Island Press, thank you. Executive editor Jonathan Cobb, who understands both the writing product and the process, waved a magic wand over the manuscript every time I got stuck. Island Press' founder and president Chuck Savitt has, by giving life to many books, opened up seas of knowledge that might otherwise have remained undiscovered. Pat Harris' editing greatly improved this work; and thanks to Emily Davis for her ready spirit and helpfulness. Jessica Heise, Senior Production Editor, ushered the manuscript through its final stages with great care, patience, and a miraculous eye for detail.

My thanks to Steven Zwerling and Gerry and Dan Perkins for their help and encouragement.

Thanks also to Alison Steele, Chris Whittier, and Felicia Nutter.

My mother has been, in presence or through prayer, a guardian spirit. My father's memory reminds me that I have been granted one of life's greatest gifts: the opportunity to work hard at what I love. Maryann and Terry Whalen have always been deep wells of encouragement and wisdom.

Noelle, William, and Anna—thank you for being there, even when I was far away.

NOTES

PROLOGUE

page

2   *closer to the raven family than to the crow:* P. C. Banko, D. L. Ball, and
W. E. Banko, "Hawaiian Crow (*Corvus hawaiiensis*)," in *The Birds of
North America*, no. 648, ed. A. Poole and F. Gill (Philadelphia, PA:
The Birds of North America, Inc., 2002). As the authors state on
page 3, "Although preliminary phylogenetic analysis places the
'Alalā closer to the Common Raven than to more typical crows, the
issue is far from resolved, and additional research is needed." See
also R. C. Fleischer and C. E. McIntosh, "Molecular Systematics
and Biogeography of the Hawaiian Avifauna," *Studies in Avian
Biology* 22 (2000): 51–60.

2   *together they leap into the afterlife:* L. C. Green and M. W. Beckwith,
"Hawaiian Customs and Beliefs Relating to Sickness and Death,"
American Anthropologist 28 (1926): 177–208; M. Beckwith, *Hawaiian
Mythology* (Honolulu: University of Hawai'i Press, 1976), 571.

2   *with only grasshoppers to eat:* M. K. Pukui, E. W. Haertig, and C. A.
Lee, *Nānū i ke kumu* (Look to the Source) (Honolulu: Hui Hanai,
1972).

5   *"through the band of cloud forests up to about 6,500 feet":* Banko, Ball, and
Banko, "Hawaiian Crow."

5   *"'alalā may have once nested in these lowlands":* Ibid.

5   *Some sixty animal species became extinct following Polynesian coloniza-
tion.:* S. L. Olson and H. F. James, "Fossil Birds from the Hawaiian
Islands: Evidence for Wholesale Extinction by Man before Western
Contact," *Science* 217 (1982): 633–635; S. L. Olson and H. F. James,
"Descriptions of Thirty-two New Species of Birds from the Hawai-
ian Islands," *Ornithological Monographs* 45, 46 (1991).

6   *Since Europeans arrived, late in the eighteenth century, thousands of species
have been introduced:* J. L. Culliney, *Islands in a Far Sea: Nature and Man
in Hawaii* (San Francisco: Sierra Club Books, 1988).

6   *Now several dozen, on average, take root annually:* S. M. Gon III, personal communication.

6 *branch tips hung with whorls of slender, sword-shaped golden yellow blossoms:* J. F. Rock, *The Indigenous Trees of the Hawaiian Islands* (Rutland, VT: Charles E. Tuttle, 1974).

6 *colorful seeds of the orange or brick red claw-shaped flowers:* Ibid.

6 *"windward side can get up to four hundred":* M. Sanderson, *Prevailing Trade Winds: Weather and Climate in Hawai'i* (Honolulu: University of Hawai'i Press, 1993).

CHAPTER 1. *Mountain of Emerald Light*

13 *"The Wood [was] impassable every where out of the common Paths":* D. G. Medway, "The Contribution of Cook's Third Voyage to the Ornithology of the Hawaiian Islands," *Pacific Science* 35, no. 2 (1981): 105–175.

13 *"The largest trees are nearly thirty feet in the girth":* J. Ledyard, *A Journal of Captain Cook's Last Voyage* (Chicago: Quadrangle Books, 1963).

15 *yelling, yakking, whooping, barking, and howling:* The approximately thirty-five different documented calls of the 'alalā have been transcribed in many different ways. Perhaps the best overview of the major calls is found in P. C. Banko, D. L. Ball, and W. E. Banko, 2002. "Hawaiian Crow (*Corvus hawaiiensis*)," in *The Birds of North America*; no. 648, ed. A. Poole and F. Gill (Philadelphia, PA: The Birds of North america, Inc., 2002).

16 *two female 'alalā welcomed him back:* U.S. Fish and Wildlife Service, "Weekly Schedule and Update," Jan. 29–Feb. 2, 1996.

17 *"Hōkū is short for Hōkū lele, which means shooting star":* A. Lieberman, personal communication.

17 *named for a rare and fragrant Hawaiian gardenia:* D. Ball, personal communication.

CHAPTER 2. *In the Beginning*

21 *In the beginning were coral polyps and starfish, sea urchins and limpets. . . . On land, Hula winds stirred the 'ie'ie vine:* Beckwith, M. W., *The Kumulipo: A Hawaiian Creation Chant* (Honolulu: University of Hawai'i Press, 1972).

21 *"Born was the 'alalā":* In her translation of the Kumulipo, Beckwith uses the term "Crow." In the translation by Lili'uokalani of Hawaii,

"An Account of the Creation of the World," (Pueo Press 1978), however, it is called the alala.

22 *the Kumulipo, or "Beginning in Deep Darkness":* M. Beckwith, *Hawaiian Mythology* (Honolulu: University of Hawai'i Press, 1976), 571; Beckwith, *Kumulipo.*

22 *a chaotic whirlwind of god-inspired life:* Keaulumoku, *The Kumulipo* (Kentfield, CA: Pueo Press, 1978).

22 *when the wiliwili bloomed along the coast, sharks would bite:* S. M. Gon III, personal communication, 2000.

23 *"the nation and its people ought to live as compatibly as they can with the fauna and flora":* H. Rolston III, "Life in Jeopardy on Private Property," in *Balancing on the Brink of Extinction: The Endangered Species Act and Lessons for the Future,* ed. K. A. Kohm (Washington, D.C.: Island Press, 1991).

23 *In the traditional Hawaiian world, four major gods reigned:* M. K. Pukui, E. W. Haertig, and C. A. Lee, *Nānā i ke kumu* (Look to the Source) (Honolulu: Hui Hanai, 1972); S. M. Gon III, personal communication, 2000.

23-24 *ancestral spirits known as 'aumākua . . . were also guides to the afterlife:* Pukui, Haertig, and Lee, *Nānā i ke kumu.*

24 *to eat one's 'aumakua could bring death:* Ibid.

24 *kapu, or forbidden, to hit anyone in the face or head:* Ibid.

24 *myriad prayers for fishing, planting, harvesting taro, cutting certain trees:* Ibid.; W. D. Westervelt, "Aumakuas, or Ancestor-Ghosts," in *Hawaiian Legends of Ghosts and Ghost-Gods* (Boston: Ellis Press, 1916).

25 *feelings for land as family are part of an ancient Hawaiian core of beliefs:* M. K. Pukui and S. H. Elbert, *Hawaiian Dictionary: Hawaiian-English, English-Hawaiian,* rev. and enl. ed. (Honolulu: University of Hawai'i Press, 1986).

25 *the families, no matter what part of the ahupua'a they happened to live on, had fish, crops, and forest resources:* S. P. Juvik and J. O. Juvik, eds., *Atlas of Hawai'i,* 3rd ed. (Honolulu: University of Hawai'i Press, 1998).

25 *Hawaiians integrated bananas, sugarcane, and other basic crops into the kalo paddies. . . . Every stage of kalo planting, harvesting, and production*

was ushered in with chants or prayers: E. Enos and K. Johnson, *A Handbook of Kalo Basics: For Its Planting, Care, Preparation, and Eating* (Wai'anae, HI: Taro Top Publication, 1996); J. Gutmanis, *Na Pule Kahiko: Ancient Hawaiian Prayers* (Honolulu: Editions Limited, 1983).

25   *Fishing for some species was banned during spawning:* L. E. Sponsel, "Is Indigenous Spiritual Ecology Just a New Fad? Reflections from the Historical and Spiritual Ecology of Hawai'i," in *Indigenous Traditions and Ecology: The Interbeing of Cosmology and Community*, ed. J. Grim (Cambridge, MA: Distributed by Harvard Press for the Center for the Study of World Religions, Harvard Divinity School, 2001).

26   *sacred drink derived from the root of the 'awa plant:* S. M. Gon III, *Visits to the Wao Akua* (Honolulu: Moanalua Gardens Foundation, 1998).

CHAPTER 3. *Captain Cook*

27   *the legendary Northwest Passage:* J. C. Beaglehole, *The Life of Captain James Cook* (Stanford, CA: Stanford University Press, 1974).

27   *"that we may cause proper examination and experiments to be made of them":* R. Hanbury-Tenison, *The Oxford Book of Exploration* (Oxford and New York: Oxford University Press, 1993).

27   *Ka'awaloa stood at the northern end of the beach:* G. Daws, *Shoal of Time: A History of the Hawaiian Islands* (Honolulu: University of Hawai'i Press, 1974). (Cook referred to this village as "kowrowa")

28   *Still farther inland they found numerous kukui trees . . . and bamboo:* B. H. Krauss, *Plants in Hawaiian Culture* (Honolulu: University of Hawai'i Press, 1993).

28   *Fields . . . may well have covered more than sixty square miles:* P. V. Kirch, *Legacy of the Landscape: An Illustrated Guide to Hawaiian Archaeological Sites* (Honolulu: University of Hawai'i Press, 1996); A. Menzies, *Hawaii Nei 128 Years Ago* (Honolulu: W. F. Wilson, 1920).

28   *Cook was escorted to a temple:* M. W. Beckwith, trans. and ed., *The Kumulipo: A Hawaiian Creation Chant* (Honolulu: University of Hawai'i Press, 1972).

28   *a railing whose posts were crowned with twenty human skulls:* J. F. G. Stokes, *Heiau of the Island of Hawai'i: A Historic Survey of Native Hawaiian Temple Sites* (Honolulu: Bishop Museum Press, 1991); J. C. Beaglehole, ed., *The Journals of Captain James Cook*, vol. 3, *The Voyage of*

the Resolution *and* Discovery, *1776–1780* (Cambridge: Cambridge University Press, 1967).

28 *a sacred stone-lined pool:* Stokes, *Heiau of the Island of Hawai'i.*

28 *the Kumulipo, the lengthy chant of more than six hundred lines:* Daws, *Shoal of Time*; Beaglehole, *Voyage of the* Resolution *and* Discovery; Beckwith, *Kumulipo.*

29 *King tried to buy them. . . . The Hawaiians . . . "refus[ed] everything I offered":* J. Cook, *A Voyage to the Pacific Ocean: Undertaken, by the Command of His Majesty, for Making Discoveries in the Northern Hemisphere: Performed under the Direction of Captains Cook, Clerke, and Gore, in the Years 1776, 1777, 1778, 1779, and 1780,* vol. 1 (London: Scatcherd & Whitaker and C. Stalker, 1788).

29 *"they calld one an Eatooa" . . . probably King's rendering of the Hawaiian* he akua, *"a god," which would include an 'aumakua:* Beaglehole, *Voyage of the* Resolution *and* Discovery; S. M. Gon III, personal communication; M. Beckwith, *Hawaiian Mythology* (Honolulu: University of Hawai'i Press, 1976), 571.

29 *"probably, the raven is the object of it":* Cook, *Voyage to the Pacific Ocean.*

30 *the lower elevations thrived:* D. G. Medway, "The Contribution of Cook's Third Voyage to the Ornithology of the Hawaiian Islands," *Pacific Science* 35, no. 2 (1981): 105–175.

30 *"shot a number of fine birds of the liveliest and most variegated plumage":* Ibid.

30 *gluey substance made from juice of the "Kepaw" (pāpala kēpau) tree and breadfruit:* Ibid.

30 *as many as two hundred birds were required for a single small feather lei:* A. J. Berger, *Hawaiian Birdlife* (Honolulu: University of Hawai'i Press, 1981).

30 *"They were delicious!":* S. M. Gon III, personal communication.

30 *"but the birds belong to my heirs":* Berger, *Hawaiian Birdlife.*

30 *Cook and his crew had a paradisaical sojourn at Kealakekua Bay:* G. Obeyesekere, *The Apotheosis of Captain Cook: European Mythmaking in the Pacific* (Princeton, NJ: Princeton University Press, 1994).

31 Resolution *sprung her foremast and had to return to Kealakekua for repairs:* Daws, *Shoal of Time.*

31 *A sailor then struck him on the head with an oar:* Ibid.

31 *As Cook headed to the water, he was struck from behind:* Ibid.

32 *on board were more than 120 crates of bird skins and other specimens:* Medway, "Contribution of Cook's Third Voyage."

CHAPTER 4. *For Love of the Gods*

34 *the missionaries rejoiced in song:* S. M. Kamakau, *Ruling Chiefs of Hawaii* (Honolulu: Kamehameha Schools Press, 1992).

34 *"Wake, Isles of the South! your redemption is near":* W. B. Tappan, "Wake, Isles of the South!" (hymn set to music by William Clarke Hauser, 1822).

35 *"were ready to exclaim, 'Can these be human beings!'":* G. Daws, *Shoal of Time: A History of the Hawaiian Islands* (New York: Macmillan, 1968); L. Thurston, *Life and Times of Mrs. Lucy G. Thurston, Wife of Rev. Asa Thurston, Pioneer Missionary to the Sandwich Islands* (Ann Arbor, MI: S. C. Andrews, 1934).

35 *Thomas Hopu, among Hawai'i's first Christian converts:* Daws, *Shoal of Time.*

35 *Hopu went ashore and proclaimed, "These white people are kahunas":* Thurston, *Life and Times of Mrs. Lucy G. Thurston*; Kamakau, *Ruling Chiefs of Hawaii.*

36 *ordered Hawaiians to abandon their old beliefs and destroy their temples:* Daws, *Shoal of Time.*

36 *"little gods who made not heaven and earth":* M. Beckwith, *Hawaiian Mythology* (Honolulu: University of Hawai'i Press, 1976), 571.

36 *missionaries turned him into the devil:* M. K. Pukui, E. W. Haertig, and C. A. Lee, *Nānā i ke kumu* (Look to the Source) (Honolulu: Hui Hanai, 1972).

36 *hunger, to the Hawaiians, was synonymous with hell:* Ibid.

36 *source of spirituality slowly shifted:* D. Abram, *The Spell of the Sensuous* (New York: Vintage Books, 1997).

36 *"hard-headed incredulity of the literal-minded English and Americans":* Beckwith, *Hawaiian Mythology,* 571.

37 *And how could one buy or sell one's own ancestors:* S. P. Juvik and J. O. Juvik, eds., *Atlas of Hawai'i,* 3rd ed. (Honolulu: University of Hawai'i Press, 1998).

37 *By 1893, non-Hawaiians owned or controlled 90 percent of the lands:* Ibid.

37 *companies ultimately came to control nearly every business associated with sugar:* Daws, *Shoal of Time.*

38 *"good for nothing but rubbish blown upon the wind":* Kamakau, *Ruling Chiefs of Hawaii.*

38 *"It can scarcely be said that there is any Native population at all":* Daws, *Shoal of Time.*

38 *where the priests were said to have recited the Kumulipo to Captain James Cook:* M. W. Beckwith, *The Kumulipo: A Hawaiian Creation Chant* (Honolulu: University of Hawaiʻi Press, 1972).

38 *only remnants of the temple's eastern and southern retaining walls remain:* J. F. G. Stokes, *Heiau of the Island of Hawaiʻi: A Historic Survey of Native Hawaiian Temple Sites* (Honolulu: Bishop Museum Press, 1991).

38 *Hawaiian version of "Holy! Holy! Holy!":* Na Himeni Haipule Hawaii (Honolulu: Hawaii Conference United Church of Christ, 1972).

CHAPTER 5. *Paniolo, Hōkū, and Mahoa*

41 *"we suspect an ʻio":* D. Ball, personal communication.

41 *"A biologist found the carcass of Hōkū":* D. Ball, personal communication.

42 *"Mahoa is gone":* D. Ball, personal communication.

CHAPTER 6. *Searching for the ʻAlalā*

45 *"LENGTH twelve inches and a half":* J. Latham, *A General Synopsis of Birds* (London: Printed for B. White, 1781).

45 *"Man is placed at the head of the animal creation":* C. von Linné and J. F. Gmelin, *A Genuine and Universal System of Natural History: Comprising the Three Kingdoms of Animals, Vegetables, and Minerals Arranged under Their Respective Classes, Orders, Genera, and Species; by the Late Sir Charles Linnaeus; Improved, Corrected, and Enlarged by J. Frid. Gmelin; Faithfully Translated and Rendered More Complete by the Addition of Vaillant's Beautiful Birds of Africa [et al.]; Methodically Incorporated and Arranged by the Editors of the* Encyclopaedia Londinensis (London: Printed for the proprietor by Lewis and Co., 1788).

46 *The toe tag of the crowlike specimen:* D. G. Medway, "The Contribution of Cook's Third Voyage to the Ornithology of the Hawaiian Islands," *Pacific Science* 35, no. 2 (1981): 105–175.

47 *the "somewhat of a naturalist" Andrew Bloxam:* S. B. Wilson and A. H. Evans, *Aves Hawaiienses: The Birds of the Sandwich Islands* (New York: Arno Press, 1974).

47 *"a disgrace to all concerned":* Ibid.

47 *J. K. Townsend, a private collector from Philadelphia:* R. Meyer de Schauensee, "Type Catalogue Manuscript" (Philadelphia, PA: Academy of Natural Sciences of Philadelphia, n.d.).

47 *Academy of Natural Sciences of Philadelphia was already one of the premier American institutions:* W. Stone, "Some Philadelphia Ornithological Collections and Collectors, 1748–1850," *Auk* 16 (1899): 166–177.

48 *the Peacock and thousands of its scientific specimens—including the ʻalalā —did not:* J. J. Poesch, *Titian Ramsay Peale, 1799–1885, and His Journals of the Wilkes Expedition* (Philadelphia, PA: American Philosophical Society, 1961).

48 *Peale received Townsend's ʻalalā specimens:* Wilson and Evans, *Aves Hawaiienses.*

48 *"Not even the Library of Congress has a copy":* Academy of Natural Sciences of Philadelphia, Card Catalog: Peale, Titian Ramsey Mammalia and ornithology. Card 2 states: "The Library of Congress has no copy of it."

50 *Cassin's version remains the voyage's official account:* Poesch, *Titian Ramsay Peale.*

50 *Peale's standing went the way of his fading profession:* W. M. Smallwood and M. S. C. Smallwood, *Natural History and the American Mind,* vol. 8, *Columbia Studies in American Culture* (New York: Columbia University Press, 1941).

50 *battles between the specialist and the generalist:* M. Rothschild, *Dear Lord Rothschild: Birds, Butterflies, and History* (Philadelphia, PA: Balaban; London: Hutchinson; Philadelphia, PA: distributed by ISI, 1983).

51 *all but broke Peale's spirit and ambition:* Poesch, *Titian Ramsay Peale.*

CHAPTER 7. *The Raven–Warrior*

54 *"Ke nae iki nei nō"—"Some breath remains":* M. K. Pukui, *ʻOlelo Noʻeau: Hawaiian Proverbs and Poetical Sayings* (Honolulu: Bishop Museum Press, 1983).

54 *'alalā is a very powerful bird, powerful enough to bring death:* "Cultural Significance of the Alala in Conservation and Recovery" (minutes of meeting at Keauhou Bird Conservation Center, February 21, 2003).

55 *a descendant of the heiau's original royal court:* B. Cook, personal communication.

57 *"supported the class system in Hawaiian society":* J. F. McDermott Jr., W.-S. Tseng, and T. Maretzki, *People and Cultures of Hawaii: A Psychocultural Profile* (Honolulu: John A. Burns School of Medicine, University Press of Hawaii, 1980).

57 *"the bones were secreted away":* S. M. Kamakau, *Ruling Chiefs of Hawaii* (Honolulu: Kamehameha Schools Press, 1992).

CHAPTER 8. *Abundance and Loss*

60 *"I found this bird numerous in the month of June":* S. B. Wilson and A. H. Evans, *Aves Hawaiienses: The Birds of the Sandwich Islands* (New York: Arno Press, 1974).

60 *the first serious ornithological exploration since Captain James Cook landed:* S. L. Olson, "On the History and Importance of Rothschild's *Avifauna of Laysan,*" online at http://www.sil.si.edu/digitalcollections/ nhrarebooks/rothschild/essays/storrs_rothschild.htm.

60 *mentor may in fact have written many of them:* Ibid.

61 *he sent a cadre of collectors there:* Ibid.; D. Amadon, "Obituary: George Campbell Munro," *Auk* 82 (1964): 256.

61 *"A friend, extremely clever at imitating sounds":* Wilson and Evans, *Aves Hawaiienses.*

62 *"They went in flocks and were most inquisitive":* G. C. Munro, *Birds of Hawaii* (Rutland, VT: Charles E. Tuttle, 1967), 192.

62 *"The necessity for the preservation of large forest tracts . . . has recently become so manifest":* H. W. Henshaw, *Birds of the Hawaiian Islands* (Honolulu: T. G. Thrum, 1902).

63 *"Though called the Kona Crow":* Ibid.

63 *entomologist R. C. L. Perkins . . . came to the islands:* Olson, "Rothschild's *Avifauna of Laysan.*"

63 *The 'alalā "feeds largely on the 'ie'ie flowers":* R. C. L. Perkins, "Notes on Collecting in Kona, Hawaii'" *Ibis* 1893:101–114.

64 *study of Hawaiian forest birds again fell into slumber:* H. I. Fisher, "Bibliography of Hawaiian Birds Since 1890," *Auk* 64 (1947): 78–97.

64 *"The birds refused to answer my call":* Munro, *Birds of Hawaii,* 192; see also S. Conant, "Hawaiian Forest Birds: A Survey of Recent Field Research," *'Elepaio* 40, no. 5 (1979): 76–79.

64 *"a grossly magnified 'meow'":* Fisher, "Bibliography of Hawaiian Birds."

65 *"Unquestionably, some areas within this range were vacated":* P. H. Baldwin, "The 'Alala (*Corvus tropicus*) of Western Hawaii Island," *'Elepaio* 30, no. 5 (1969): 41–45.

65 *"The effects of avian malaria on populations of resident Hawaiian birds":* Ibid.

66 *"During our first night, in the pre-dawn hours of June 18":* E. Eisenmann, "Observations on Birds on the Island of Hawaii," *'Elepaio* 21, no. 9 (1961): 66–70.

66 *a roll call of the damned:* W. E. Banko and P. C. Banko, *History of Endemic Hawaiian Birds, Part I, Population Histories—Species Accounts. Forest Birds: Hawaiian Raven/Crow ('Alala),* CPSU/UH Avian History Report 6B (University of Hawai'i at Manoa, Cooperative National Park Resources Studies Unit, 1980).

66 *All the nests "were in ohia trees":* Q. P. Tomich, "Notes on Nests and Behavior of the Hawaiian Crow," *Pacific Science* 25 (1971): 465–474.

68 *"Ka'ū would be graced by 'alalā no more":* S. M. Gon III, personal communication.

68 *painstakingly compiled by Winston Banko and his son Paul:* Banko and Banko, *History of Endemic Hawaiian Birds.*

68 *"The birds seemed fairly tame":* B. Benham, *Hawaii Tribune-Herald* (1971).

69 *The 'alalā had "plummeted from hundreds to a scattered few":* W. E. Banko, "Endangered Birds in Hawaii," *'Elepaio* (1972).

69 *last documented sighting of the 'alalā in Ka'ū:* Anon., *'Elepaio* (1975): 37.

69 *fewer than fifteen birds were known to exist in the wild:* P. Banko, "Report on Alala" (unpublished manuscript, 1976).

CHAPTER 10. *Escape to Captivity*

82 *the federal Endangered Species Preservation Act:* M. J. Bean and M. J. Rowland, *The Evolution of National Wildlife Law*, 3rd ed. (Westport, CT: Praeger, 1997).

83 *"We do not anticipate further problems":* E. M. Dustman, letter to M. Takata, August 5, 1970.

83 *And set them he did:* W. Banko, personal communication.

83 *the charismatic birds would play tricks on him:* "Cultural Significance of the Alala in Conservation and Recovery" (minutes of meeting at Keauhou Bird Conservation Center, February 21, 2003).

85 *"doing well in captivity with excellent appetites and glossy, smooth plumages":* L. K. Katahira, field notes, September 13, 1975.

86 *loud "Aaoow-whop!" cries:* D. Ball, personal communication.

86 *housed by the Bankos at Hawai'i Volcanoes National Park:* P. Banko, personal communication.

87 *Some biologists branded the father and son troublemakers:* C. J. Ralph, letter to S. A. Temple, June 30, 1978.

87 *"we would welcome your assuming responsibility for a Crow propagation project":* A. O'Connor, letter to M. Takata, June 19, 1975.

87 *"We would be more than willing to accommodate the birds":* R. L. Walker, letter to L. A. Greenwalt, July 18, 1975.

88 *a costly, unsustainable race:* P. Banko, personal communication.

88 *"All three crows bit me":* E. Kosaka, memorandum to R. L. Walker regarding transfer of crows from national park to Pōhakuloa.

CHAPTER 11. *Mountain of Sorrow*

90 *a place called Pu'uwa'awa'a, Hawaiian for Furrowed Hill:* M. K. Pukui, S. H. Elbert, and E. T. Mookini, *Place Names of Hawaii* (Honolulu: University of Hawai'i Press, 1976), 289.

90 *open fields interspersed with islands of trees:* Hawai'i Department of Land and Natural Resources, Division of Forestry and Wildlife, "Draft Management Plan for the Ahupuaa of Puuwaawaa" (Honolulu: Hawai'i Department of Land and Natural Resources, Division of Forestry and Wildlife, 2002).

90 *among the best feeding habitats the 'alalā ever knew:* J. Giffin, "Hawaiian Crow Habitat Use," *Journal of Wildlife Management* 51, no. 2 (1987):

491; National Research Council, *The Scientific Bases for the Preservation of the Hawaiian Crow* (Washington, DC: National Academy Press, 1992), 136.

90 *a huge cinder cone mound:* S. Carlquist, *Hawaii: A Natural History* (Garden City, NY: Natural History Press, 1970), 463.

90 *"the richest floral section of any in the whole Territory":* P. Tummons, "Pu'uwa'awa'a Burns, and DLNR Fiddles," *Environment Hawai'i* 1, no. 9 (1991).

90 *"a veritable bonanza for the delight of the delving botanist":* Ibid.

90 *"A crow was heard to give a two-tone 'caw' ":* P. H. Baldwin, "The 'Alala (*Corvus tropicus*) of Western Hawaii Island," *'Elepaio* 30, no. 5 (1969): 41–45.

90 *Three years later, he hiked across the northern side of Hualālai:* Ibid.

92 *At the summit two crows flew up and over the cone:* Ibid.

92 *bright reddish yellow fruit that was sought by the native Hawaiians and the 'alalā alike:* J. F. Rock, *The Indigenous Trees of the Hawaiian Islands* (Rutland, VT: Charles E. Tuttle, 1974); J. Giffin, "Alala Investigation," unpublished manuscript, 1983 (compilation of the Pittman-Robertson Project No. W-18-R, Study No. R-II-B, 1976–1981, Hawai'i Department of Land and Natural Resources, Division of Forestry and Wildlife, Honolulu).

93 *industriously mining the seed capsules.* "Nearly 80 percent of all the capsules . . . were eaten": Rock, *Indigenous Trees.*

93 *the sound ricocheted through the forest:* Ibid.; Carlquist, *Hawaii: A Natural History.*

93 *the hau kuahiwi, already extremely rare:* Rock, *Indigenous Trees*; Tummons, "Pu'uwa'awa'a Burns."

93 *specimens today can be found only in botanical gardens or under cultivation:* Rock, *Indigenous Trees.*

93 *the native red cotton tree:* Tummons, "Pu'uwa'awa'a Burns."

93 *cotton tree survives only in botanical gardens:* Rock, *Indigenous Trees.*

93 *The 'aiea:* J. L. Culliney, *Islands in a Far Sea: Nature and Man in Hawaii* (San Francisco: Sierra Club Books, 1988); Rock, *Indigenous Trees.*

93 *globose orange fruit was favored by the 'alalā:* H. F. Sakai and J. R. Carpenter, "The Variety and Nutritional Values of Foods Consumed

by Hawaiian Crow Nestlings, an Endangered Species," *Condor* 92 (1990): 220–228.

93 *sticky sap that early Hawaiians applied to branches to catch birds:* Rock, *Indigenous Trees.*

93 *the dry forests were also slower to recover:* Giffin, "Hawaiian Crow Habitat Use."

94 *Once he saw eight and heard a dozen more on the ranch:* W. E. Banko and P. C. Banko, *History of Endemic Hawaiian Birds*, Part I, *Population Histories—Species Accounts. Forest Birds: Hawaiian Raven/Crow ('Alala)*, CPSU/UH Avian History Report 6B (University of Hawai'i at Manoa, Cooperative National Park Resources Studies Unit, 1980).

94 *placed a ten-year kapu, or prohibition, on them:* Culliney, *Islands in a Far Sea.*

94 *"The toothsome 'ie'ie vines":* C. S. Judd, "The Natural Resources of the Hawaiian Forest Regions and Their Conservation" (unpublished manuscript, 1926).

94 *parties three thousand strong gathering sandalwood. . . . Beginning in the 1800s, the forests were further exploited:* Ibid.

95 *by 1850 the abundance of free-ranging cattle supported "boiling plants":* Ibid.

95 *Goats and sheep browsed on trees and bushes:* National Research Council, *Scientific Bases for the Preservaton of the Hawaiian Crow* (Washington, D. C.: National Academics Press, 1992), 136.

95 *"In general, this area needs more sunlight":* P. Tummons, "Cattle, Sheep, Goats Trample Pu'uwa'awa'a Treasures," *Environment Hawai'i* 11, no. 3 (September 2000).

95 *state-owned land could "be easily reserved":* Tummons, "Pu'uwa'awa'a Burns."

95 *many plants and trees at Pu'uwa'awa'a were the last of their kind. . . . "If we are to be assured of success . . . the only solution will be to protect these trees in their natural habitat":* Tummons, "Pu'uwa'awa'a Burns."

95 *"It will afford a place where native species can be replanted or encouraged to propagate themselves":* Tummons, "Pu'uwa'awa'a Burns."

95 *F. Newell Bohnett, cofounder of the once popular Sambo's restaurants:* R. J.

Lagomarsino, "Tribute to Sam Battistone" (extension of remarks by Hon. Robert J. Lagomarsino in the House of Representatives, July 1, 1992), E2059.

96 *a commensurate increase in leasing fees:* Tummons, "Puʻuwaʻawaʻa Burns."

97 *like "entrusting the welfare of a beloved invalid . . . to Jack the Ripper":* Ibid.

97 *by 1974 only two ʻalalā were documented on Hualālai:* National Research Council, *Scientific Bases.*

98 *His only fault, he said, was in overlooking a technicality:* Tummons, "Puʻuwaʻawaʻa Burns."

98 *confirmed that the construction . . . had been done without permission:* Ibid.

98 *recommending that "the matter be filed":* Ibid.

98 *"We believe that this response to Senator Jean King will answer her request":* Ibid.

99 *The lease gave the state the right to conduct research:* Ibid.

99 *"please contact your friend Giffin and suggest he keep his findings quiet. . . . They are still killing crows in Iowa":* Ibid.

99 *"grazing of cattle was in accordance with the theory of evolution's basic premise":* F. M. Miller, "Rancher Discounts Allegations," *West Hawaii Today* (August 23, 1984).

99 *"I do not know what these plants look like. . . . This proposal is a classic example of an irresponsible suggestion":* Tummons, "Puʻuwaʻawaʻa Burns."

100 *"ʻAlalā habitat at Puʻuwaʻawaʻa Ranch was seriously damaged":* Ibid.; Anon., *West Hawaii Today* (October 14, 1984), 6.

100 *Trees were being sawn into planks and shipped to Honolulu:* Tummons, "Puʻuwaʻawaʻa Burns."

100 *biologists were still finding "evidence of recent logging activity":* Ibid.

101 *the only ʻalalā remaining in the area was a single aged female:* Ibid.

101 *"I felt comfortable and confident" . . . DLNR rejected the idea:* Ibid.

101 *"told the Land Board he had ʻadmittedly been indiscreet'":* H. Clark, "Board Cracks Down Hard on Kona Rancher," *Honolulu Advertiser* (1984): A-4.

101 *"most serious concern is for . . . a better and financially independent*

Kona": Tummons, "Pu'uwa'awa'a Burns"; Anon., *West Hawaii Today* (1984), 19.

102 *three suspicious fires were set:* Tummons, "Pu'uwa'awa'a Burns."

104 *"Fear falls upon me on the mountain top"*: M. W. Beckwith, *The Kumulipo: A Hawaiian Creation Chant* (Honolulu: University of Hawai'i Press, 1972).

CHAPTER 12. *Barbara Churchill Lee*

107 *King 'Umi had numerous children:* S. M. Kamakau, *Ruling Chiefs of Hawaii* (Honolulu: Kamehameha Schools Press, 1992); A. Fornander, *An Account of the Polynesian Race: Its Origins and Migrations* (Rutland, VT: Charles E. Tuttle, 1980).

108 *"I couldn't become this friendly with them"*: R. Kroese, "Endangered Hawaiian Birds Find . . . Dedicated Helpers, a Sanctuary," *West Hawaii Today* (1980).

110 *Lee pronounced Kekau dead at 8:45 P.M.:* B. Lee, personal notes on Kekau, June 12, 1979.

112 *"Your role in the recent disposition of an Hawaiian crow . . ."*: R. L. Walker, memorandum to B. Lee, July 1979.

116 *in a place known only to the morning star:* B. Lee, memorandum to R. L. Walker, July 22, 1979.

116 *"She also is the first person ever to succeed in getting 'alalā to breed and lay eggs in captivity"*: Kroese, "Endangered Hawaiian Birds . . . Find Dedicated Helpers." Kroese, Ron. *West Hawaii Today.* Aug. 28, 1980.

117 *Ah Fat himself, now seventy, soon retired:* M. Melrose, "Ah Fat Lee: Kohala Boy Who Did Good," *Big Island Trading Post, West Hawaii Edition* 3, no. 17 (1985).

117 *fewer than thirty 'alalā were believed to remain in the wild:* Complaint for a Declaratory Judgment and Injunctive Relief; Exhibits "A" and "B"; Summons; in United States District Court for the District of Hawai'i, Civ. no. 91-00191 DAE (Honolulu, 1991).

118 *"private petting zoo"*: P. Tummons, "Saving the Alala: A Test of Commitment," *Environment Hawai'i* 1, no. 10 (1991).

CHAPTER 13. *The Bird Catcher*

122 *permit allowed biologists to rescue only sick or injured ʻalalā:* R. L. Walker, letter to M. Dillon, June 16, 1977.

122 *Fish and Game applied to the Service for a permit to capture healthy ʻalalā fledglings:* U.S. Fish and Wildlife Service, Federal Fish and Wildlife License/Permit Application, April 1, 1977; M. Takata, letter to director of U.S. Fish and Wildlife Service, March 29, 1977.

123 *Some two months after this application was filed . . . Giffin captured two young ʻalalā in the wild:* U.S. Fish and Wildlife Service, License/Permit Application; J. Giffin, "Notes on Capture of Two Alala (Eleu and Ulu)," June 15, 1977.

123 *"I trust that this letter and the phoned report satisfy the conditions of the permit":* R. L. Walker, letter to M. Dillon, June 16, 1977; U.S. Fish and Wildlife Service, License/Permit Application.

123 *"none of the fledglings . . . showed any indication of parasitism or illness":* State of Hawaiʻi, "Job Progress Report, Statewide Non-Game and Endangered Species Program: Limited Surveys of Forest Bird Habitats on the Island of Hawaiʻi, Segment, Alala Investigation," project no. W-18-R-2, job no. R-II-B. This report, covering the period of the 1977 breeding season, states that a total of nine fledglings were seen, including four on Hualālai. Three of these, which included Ulu and ʻEleʻū, were "removed from the population for captive breeding stock." The same report states that "none of the fledglings handled showed any indication of parasitism or illness" (p. 11). The same report goes on to state that "there was sufficient justification for taking these birds because their chances for survival were [thought] to be slight. All three had dropped to the ground and were vulnerable to mongoose and feral animals" (p. 5).

123 *"As you know, we have salvaged two fledglings":* M. Takata, letter to H. A. Hansen, August 5, 1977.

124 *Giffin captured a third ʻalalā fledgling:* E. Kosaka, "Annual Report on the Alala by Ernest Kosaka: 10-1-1976 through 09-30-1977," table I, "Weight Recorded from Captive Alala" (Honolulu: Hawaiʻi Department of Land and Natural Resources, Endangered Species Restoration Project).

124 *When the required permit finally arrived:* U.S. Fish and Wildlife Service,

Federal Fish & Wildlife Permit 2-727, August 19–December 31, 1979.

124 *"we have two more to go to fill our quota"*: Ibid.; R. L. Walker, letter to E. Kosaka et al., August 26, 1977.

124 *"the keel bone of the fledglings was prominent"*: J. Giffin, field notes, in longhand, on capture of Imia; E. Kosaka, "Progress Report, Endangered Species Restoration Project" (Honolulu: Hawai'i Department of Land and Natural Resources, June 1978).

124 *the fledgling was taken from a nest on McCandless Ranch:* Taken from nest 78-5 #374 on McCandless Ranch.

125 *"The authorizations . . . are to be strictly construed"*: U.S. Fish and Wildlife Service, 50 CFR 13.42.

126 *a particularly inopportune time for Giffin:* M. Buck, personal communication.

126 *was promoted to chief biologist:* Ibid.

CHAPTER 14. *Scientists to the Rescue*

127 *research biologist for the World Wildlife Fund and the International Council for Bird Preservation:* S. A. Temple, curriculum vitae, 1978.

128 *Temple fed tambalacoque seeds to domesticated turkeys:* S. Valdes-Cogliano, "A Lost Piece of the Puzzle," *Endangered Species Bulletin* 21, no. 6 (1996): 11; D. R. Herhey, "The Widespread Misconception That the Tambalacoque or Calvaria Tree Absolutely Required the Dodo Bird for Its Seeds to Germinate," *Plant Science Bulletin* 50, no. 4 (2004): 105.

128 *His conclusions . . . soon came under vigorous scientific attack:* Herhey, "Widespread Misconception"; A. W. Owadally, "The Dodo and the Tambalacoque Tree," *Science* 203, no. 4387 (1979): 1363–1364.

128 *Subsequent researchers pointed out flaws. . . . Today, Temple's hypothesis regarding the dodo and the tambalacoque is largely discredited:* Herhey, "Widespread Misconception."

128 *He proposed to set up time-lapse cameras near 'alalā nests:* S. A. Temple, memoranda to USDA Forest Service, May 12, 1978.

130 *"the roof rat . . . may have been a predator on the eggs"*: Q. P. Tomich, "Notes on Nests and Behavior of the Hawaiian Crow," *Pacific Science* 25 (1971): 465–474.

130 *"intensive studies of 'alalā breeding biology were postponed"*: W. E. Banko and P. C. Banko, "Progress Report of Alala (*Corvus tropicus*): Population Studies" (unpublished manuscript, 1975).

131 *"When the observer returned fourteen days later, the nest was abandoned"*: J. Giffin, "'Alala Investigation, Job Progress Report, July 1, 1976 to June 30, 1977."

131 *"In several instances it appeared as if a pair might attack"*: Ibid.

131 *"disturbances by this investigator played no part in the nest failures"*: Ibid.

131 *"These birds will . . . seldom abandon after incubation is well in progress"*: Ibid.

132 *if recent observations are a measure of the bird's nesting behavior*: D. Ball, personal communication.

132 *Giffin listed a number of "inimical factors" to the 'alalā in the wild*: J. Giffin, "Alala Investigation," unpublished manuscript, 1983 (compilation of the Pittman-Robertson Project No. W-18-R, Study No. R-II-B, 1976–1981, Hawai'i Department of Land and Natural Resources, Division of Forestry and Wildlife, Honolulu).

132 *Nowhere in his 1977 field report, however*: J. Giffin, "Interim Report, Phase 2."

132 *In the spring of 1978*: May 2–June 23, 1978.

132 *set up a surveillance camera about forty-five feet away from one active nest*: Nest 2A (78-8a), May 2; Giffin, "'Alala Investigation, Job Progress Report."

133 *the birds were nowhere to be found*: H. F. Sakai and C. J. Ralph, "A Study of the Hawaiian Crow (*Corvus tropicus*) in South Kona, Hawaii" (unpublished manuscript, 1978).

133 *the 'alalā had again apparently deserted*: Ibid.

133 *"This bodes ill . . . for nest manipulations early in the cycle"*: C. J. Ralph, letter to S. A. Temple, June 30, 1978.

133 *"time-lapse cameras cause minimal disturbance"*: S. A. Temple, memorandum to USDA Forest Service, May 12, 1978.

133 *"The click of a camera shutter at close range has been known to produce a fright response"*: J. Giffin, memorandum to D. H. Woodside, May 30, 1978.

134 *in the only nest without a camera mounted nearby*: David Jenkins, memo to Ernest Kosaka, June 22, 1979.

134 *the question of whether the noisy camera and its eyelike lens caused the chick*

to flee from the nest: S. A. Temple, memorandum to the USDA Forest Service regarding continuation of support for studies of the endangered Hawaiian crow, table 1, November 29, 1979.

134 *that nest, too, had been abandoned:* Ibid.

134 *ʻalalā abandoned that nest, too, a few days after researchers visited:* Ibid.

135 *in effect supporting what had long been suspected:* W. E. Banko and P. C. Banko, *History of Endemic Hawaiian Birds*, Part I, *Population Histories—Species Accounts. Forest Birds: Hawaiian Raven/Crow (ʻAlala)*, CPSU/UH Avian History Report 6B (University of Hawaiʻi at Manoa, Cooperative National Park Resources Studies Unit, 1980).

135 *"Furthermore, the unhatched eggs which we recovered were found to be infertile":* S. A. Temple and C. D. Jenkins, memorandum to USDA Forest Service, 1979.

135 *the eggs "appeared" to be infertile—a less than certain conclusion:* S. N. Wiemeyer, research biologist, memorandum to N. Coon, staff specialist, September 19, 1979.

135 *"contrary to the statement made by the two scientists":* Record of telephone conversation between E. Kosaka and W. White, U.S. Fish and Wildlife Service, Region 1, January 30, 1980; file reference: "Amendment to Permit Application by CKJ Ralph/Temple."

135 *Some two thousand feet of film had been captured:* S. A. Temple and D. Jenkins, "Final Progress Report: 1979 and 1980 Alala Research" (unpublished manuscript, 1981), 9.

136 *According to Jenkins, the film . . . was never completely analyzed:* D. Jenkins, personal communication.

136 *"this poor rate at fledging young has some very readily identifiable causes":* S. A. Temple, transcript (with audience questions) of speech given at Third Conference in Natural Sciences, Hawaiʻi Volcanoes National Park, June 1980.

136 *"the type of disturbance that we have been causing . . . doesn't appear to cause any observable problems at all":* Ibid.

136 *fewer than two dozen ʻalalā remained:* J. Giffin, "'Alala Investigation, Final Report" (Honolulu: Hawaiʻi Department of Land and Natural Resources).

139 *he blamed it on ranch activities:* S. Temple, personal communication.

CHAPTER 15. *Kapu*

141 *In 1980 she placed a kapu . . . on McCandless Ranch:* National Audubon Society, "'Wild' Alala (Hawaiian Crow) Down to 10," Audubon Action Alert, May 31, 1989.

142 *inquiring "what authority we have to enter private property":* W. W. Paty, memorandum to W. Price II, September 21, 1989.

142 *"We do not feel DLNR can enter onto McCandless Ranch property":* R. Y. K. Young, letter to W. W. Paty, December 20, 1989.

142 *fear of "alienating" large landowners:* National Audubon Society, "'Wild' Alala."

142 *"Endangered Species Act . . . does not empower the Service to enter private lands":* J. F. Turner, letter to P. Saiki, February 6, 1990.

143 *"The hasty and ill-advised actions":* B. Lee, letter to H. E. Woodsum Jr., May 18, 1989.

143 *"I don't like the new ideas of experimental manipulations":* S. Haight, letter to P. A. A. Berle, June 22, 1989.

144 *"should be an action where the State, not the McCandless Ranch, calls the shots":* S. Conant, letter to W. Paty, June 30, 1989.

144 *"I am in total support of the Hawai'i Audubon Society's resolution supporting the captive rearing of the 'Alalā":* A. A. Lieberman, letter to W. Paty, July 17, 1989.

144 *"Wild birds must be brought into captivity and brought into captivity now":* S. L. Pimm and M. Hofer, letter to J. Waihee, August 4, 1989.

144 *"The owners are afraid that if biologists get in . . . they'll invoke the Endangered Species Act":* Anon., "Let It Pau Out?" *Audubon* (November 1989): 14–15.

144 *allowing "personal opinion and petty politics to intrude into the realm of scientific fact":* Ibid.

145 *"We believe that the legal tools are available":* P. Berle, *Maui News* (November 12, 1989).

145 *"I am writing to request your permission":* J. Waihee, letter to C. Salley, June 12, 1990.

145 *"No research . . . has accomplished the goals set forth in your letter":* C. Salley, draft letter to J. Waihee, June 12, 1991. According to Salley, this draft was the same as the letter sent to Governor Waihee.

146 *the National Audubon Society began soliciting funds for its war chest:* D. Kokubun, letter to Hawai'i Audubon members, February 1991.

147 *"We . . . don't give a hang for scientific research":* P. Wagner, "Alala Count Effort Faces Obstacles," *Honolulu Star-Bulletin* (June 22, 1989).

CHAPTER 16. *Yahoo!*

148 *He eventually obtained the equivalent of a Ph.D. degree in zoology:* Deposition of Dr. F. P. Duvall II, December 11, 1991.

149 *Duvall was determined to solve "the majority of the problems facing the propagation project":* F. Duvall, "Captive Propagation of the Alala, Job Progress Report, July 1, 1984 to June 30, 1985" (Honolulu: Hawai'i Department of Land and Natural Resources).

149 *"I must report to you, with great discontent":* F. Duvall, memorandum to S. Ono, June 19, 1985.

150 *Nor did the 1986 breeding season produce any chicks:* F. Duvall, "Job Progress Report: E-W-2; Study No. 1, Job No. 1 Captive Propagation of Endangered Birds (Alala), July 1, 1985 to June 30, 1986" (Honolulu: Hawai'i Department of Land and Natural Resources).

150 *"all nine individuals were reproductively active and built nests":* Duvall, "Job Progress Report, July 1, 1985 to June 30, 1986."

150 *Hi'ialo and Kalani . . . produced two eggs:* Ibid.

150 *'Umi and his mate, Lu'ukia, also nested and produced two eggs:* Ibid.

150 *"They make a tremendous noise before the sun rises":* Anon., "Why Try? Call of the 'Alala Is Like No Other in the World," *Maui News,* December 15, 1986.

151 *"we are now well prepared to breed 'alalā":* W. Paty, letter to C. Salley, February 24, 1987.

151 *blamed the low egg production and lack of chicks on "a big rainstorm":* J. TenBruggencate, "Wildlife Experts Hope Isle Crow Makes Comeback," *Honolulu Star-Bulletin* (May 17, 1987).

151 *the pairs had not yet become "confident" enough to breed in their new aviaries:* J. TenBruggencate, "One of Nine Native Crows Dies on Maui," *Honolulu Advertiser* (July 3, 1987), A-14.

151 *his contention that no eggs had hatched under her care:* F. Duvall, letter to B. Lee, June 3, 1987.

151-152   *"I found it quite presumptuous"*: F. Duvall, letter to B. Lee, June 3, 1987.

152   *"the now apparent sluggish non-normal behavior"*: F. Duvall, memorandum to M. Ueoka, June 16, 1987.

152   the bird's *"status [was] very serious"*: F. Duvall, memorandum to M. Ueoka, June 16, 1987.

152   *Hiʻialo was dead*: F. Duvall, memorandum to M. Ueoka, June 16, 1987.

152   *pathology report concluded that Hiʻialo had died from infection*: Pathology report, National Wildlife Health Center, June 13, 1987.

153   *"although the report may be accurate, it may not be complete"*: E. Kosaka, letter to A. F. Lee and B. Lee, October 9, 1987.

153   the death left only *"eight others in the state's captive propagation program"*: TenBruggencate, "One of Nine Native Crows Dies."

153   *detailed rebuttals on five of Duvall's points*: B. Lee, letter to F. Duvall, June 13, 1987.

153   *"It is my belief that time ran out for the species"*: B. Lee, letter to F. Duvall, June 13, 1987.

154   *"I now feel comfortable that there was one nestling ʻalalā that hatched during your tenure"*: F. Duvall, letter to B. Lee, 1987.

154   *"'Yahoo, we saved another endangered species'"*: Anon., "Score One to Keep Rare Crow from Extinction," *Honolulu Advertiser* (June 13, 1988).

154   *"A welcomed event in the State's captive propagation program"*: F. Duvall, memorandum to S. Ono, June 19, 1985.

155   *"we think we've got it figured out"*: K. Miller, "Maui's Reluctant Crows Fight against Extinction," *Honolulu Star-Bulletin* (May 3, 1989), A-4.

155   *"too little and much too late"*: A. J. Berger, letter to M. R. Sherwood, September 12, 1989.

155   *"didn't know much about endangered birds, and especially passerine birds"*: Ibid.

155   *"I begin to doubt that he knows very much"*: Ibid.

156   *Waʻalani, trying to nest, would eventually drive . . . Hoikei away*: N. C. Harvey and S. Farabaught, "Effects of Early Rearing Experience on Behavior and Nesting in Captive ʻAlala (*Corvus hawaiiensis*)" (unpublished document, San Diego: Zoological Society of San Diego, Center for Reproduction of Endangered Species, July 1999).

156 *violent fits of flopping on his side:* Ibid.; C. Kuehler, personal communication.

156 *"inherent very likely genetic-lethal factors":* F. Duvall, "Annual Performance Report, Statewide Endangered Species Program, July 1, 1990 to June 30, 1991" (Honolulu: Hawai'i Department of Land and Natural Resources).

157 *"it is a very difficult task":* U.S. Fish and Wildlife Service, The Peregrine Fund, and Hawai'i Department of Land and Natural Resources, joint press release, September 3, 1998.

CHAPTER 17. *Helicopter Dreams*

159 *something Duvall didn't deny and was delighted to take credit for:* When I put the question to him, he smiled and said, "Let's say I was a strong advocate."

161 *Paty canceled the state plans:* J. TenBruggencate, "Ranch Vetoes State Plan to Corral Last Alala," *Honolulu Advertiser* (May 5, 1989).

161 *ranch flock represented the much-needed new blood:* Ibid.

162 *first step in justifying the need for new management:* A. Lieberman, personal communication.

162 *tactful on the surface and blunt between the lines:* C. Kuehler, "Recommendations for Alala (*Corvus hawaiiensis*) Recovery Project" (Honolulu: Hawai'i Department of Land and Natural Resources, Division of Forestry and Wildlife, 1990).

162 *"a last ditch attempt to increase productivity":* F. Duvall, memorandum to M. Buck, December 9, 1990.

162 *"radiographing of late term 'alalā eggs to determine embryo positioning":* F. Duvall, "Annual Performance Report, Statewide Endangered Species Program, July 1, 1990 to June 30, 1991" (Honolulu: Hawai'i Department of Land and Natural Resources).

162-163 *one should "allow females to incubate for five to seven days":* Kuehler, "Recommendations for Alala Recovery Project."

163 *doing so "could jeopardize production likelihood":* F. Duvall, memorandum to M. Buck, December 9, 1990.

163 *"not only improve hatchability but decrease the incidence of egg predation and breakage":* Kuehler, "Recommendations for Alala Recovery Project."

163   *argued that the males were needed to help the females with family responsibilities:* F. Duvall, memorandum to M. Buck, December 9, 1990.

163   *"Egg normality and hatchability . . . has been very poor":* F. Duvall, memorandum to C. Terry, 1991.

CHAPTER 18. *Aliʻi Neo*

164   *"Plaintiff Hawaiian Crow . . . brings this action by its next friends":* Complaint for a Declaratory Judgment and Injunctive Relief; Exhibits "A" and "B"; Summons; in United States District Court for the District of Hawaiʻi, Civ. no. 91-00191 DAE (Honolulu, 1991).

164   *not required by law to implement every provision of a recovery plan:* E. Ching, "Analysis of Section Four of the Endangered Species Act as an Offensive Tool in the Conservation of Endangered Species on Private Land as Illustrated by Recovery Efforts for the ʻAlala" (unpublished manuscript).

166   *Judge Ezra sat in his lofty perch:* R. P. Smith, personal communication.

167   *Pence . . . was the first permanent federal judge confirmed in Hawaiʻi:* H. Morse, "Martin Pence, Senior Federal Judge, Retiring," *Honolulu Star-Bulletin* (January 22, 2000).

167   *Ezra had left the underlying legal point . . . unresolved:* Ching, "Analysis of Section Four."

167   *committee was to "review all the available information on the ʻalalā":* National Research Council, *The Scientific Bases for the Preservation of the Hawaiian Crow* (Washington, DC: National Academy Press, 1992), 136.

168   *she had written a negative letter to the governor of Hawaiʻi:* C. Kuehler, letter to W. Paty, 1989.

168   *NRC committee ultimately included many respected ornithologists and biologists:* National Research Council, *Scientific Bases.*

169   *"addition of new wild-caught adult birds . . . should have a very low priority":* Ibid.

169   *taking wild eggs "allows for simultaneous augmentation of the captive and wild populations":* Ibid.

170   *"creativity and experimentation should always be encouraged":* Ibid.

170   *report also restated the importance of allowing the birds to sit on their eggs:* Ibid.

170   *"All human contact is kept to a minimum":* K. Miller, "Hatching of

Endangered Island Crow Is Imminent," *Honolulu Star-Bulletin* (May 20, 1989).

171 *"sanitation in the enclosure would also be improved substantially":* National Research Council, *Scientific Bases.*

171 *report recommended that "a full-time director . . . be hired:* Ibid.

171 *The agreement was signed in July 1993:* E. Ching, personal communication.

171 *Duvall and Giffin would be prohibited from ever setting foot on the ranch:* C. Salley, personal communication.

172 *"And that is what came to pass":* C. Salley, "The Rose and the Dragon: McCandless Ranch: An Historical Anecdote" (unpublished manuscript, n.d).

CHAPTER 20. *Hope–At Last*

179-180 *Cade thought that . . . his organization would succeed where the state had failed:* T. Cade, personal communication.

180 *Several other collaborators . . . would fill in the remaining political and cultural gaps:* The Peregrine Fund and the Zoological Society of San Diego, *Hawaiian Endangered Bird Conservation Program: Report to U.S. Fish and Wildlife Service and State of Hawai'i, July 1, 1999–September 30,* 21810 (San Diego: Zoological Society of San Diego, 2000).

181 *In 1993, that first year of TPF's involvement, seven chicks were thus hatched:* A. A. Lieberman, "Alala Hatching Table 1988–2005" (unpublished document, 2005).

181 *recommendation that Kuehler had made . . . four years earlier but that Duvall had rejected as unsound:* F. Duvall, memorandum to M. Buck, December 9, 1990.

181 *largest single crop in the captive flock's history. Several birds who had never before produced young were suddenly parents:* Lieberman, "Alala Hatching Table 1988–2005."

181 *breaking out had become a common practice at Olinda:* P. Shannon, personal communication.

182 *"You must always be prepared to adapt your techniques":* P. Shannon, personal communication.

182 *the wild birds contributed twelve new chicks, while the captive flock added another four:* Lieberman, "Alala Hatching Table 1988–2005."

182 *That same year, but a single chick was produced at Olinda:* Ibid.

183 *early that year the new state-of-the-art breeding facility . . . had been built:* The Peregrine Fund and the Zoological Society of San Diego, *Hawaiian Endangered Bird Conservation Program: Report to U.S. Fish and Wildlife Service and State of Hawai'i, October 1, 2001–September 30, 2002* (San Diego: Zoological Society of San Diego, 2002).

184 *the facility became home to . . . other struggling forest bird species:* A. Lieberman, personal communication; Peregrine Fund and Zoological Society, *Report, July 1, 1999–September 30, 2000.*

CHAPTER 21. *A Cruel Kindness*

185 *In August 1997, Hilu . . . was found dead:* The Peregrine Fund, "Survivability of Alala Released by The Peregrine Fund 1993–1999" (unpublished document, n.d.).

185 *"We will be watching":* U.S. Fish and Wildlife Service, "Update, August 25–29, 1997."

185 *"The remains of HiwaHiwa were recovered":* U.S. Fish and Wildlife Service, "Update"; U.S. Fish and Wildlife Service, "Weekly Schedule and Update, September 1–5, 1997."

185-186 *the number of 'alalā in the wild soon grew again:* The Peregrine Fund, "Release and Death Chart," n.d.

186 *release of the four was quickly followed by the death of Nānū:* U.S. Fish and Wildlife Service, "Update"; U.S. Fish and Wildlife Service, "Weekly Schedule and Update, September 15–19, 1997."

186 *Uila's carcass was found in a burrow:* Peregrine Fund, C. Kuehler, "Survivability of Alala released by the Peregrine Fund (1993–1999)" (unpublished data n.d.); U.S. Fish and Wildlife Service, "Weekly Schedule and Update, November 3–7, 1997."

186 *ten of the twenty released 'alalā had died:* C. Kuehler, "Survivability of Alala Released by The Peregrine Fund (1993–1999)" (unpublished table, n.d.).

188 *"We believe this action will be viewed as a general step backwards":* C. Kuehler and A. Lieberman, letter to K. Rosa, U.S. Fish and Wildlife Service, January 25, 1999.

189 *TPF warned that "if the release program does not continue":* Ibid.

189 *having the birds pay their way . . . would amount to sustainable conservation:* G. Klingler, personal communication.

190 *"we are spinning our wheels in Hawaii"*: C. Kuehler, personal communication.

190 *four of 'Umi's great-grandchildren were sent into the wild:* C. Kuehler, "Survivability of Alala (1993–1999)."

CHAPTER 22. *Dead Ravens Flying*

193 *wings, pelvis, and legs had been "picked clean"*: D. Ball, memorandum to 'Alalā Recovery Team participants regarding U.S. Fish and Wildlife Service, "Weekly Schedule and Update, January 5–9, 1998."

193 *a project volunteer discovered one of the earlier releases, Hiapo, lying on his side:* U.S. Fish and Wildlife Service, "Weekly Schedule and Update, April 6–12, 1998."

193 *the carcass of Hulu was discovered:* U.S. Fish and Wildlife Service, "Weekly Schedule and Update, June 29–July 3, 1998."

193 *scat of a small cat or mongoose:* U.S. Fish and Wildlife Service, "Weekly Schedule and Update, July 27–31, 1998."

193 *Noe, one of the most experienced of the releases, was killed:* U.S. Fish and Wildlife Service, "Weekly Schedule and Update, June 29–July 3, 1998."

194 *In September came more deaths:* D. Ball, personal communication; U.S. Fish and Wildlife Service, "Weekly Schedule and Update, September 7–11, 1998."

194 *Eight of these birds had died since that time:* U.S. Fish and Wildlife Service, The Peregrine Fund, and Hawai'i Department of Land and Natural Resources, joint press release, September 3, 1998.

194 *Alahou, who grew ill, was recaptured but died shortly after. Meanwhile, Makoa had also passed away:* The Peregrine Fund, "Survivability of Alala Released by The Peregrine Fund 1993–1999" (unpublished document, n.d.); U.S. Fish and Wildlife Service, "Weekly Schedule and Update, July 17–23, 1999."

195 *twenty-seven released since 1993 . . . twenty-two now dead:* D. Ball, personal communication; Peregrine Fund, "Survivability of Alala 1993–1999."

195 *"The 'alalā program continues to be a disaster"*: C. Kuehler, personal communication.

CHAPTER 23. *The 'Alalā from Hell*

199 *Work presented his findings in a "good-faith attempt"*: T. M. Work, memorandum to 'Alala Recovery Team, November 14, 1998; J. Burgett, faxed memorandum to C. Kuehler with draft reply to 'Alala Recovery Team, February 23, 1999.

199 *"It makes it sound like the Peregrine Fund is doing a bad job"*: 'Alala Partnership meeting minutes, February 9, 1999.

200 *Work's information was "inaccurate, incomplete and incorrectly analyzed"*: The Peregrine Fund staff, memorandum to D. Ledig regarding November 4, 1998, memorandum to 'Alala Recovery Team, January 15, 1999.

200 *he blamed the Service field team for giving him bad data*: 'Alala Partnership, memorandum to 'Alala Recovery Team, February 19, 1999.

200 *Later he admitted that his analysis "may depict a misleading picture"*: T. M. Work, memorandum to 'Alala Recovery Team.

200 *Kuehler and Lieberman responded that they were, understandably, "hesitant"*: C. Kuehler and A. Lieberman, letter to K. Rosa, U.S. Fish and Wildlife Service, January 25, 1999.

200 *"We can breed, hatch and raise them but the habitat cannot support them"*: C. Kuehler, personal communication.

CHAPTER 24. *Regrets*

204 *"We're also going to lose our two best breeders"*: Hoikei and Wa'alani.

CHAPTER 25. *Heart of Koa*

210 *Rock named the "beautiful species" Cyanea marksii in honor of Cynthia Salley's father*: J. F. Rock, "Some New Hawaiian Lobelioids," *Occasional Papers of Bernice P. Bishop Museum* 22, no. 5 (1957): 35–66.

212 *the secretary "shall develop and implement" these plans*: See Section 4 of the Endangered Species Act of 1973, "Determination of Endangered Species and Threatened Species," 16 USC 1531.

213 *Hōkū-hoʻokele-waʻa—better known as Sirius*: M. K. Pukui and S. H. Elbert, *Hawaiian Dictionary: Hawaiian-English, English-Hawaiian*, rev. and enl. ed. (Honolulu: University of Hawaiʻi Press, 1986).

213 *Makaliʻi—Little Eyes, or the Pleiades*: S. E. Rhoads, *The Sky Tonight: A*

Guided Tour of the Stars over Hawaii, rev. ed., Bishop Museum Special Publication 96 (Honolulu: Bishop Museum Press, 1996); Pukui and Elbert, *Hawaiian Dictionary*.

CHAPTER 26. *Kahuna 'Alalā*

215 *the warrior Keʻeaumoku cut the throat of Kamehameha the Great's main rival:* M. K. Pukui, S. H. Elbert, and E. T. Mookini, *Place Names of Hawaii* (Honolulu: University of Hawaiʻi Press, 1976), 289.

218 *"confessed that he was the one that fired the gunshot":* Lawsuit, Civ. no. 92-185K, Exhibit 1362–1366.

219 *Clarence Jr.'s great-great-granduncle, Lapawila:* Also spelled Lapauila.

220 *The Medeiros family believes:* His family's claim to ahupuaʻa Kalāhiki is in the will of Clarence's ancestor Kinimaka, a copy of which was submitted to the court in support of the suit to reclaim part of McCandless Ranch. As was often the case with the descendants of island royalty, Kinimaka owned parcels of land throughout the islands. This included not only Kalāhiki—one of the parts of McCandless Ranch that Clarence Sr. and Clarence Jr. were seeking —but also ahupuaʻa elsewhere throughout the islands.

The Medeiroses' claim to ahupuaʻa Hoʻokena came through Ruth Keelikolani. In her will of January 30, 1871, she bequeathed ten properties to her adopted son William Pitt L. Kalahoolewa (aka William Pitt Leleiohoku), who was the younger brother, according to Clarence Jr., of King Kalakaua and Queen Liliuokalani. According to the genealogy, Clarence Jr. is the third great-grandnephew of William Pitt Leleiohoku.

220 *"For over 6 generations, my family have seen the 'Alalā":* C. Medeiros Jr., "Cultural Significance of the Alala in Conservation and Recovery" (handout for meeting at Keauhou Bird Conservation Center, Volcano, HI, February 21, 2003).

222 *the more recent territory of their familiars:* "Liloa and Akahi-a-Kuleana begat Umi-a-liloa; Umi-a-liloa and Kapukini-a-Liloa begat Kealiia-kaloa; Kealiiakaloa and Makuahine-a-Palaka begat Kukailani. Ku-kailani and Kaohukiokalani begat Makakaualii. Makakaualii and Kapu-Kamola-a-Walu begat Iwikauikaua. Iwikauikaua and

Keakamahana begat Kahalekai Iwikauikaua. Kahalekai Iwikaui-
kaua and Pae of Kalakiki, Waiea and Tahiti begat Oi Umauma
Kahalekai. Oi Umauma Kahalekai and Kawahineailaau Ipaapuka
begat Kaaua Oi Umauma. Niau and Kaaua Oi Umauma begat
Kaaumoana Moa Niau. Zen Man Sing and Kaaumoana Moa Niau
begat Annie Man Sing Zen. Charles Hua Kalalahua and Annie Man
Sing Zen begat Pansy Wiwoole Hua. Clarence A. Medeiros, Sr. and
Pansy Wiwoole Hua begat Clarence Jr. and Jimmy Sr." C. A.
Medeiros Jr., "Genealogy of Liloa and Akahi-a-Kuleana,
Researched and Compiled by Clarence A. Medeiros, Jr." (unpub-
lished documents, n.d.).

220 *his family was also woven into the vast genealogy of . . . the Kumulipo:*
Clarence Jr. states his connection to the Kumulipo as follows:
Lonoikamakahiki; Keawe; Elehiki; Kainoa; Ihalau; Kanuha;
Kahae; Kanuha; Uweloa; Kaupeau; Ahu; Kepookalani; Kama-
nawa; Kapaakea; Keohokalole; Keakamahana; Iwikauikaua; Kea-
kealaniwahine; Kalaniopuu.

223 *"She barely made it out of her house alive":* Lawsuit, Civ. no. 92-185K
and BOA 04-013-014.

CHAPTER 27. *Broken Home*

224 *it became necessary to partition the ranch:* C. Salley, personal communication.

225 *They decided to sell part of Kai Malino to pay it:* C. Salley, personal communication.

225 *Congress earmarked funds:* G. Shirilla, personal communication.

225 *TNC . . . allowed the option on the property to expire:* G. Shirilla, personal communication.

226 *it was sure to light a fire under the Service:* J. TenBruggencate, "Last
Habitat for Crow Endangered," *Honolulu Advertiser* (February 15,
1996), A1.

226 *"but the Fish and Wildlife Service doesn't have the money":* Ibid.

226 *whose reputation in the environmental community preceded him:* Ibid.

226 *"remembered for clear-cutting the area":* P. Tummons, "Ranch Plans to
Manage 'Alala Habitat May Put Public Purchase on Hold,"
Environment Hawai'i 6, no. 9 (1996).

226 *the Sierra Club Legal Defense Fund sued the ranch:* Sierra Club Legal Defense Fund, "Endangered Alala (Hawaiian Crow) Threatened by Koa Logging," *News from the Sierra Club Legal Defense Fund,* March 28, 1996.

227 *cutting shouldn't start in the middle of the 'alalā habitat:* Ten Bruggencate, "Last Habitat."

227 *Anyone who trespassed would be arrested:* G. Shirilla, personal communication.

227 *Fearing a similar suit, she stopped:* C. Salley, personal communication.

227 *a dozen or more people in a day—at $200 each:* G. Klingler, personal communication.

228 *government could preempt complicating claims of landownership:* G. Shirilla, personal communication.

228 *David and Lucile Packard Foundation promised the Service $1.1 million:* G. Shirilla, personal communication.

228 *"there might not have been a forest worth purchasing or any 'alalā left in the wild":* Sierra Club Legal Defense Fund, "Citizens Preserve Habitat for Critically Endangered Alala," press release, October 1, 1997.

228 *"Our lawsuit demonstrates the important role citizens play":* Ibid.

228 *"There is something missing here":* K. Unger, "Give Credit Where Due at Kai Malino," *West Hawaii Today* (October 7, 1997).

229 *additional mile of new road along the refuge's northern boundary:* G. Shirilla, personal communication.

230 *"all contents within all lava tubes":* J. Santimer, letter to G. Shirilla, August 24, 1998; B. Rosehill, letter to G. Shirilla, November 20, 1998.

230 *"We offered what we felt was a fair price":* G. Shirilla, personal communication.

231 *When Salley got word of the episode:* C. Salley, personal communication.

231 *At the meeting were Ledig and Burgett:* Noticeably absent was Robert Smith, who had left the Service in 2000 to become director of the new Northwestern Hawaiian Islands Coral Reef Ecosystem Reserve, part of the National Marine Sanctuary Program.

231 *"Keālia Ranch should not be the 'sacrificial lamb'":* C. Salley, personal communication.

232 *researchers were henceforth prohibited from bringing cameras onto the ranch:* C. Salley, personal communication; R. P. Smith, personal communication.

232 *also prohibited from taking notes:* J. Burgett, personal communication.

233 *promising not to gather any evidence "to build a case or another lawsuit against us":* C. Salley, personal communication.

233 *a matter of "prudent business":* D. Ledig, personal communication.

233 *only a short stretch was across McCandless property:* D. Ledig, personal communication.

233 *"torn up by Service people who didn't know how to drive their 4-wheel drive vehicles":* P. Henson, personal communication.

234 *"Our family has been managing this land for eighty years":* D. Ledig, personal communication.

234 *"We can't be bulldozing next to crows' nests":* Ibid.

236 *"Make no mistake: I minded the biologists' being on the ranch":* D. Ledig, personal communication.

237 *the Packard Foundation finally withdrew its grant:* 'Alalā Partnership meeting minutes, February 9, 1999.

CHAPTER 28. *Quagmire*

239 *while the Service owns the refuge, the sellers still insist on controlling it:* P. Tummons, "Government Pays $8 Million for Refuge in South Kona, But Has No Legal Access," *Environment Hawai'i* 14, no. 4 (October 2003).

CHAPTER 29. *Last Light*

243 *the hills of 'Āinapō—Land of Darkness:* R. W. Hazlett and D. W. Hyndman, *Roadside Geology of Hawai'i* (Missoula, MT: Mountain Press, 1996).

EPILOGUE

246 *the extinction of human experience:* R. M. Pyle, "The Extinction of Experience," *Horticulture* 56 (1978): 64–67.

246 *"When we hold a bird what is in our hands":* W. S. Merwin, *The Folding Cliffs: A Narrative* (New York: Knopf, 1998).

INDEX

MARK JEROME WALTERS is author of the widely acclaimed books *A Shadow and a Song*, on the extinction of the dusky seaside sparrow, and *Six Modern Plagues and How We Are Causing Them*, recipient of the 2004 Independent Publisher Book Award. He is a contributing editor of *Orion* magazine, and his work has appeared in *Audubon*, *Reader's Digest*, and numerous other publications. Walters earned a master's degree from the Columbia University Graduate School of Journalism and a Doctorate in Veterinary Medicine from Tufts University. A professor of journalism and media studies at the University of South Florida, he lives on Florida's Gulf Coast.